The Real
Freshman
Handbook

The REAL FRESHMAN HANDBOOK

A Totally Honest Guide to Life on Campus

JENNIFER HANSON
& Friends

HOUGHTON MIFFLIN COMPANY
Boston   New York   2002

For information about permission to reproduce selections
from this book, write to Permissions, Houghton Mifflin Company,
215 Park Avenue South, New York, New York 10003.

Visit our Web site: www.houghtonmifflinbooks.com.

Library of Congress Cataloging-in-Publication Data
Hanson, Jennifer.
    The real freshman handbook : a totally honest guide to
life on campus / Jennifer Hanson and friends.
    p.   cm.
    Previous ed.: 1996.
    ISBN 0-618-16342-5
    1. College student orientation—United States—Handbooks,
manuals, etc. I. Title.

LB2343.32 .H36   2002
378.1'98—dc21   2001051886

Illustrations courtesy of Lynn Jeffery

Printed in the United States of America

QUM 20 19 18 17 16 15 14 13 12 11 10

Contents

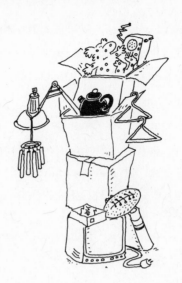

WELCOME TO OL' BIG U

Introduction

Welcome to college!!! You're in for the ride of your life—enough '70s parties to wear down the seat of those vinyl camouflage pants your dad gave you for graduation; all-night rap sessions about men, women, and Pat; moonlight kisses on the football field after the lights have been extinguished. If you're especially photogenic, you may even find yourself having an animated conversation with a professor in front of a blazing maple tree and, later, in an admissions brochure.

In the above endeavors you don't need much guidance; just follow your libido and the fashion dictates of Abercrombie & Fitch. But college isn't all *Felicity*-style hangin'; as the stacks of forms colleges send incoming freshmen attest, there's a lot of practical stuff to deal with. How do you go about choosing four classes from a catalog of three thousand, let alone how do you survive them? How do you get a vomit stain out of your comforter and the neighborhood cockroaches out of your Tupperware? What should you do if your roommate develops severe stomach pains and is too weak to get to the infirmary? How can you avoid spending more on books than you did on plane fare? How do you build a loft? How can you maintain full-body fitness without leaving your Barcalounger? And, most important of all, how can you ensure that your nocturnally foraging roommate is out cold, his coonskin cap covering his face, by midnight the evening before your "rocks for jocks" exam?

We know the solutions to these and other pressing problems because we've been there; we've been through freshman year and the memory is still fresh as dog doo. You see, my friend, we're college students just like you, only a little older (juniors), a little wiser, and a little more obsessed with corn. We know that you could find out everything in this book by yourself if you had to and that many of your less literate classmates will, and more. But there is just so much fun to be had . . . why reinvent the wheel when you could be out burning up the road?

We come originally from Minnesota, where we rose out of the cornfields of our youth to attend high school in the lovely but unfortunately crop-free city of Minneapolis. There we lived in friendship, gossip, and a pizza restaurant called Sydney's; there we parted, each bound for a different part of the country and a different type of collegiate environment. Two years later we came together again, possessed by a mission to spread the lessons we learned from our mistakes and experiences, and the gospel of grain. The result of our reminiscences, Jolt-fed brainstorming, and piety: the book you now hold in your trembling hand.

From our class, our campuses, and our fields to yours, then, our gift.

The Real
Freshman
Handbook

1

Avoiding Ex-cons: How to Make the Rooming Questionnaire Make Your Year

If you decide to live off campus, please see chapter 8. If you decide to live on, the first day of the rest of your life will be the day you fill out . . . the *rooming questionnaire*. You can't get through a year of college without hearing the stories—the roommate from Burbank with a psychiatric record longer than Hannibal Lecter's; the klepto with a yen for boxers; the obsessive-compulsive who sets five alarm clocks, each to a different track on Eminem's latest release; the girl who returns from her boyfriend's room via the fire escape, yet plays dumb when you ask her for cat-burgling tips; the dude who likes to make love vicariously by listening to your phone conversations with your girlfriend.

September's charming eccentricities are May's motives for mastering voodoo: your roommate situation, and how you deal with it, can make or break your freshman year. Not surprisingly, however, colleges give you very little voice in the important decision of whom you'll be living with. Some colleges don't even make a pretense of thoughtful matching; if your school is one of these, you may well mistake your roommate questionnaire for a piece of stationery. But before you excitedly use it to begin a letter to your Estonian pen pal, read that brief text at the top—it probably asks you the two questions most colleges find they have to ask: whether you're a smoker, and whether you're willing to live with one. But even colleges that seem to take a profound interest in your hobbies and personal quirks may be putting on a bit of a show; most colleges we know base their arrangements on only the most general of information about you. Forget the tearjerkers about your kitty's battle with depression and devote your attention to the basics.

Type of Dorm

Depending upon your college's facilities, you may have the option of living in various "special dorms." Chances are, you won't be assigned to one of these unless you ask to be, but be on your guard if you happen to know that your college has such dorms. One of us, either randomly or because of the autobiographical info we provided, got assigned to a 24-hour quiet dorm. It turned out all right—and turned out to be something less than 24-hour quiet—but it could easily have been graveyard city. If you would definitely not want to be in one of these special dorms, say so:

Single-sex dorms (mandated on some campuses, particularly those with religious affiliations). Unfortunately, such dorms have gained the reputation of being "virgin vaults" and/or bastions of homosexuality—neither of which they necessarily are. While it's true that nymphos and homophobes might find a stay in a single-sex dorm uncomfortable, these buildings can also simply provide a comfortable atmosphere for the conservative, the shy, or those who prize the privilege of being able to walk to the bathroom in nothing but a birthday suit.

Quiet dorms. Two types of dorms fall into this category: 1) dorms in which there are actual rules mandating silence at certain hours or all hours, and 2) dorms that are quiet by reputation or by virtue of their distance from campus centers. Both types have their advantages for naturally outgoing people who simply can't concentrate in the presence of distractions: If you can count on making friends quickly outside your dorm, then these may be for you. But if you tend to hang back, it may be in your interest to put yourself in a more sociable environment where you won't be able to help meeting people. Many freshmen make most of their friends through their dorms, and if yours disallows talking in the halls, bonding becomes *très difficile*.

Chemical-free dorms. Such dorms often end up being kind of a compromise between regular and quiet dorms. Since alcohol isn't allowed, the parties will be elsewhere—yet in the absence of noise restrictions, conviviality flourishes.

Mixture of Classes

The freshmen live together, eat together, and sow corn together at some schools; at others, there are more opportunities to mix. If you're offered the choice between an all-freshman dorm and a mixed-class one, consider the following before deciding:

Two breeds of party animals. Both types of dorm can be very social, but in different ways. All-freshman dorms tend to resemble the setting of *The Real World* minus the cameras—people are continuously lounging in common areas, expounding upon their philosophies of life with newfound friends, and gossiping about each other. Buildings with upperclassmen, on the other hand, tend to be less feverishly open and friendly, but with more actual parties.

Dad #2? Living in a mixed-class dorm, you're more likely to get the inside scoop on professors, hangouts, and college in general. But if the thought of dorming with a living version of this book is a little nightmarish, the vast communal ignorance of an all-freshman dorm may be more your cup of tea. Upperclassmen, too, can be less interested in random social interactions and more preoccupied with existing friends, classes, and work.

Number of Roommates

Depending upon your college's facilities, there may not be much choice on this one. But if you do have a chance to express a preference, keep in mind the following pros and cons of each type of configuration:

Single. Unless your college is riding the trend of converting closets into bedrooms, you've got some space, peace, and quiet. But at a stiff price: A lot of the freshmen we knew with singles spent their evenings lurking around laundry rooms, desperate to make friends over a box of Tide. Once you snag a honey, however, it's all good.

Double (usually one room, occasionally two). Doubles work out one of three ways: 1) bond like Krazy Glue and a hungry tot's teeth; 2) get along, but don't hang out together or consider rooming together again; 3) hate each other more than *Survivor*'s Kelly and Sue. To those fearing loneliness above all else, the first might seem the ideal situation for a college freshman, but even it has its disadvantages. Just ask Siamese twins.

Triple (one to three rooms; usually two). Bad luck comes in threes . . . 'nuff said. Almost inevitably, your waking hours will be spent in demolition derby–style bonding, competing for the favor of the most well-liked musketeer.

Quad+ (three to four rooms; probably three). Frat houses are the only places you can find such suites on some campuses, but if you've got the option, go for it. Big rooms tend to be noisier and messier than smaller ones, but when it comes to the bonding scene, you're set. You're almost bound to like at least *one* of your roommates, and even if you don't, you may be able to snag one of their proto-friends when they visit the room. By the same token, you're likely to detest at least one of your bedbuddies as well, but in a big suite there'll be ample opportunity to avoid him or her.

Personal Habits

You may think you're flexible, but how do you feel about sleeping with the lights on every night while your nocturnal roommate plans garbage can conquests and other raccoonesque diversions? Similarity in personal habits is more crucial than you think. But before you provide a "cheers and jeers" guide to your tastes in music, pizza consumption (crust first?), and lava lamps, remember that colleges' interest in your life is limited. Confine your remarks on the questionnaire to the following topics:

Sleeping habits. If you're a morning person at home, you're probably going to stay one at college; it's just that "A.M." will now be used to describe anything before dinner. If you're "late" at home, get a pet bat and prepare to become nocturnal; if you're a swimmer, learn the sleep-stroke because you're not going to get many z's before predawn practice. The questions about sleeping behavior are fairly straightforward, but if your schedule is rigid, if you require a lot of sleep (more than seven hours per night), or if you have trouble getting to sleep (overhead lights and Eminem are a problem), you'll want to emphasize your desire to room with someone of similar habits.

What, me messy? The jury's still out on whether, if you're a reform-minded pig, you should claim to be neat in order to be assigned someone who will force you to tidy the sty. Change is possible, certainly, but if it doesn't happen for you, you may drive your roommate bananas. If you're a die-hard oinker, it still may be in your interest to attract a cleaner roommate—provided you're willing to sacrifice a potential friendship. Less mess from him or her means more room for yours. There's less ambiguity about course of action if you're a neat freak: Say so, in no uncertain terms! People, whether innocently or for the devious reasons suggested above, tend to claim to be cleaner than they are. If order's really a passion with you, don't conceal your ardor.

Social atmosphere. As we suggested in the section on special dorms, the choice between a quiet environment and a loud one can be tough. Peace is a valuable commodity, but it's easy to get the blues freshman year, and there's a tendency to feel that you're falling behind anytime you're not with people. Besides, quiet types aren't always the easiest to get along with—who wants to haul out earphones every time you want the volume above 2? On the other hand, though a social room will allow you to meet lots of people, if you sign yourself up as a party animal you may find your sleep disturbed by activities more bestial than you imagined.

Speaking the Language: The Roommate Questionnaire

So you've decided what you want in a room and roommate(s); now it's time to spit it out. In general, straightforwardness is sufficient, but there are a few traps into which the unwary can fall. You'll be okay as long as you realize that the dean in charge of housing at every college speaks a slightly aberrant dialect. Witness the following examples, taken from our friends' experiences, of what can be lost in translation:

You write:

"I guess I wouldn't *mind* rooming with a smoker, as long as he doesn't do it in the room constantly."

They read:

"I have invested all my lawnmowing money in R. J. Reynolds, and plan to compete for the part of the Marlboro Man when this self-tanning cream has aged my skin sufficiently. See you at the auditions in '08!!!"

"My friends call me 'Friendly Sue,' I guess because I'm always so *bubbly!* Gosh, I think I could get along with *anyone!*"

"I've never roomed with an ex-con, and would like to."

"I'm what you'd call an individual, and I like it when the people around me are, too."

"Down, homophobia! I'll be the third in a triple with that lesbian couple."

"Music is my passion. As some hearts hearken to romance, some to nature, and some to religion, so mine to music. As there is no creature on this earth I would harm, there is no note I shun."

"I study best to bagpipes."

Getting Acquainted

Sometime between the Fourth of July and Labor Day, depending on the efficiency of your college's lottery system (er, thoughtful housing officers), you'll get a slip of paper in the mail with your roommate's name, address, phone number, and e-mail address. For a number of reasons—pre-bonding, curiosity, and assignation of refrigerator responsibility, if nothing else—it's probably a good idea to get in touch with the person.

E-mail is safe; the phone is friendlier. However you decide to open communication, it's probably best to avoid displaying your eccentricities, charming as your friends from home may find them. One of us wrote roommates that we were bringing an uncaged, "outgoing" pet frog with us. At the time it seemed like a delightful display of wit, but as weeks passed and no reply arrived, it began to seem more like a proclamation of lunacy. There'll be plenty of time to "be yourself" later; restrictive though it sounds, we counsel restraint, and respect for those who would rather eat amphibians than contemplate living with them. First impressions count for a lot.

Odd but true: Among our friends one of the most burning questions people had about their future roommates concerned sexual orientation. We all resisted the temptation to ask, but one of our roommates did not. It's probably an inappropriate question, and can cause unnecessary worry. With few exceptions (see "They read" on previous page), we've never heard of a situation made unbearable by one roommate's sexuality alone.

Your first contact with your future roommate may be a great success —congratulations! But if you're in a triple+ and think your suite will have more than one bedroom, we'd advise not deciding on the spot to room with the first person you contact no matter how charming his or her phone voice is. Maybe they've just got DJ experience.

Personal compatibility aside, there are some practical matters to make sure to talk about. If your roommate's bringing a full stereo setup, for example, there may not be need or room for you to bring any kind of boom box. Same with printers, too: depending on whether you have the same kind of computer, you may not need more than one. TVs, microwaves, futons, rugs, coat trees, and to a lesser extent, refrigerators are luxuries; lamps, telephones, and answering machines are not. If you're dividing up responsibilities, it may make sense for the person who lives nearer to bring the bulkier items, but if you're planning to go shopping near campus with your parents anyway, it may make no difference.

2
Narrowing the Field: Course Selection

It looked like a phone book, so you tossed it in the general direction of your paper-chewing pit bull. But as shreds began to fly from his jaws, you noticed that not only were they not yellow, but the text fragments wafting your way referred more often to "patriarchy" and "the oppressor" than the average plumbing ad.

Luckily for you, Max started at the back of your course catalog and only tore his way through a couple of graduate-level Women's Studies courses. But in some ways, you wish his canines had done a little more arbitrary pruning, because you're left with a couple of hundred classes from which to choose four or five—and if your school is like most of ours, you've got to make the decision weeks before you even get on campus. You're tempted to turn to tarot cards or, worse, the collective wisdom of your extended family, but in the nick of time you recover your sanity enough to consult the following guide:

Choosing Your Courses

Find out what the requirements are for graduation at your college. You have a lot of time to fulfill them, but if you're unsure what to take, it never hurts to get requirements out of the way. Your college may also have freshman-specific requirements to take into account.

If your college has a foreign language requirement that your projected placement test score will not exempt you from, and if you plan to fulfill it by taking the same language you took in high school, begin to do so first semester. If you wait, your memory of the *plus-que-parfait* will be even foggier.

Keep in mind that foreign language courses, particularly those in East Asian languages, are among the most difficult, though social, classes at many colleges (and you may have to contend not only with a new alphabet, but with near-native speakers who are in the class primarily to learn the language's written form). Meetings can be as frequent as five times a week—sometimes even twice in a single day. Constant vocab quizzes. *Mama mia!*

In other departments, too, you may find that the introductory courses tend to be offered first semester, followed by intermediate companions in the spring which require the intro course as a prerequisite. Having said that, however, there's no need to confine yourself to introductory survey-style classes; many interesting, focused courses have no prerequisites, particularly in humanities fields.

Not only are many courses offered only in alternate semesters, but some are offered only in alternate years. Junior year might be a long time to wait for a course crucial to your studies; plan ahead and consider taking the course now.

If you are even remotely considering going premed, begin taking a couple of the courses—basic chemistry, perhaps a math course—right away. In addition to getting you on track—see warning above about the timing of introductory courses—and ensuring that you'll be ready to take the MCAT by the summer after junior year at the latest, taking premed courses first semester can actually be a bonding experience. The introductory classes tend to be large and freshman-full, and many departments encourage collaboration on problem sets. Even if you end up bagging med school, the courses will probably still fulfill distribution requirements.

If you won't be getting a start on fulfilling reqs by taking premed courses, it's a good idea to do so by taking other introductory courses. You've thought from toddlerdom that you wanted to major in astro-

The Premed Track

Pre-law has no official or even unofficial requirements; other majors or pre-professional programs vary from school to school; but med schools are very consistent in their demands. If you're even vaguely considering med school, you might as well jump on the track now while lots of your dormmates and friends will be doing so; at a minimum, you'll fulfill some science distribution reqs for graduation. Most people take inorganic chemistry, math and conceivably physics (depending on whether you want to actually major in science) freshman year. Here's what you have to look forward to, in all:

Two semesters, inorganic chemistry.
Two semesters, organic chemistry.
Two minutes, physical chemistry.
Two semesters, biology.
Two semesters, physics.
One semester, mathematics.
One semester, English.

physics, but a course you take to fulfill distribution requirements may prove that your true interest is in the study of Zoroastrian burial rites. It's better to hear the call of the dead first semester than fourth.

Having said that, don't worry too much about majors at this point. Your school probably won't ask you to declare until the end of sophomore year, and even after that it's generally easy to switch.

Register for one or two more courses than you plan to take, if possible. Attend all of them for the first week, checking out their workload, professor, size, and exam schedule. Drop those that don't grab you, or—attention *E.R.* fans and barflies—those with Friday paper deadlines.

No matter how many Nobel Prizes you plan to garner by the end of freshman year, don't overload first semester. If your college recommends taking four classes, don't take five; if taking organic chemistry, multivariable calculus, introductory Chinese, and a graduate seminar

Choosing the Appropriate Level

If the course catalog lists prerequisites only in terms of other college courses, it's pretty hard to know what to do. If you've taken achievement tests or APs, these may help you to place yourself; otherwise, you can call the appropriate department for advice or try to hold off making a firm selection until you've been able to take a placement test in the fall. If such a test can get you out of requirements, it's certainly in your interest, lame as it sounds, to study for it. If you might want to jump ahead to a fairly high level of the subject, also bring high school notebooks to school to refresh your memory. If you decide to stay at a lower level than your score allows you, you'll still have that option.

Course difficulty varies with the school, but for rough-and-ready figuring, assume that a college course moves about twice as fast as a high school one—three years of high school German, then, would prepare you for the fourth-semester course at college. Sometimes rather than take such a course, you may want to take an accelerated version of a lower-level course; accelerated introductory chemistry, say, if you had a year of AP chemistry in high school.

If you're shaky on a subject integral to your intended major, it's probably in your interest to retake it in college.

on *Ulysses* sounds like a piece of cake, a few weeks of *kanji* and polymers will banish all thoughts of Duncan Hines. As one of our friends found out, it's a lot easier to fail college courses than high school ones. Not only that, but bonding requires all the free time you can devote to it. James Joyce isn't going anywhere, but if you don't watch out, your dormmates may make travel plans that don't include you.

Some colleges offer special only-for-freshmen classes; if yours does, seriously consider taking one, even if it requires application. Not only are such courses often on interesting, offbeat topics, but they provide a good way of meeting people outside your dorm. If you go to a large university, you'll especially prize these seminars' intimate settings.

Along these same lines, try to achieve balance in your schedule as a whole—of large and small classes, science and humanities classes, and, of course, meeting times. Sure, it's cool to have every weekend last three days—as you sometimes can arrange to do by choosing classes that don't meet on Fridays or Mondays—but if it means you'll be taking notes from ten till two every Tuesday and Thursday, it may not be worth it. Four classes in a row was no problem in high school, but in college, for some reason, it's less than fun (hey, you're getting older).

If the course catalog (check online for updated syllabi, also) somehow provides information on final exam times, take that into consideration. If an interesting course has its exam the same day as another course you're taking, or if its exam falls at the end of the period, that's not necessarily a reason to turn your back on it, but it's a disadvantage you should keep in mind. The same goes for midterms and paper deadlines, if they are indicated at this stage; if not, the dates will be on the syllabus you get on the first day of class and you can shuffle classes then if you like.

It's important that you consider seriously your course selection now, but keep in mind this statement, which also applies to college life in general: Everything Is Negotiable. If, when you arrive in the fall, you hear about an incredible class that you'd passed over in the catalog, try going to the professor and wheedling your way in—tell him or her of your interest, say that you're considering majoring in the department (even if you aren't, you may be by the time the class ends). By the same token, if you hear from several sources that a class you've registered for is terrible, either drop it cold or find some excuse to—athletic practice, your job, the schedule of your sacrificial obligations, etc.

Remedial Reading

Even after you've memorized the above advice, you may find it difficult to apply; course descriptions are written in a code that's a bit of a chore to crack. Luckily, we've done it for you. We take the following synopsis as an example:

Dead Poets Society–*like*
attempt to get in with
students

Fairly
high-level course

indicates there is a
second half to the
course; check whether
you need to take "a"
to take "b" (which
could be better)

Agricultural Sciences 110a. New Techniques of
Corn Cultivation

Professor "Pop" Prieb

grammar and lan-
guage error, sug-
gesting your status
as a non-speaker
of English should
not keep you
from an A

may suggest he has
personal agenda

Course examines the biological bases of corn re-
production, including recently developed "micro-
wave-ready" strains. Moves to discussion of irrigation
and fertilization options, culminating in demonstra-
tion of how to turn that dod-blasted lawn of your
neighbor's into ingredients for the best whiskey this
side of Oscaloosa!

say…who gave
this guy his Ph.D.?
Redenbacher
University?

Still thinks Prohibition
is in effect; don't ask to
use his bathroom when
he has a class dinner or
he may think you're FBI

M, W, F, 5:30 A.M. In the field. Labs (2x/wk.) to be
arranged. Exam: none.

"Pop" probably
hails from
Oscaloosa, and
favors natives

TOO
EARLY

can't hurt

What?! Along with
three lectures? This
course is only for
the die-hard crop
analyst

3
The Ultimate
Packing List

You've been to slumber parties, you've been to camp, you may even have studied abroad, but you've never really moved your *life* outside a fifty-foot radius of your parents' toolbox/pantry/linen closet/medicine cabinet. Okay, so your parents' house is essentially Wal-Mart compared to what you're moving into.

You need stuff . . . and if you bring it, in addition to living in the lap of luxury yourself you will be the toast of the dorm (see chapter 8 for additional apartment-specific items). Everybody knows the guy who thought to bring scissors, let alone a nice lug wrench. There are probably stores near your campus, but they may not be good ones, and why start paying now when you can mooch stuff off your parents (or their credit card) before you leave?

For Your Closet

Of course, only you can be the judge of what and how many clothes you'll need. Depending on whether you consider a quick wallow in a puddle a wash, you may be able to get by with only one or two pairs of jeans and a few Hanes Beefy-T's. College *is* casual, and closets tend to be tiny and shared with roommates; the tradeoff is that the more

Advice for Those Planning
Arctic Expeditions
(i.e., trips to schools above the Mason-Dixon line)

No, honey, that li'l halter top ain't gonna pull you through January in Massachusetts, 'lessn your idea of fighting the freshman fifteen is to sacrifice a couple of appendages to frostbite. You're going to need some new clothes—depending on the location of your school and whether you're likely to transfer southward by October, perhaps a whole new wardrobe. While it may be easier to wait to buy until you arrive at school, the muffler trade in Hot Springs being sluggish (and few Copperhead schools offering winter clothing grants to displaced Dixies), you don't want to wait *too* long. The first snowfall can come suddenly, and you may want to get a start on your shopping while your parents' credit cards are still within grabbing distance. Here's what you'll need:

Winter jacket or coat. Jackets—the warmest ones are covered in Gore-Tex and/or lined with Thinsulate—run about $75–$200 and are available in sporting goods stores and through catalogs like Lands' End and L.L. Bean. If you want something more formal, unlined leather keeps you warm through the 40s; lined leather or wool should do you into the 20s. Below that, you'll want a warm jacket for any length outside.

Boots. Some degree of water resistance is really important, but that doesn't necessarily mean rubber; leather and synthetics can be treated with sprays or creams. Sidewalks in college towns aren't exactly groomed like Park Avenue; if you have to choose between rugged and stylish, go for the former.

Gloves or mittens. As above, Gore-Tex and Thinsulate are the best; leather on the outside is great if you'll be driving. Mittens are warmer than gloves; gloves let you do more.

Long johns. Available in a host of colors, not just silver. Useful for bedtime when the dorm gets cheap with the heat, skiing down the library steps, snow angels.

clothes you have, the less often you'll have to do laundry and/or attract neighborhood dogs with your aroma.

We list here just a few of the items you might forget:

formal outfits or dresses from high school, if you'd ever consider
wearing them again
hangers (including special ones for skirts and pants, if desired; ones
that hold five skirts or pairs of pants at once are especially good
for small closets)
jewelry boxes, shoe boxes, crates for storage
laundry bag (one with straps so you can carry it like a backpack is
nice; the plastic crates are good but take up a lot more room in
your closet)
laundry detergent
mirror, handheld or standup; full-length if you need one (there
probably won't be a mirror of any kind in your bedroom)
pajamas
fold-up rack for drying clothes
raincoat, shoes that can handle water (you'll be walking between
classes rain or shine)
Rollerblades, if you have them (good for transportation and less susceptible than bikes to theft)
shoe polish
slippers (dorm floors don't tend to be clean)
socks, underwear, hose—good stocks of each (may not be available
cheaply nearby; you want to be able to wait a good two weeks at
least between laundry loads)
umbrella

For Your Desk

Stock these essentials and your desk will be the nexus of the entire
dorm, scantily clad members of the opposite sex circling it like fish in
heat, ready to do anything to seduce you into lending them a couple
of, mmmm, rubber bands. . . .

address book
batteries
calculator
duct tape (useful for taping
    over cords; also for decora-
    tion, see chapter 9)
envelopes
extension cords, including
    one for your phone and/or
    modem/Ethernet adapter
flashcards/note cards
flashlight
floppy disks, zip disks
folders
glue/glue stick
hammer
highlighters
ink cartridges/toner if you
    have a laser printer
legal pads/notebooks
light bulbs
markers
matches/lighter
nails
needle, thread, and extra buttons
packing tape, Scotch tape
paper clips
pencil sharpener
pens, pencils
Post-Its/tabs
poster gum
power strips and plug adapters (three-prong to two),
outlet expanders
rolls of quarters for laundry
rubber bands
safety pins
scissors (make sure not to pack them in a box—you'll need them to
    open your boxes)

Flexibility

Too cheap to buy posters?
Alternate uses for poster gum:

* "no-cal" chewing gum
* plug for mouth of gabby
  roommate/pet
* to make a Tupperware
  o'ramen serve eight instead
  of one, shape into cubes
  and toss in as matzo balls
* your way to say "no more
  tears" when your friend's
  Silly Putty is misplaced
* drain stopper

screwdriver/tool set (even if you're not Mr./Ms. Handy, you
    may need it for assembling furniture)
stamps
stapler, staples, staple remover
string
surge suppressor for computer (regular power strips don't
    protect)
Swiss Army knife (also very useful for opening boxes)
tape measure
thumbtacks
Wite-out
wrapping paper, ribbon
wrench

For Your Bookshelf

If you didn't hold a ceremonial burning of your high school texts,
notes, and papers after graduation, you may want to bring them—or
at least those pertaining to placement tests you'll be required to take,
or courses you'll be taking first semester. Just to be safe, you may also
want to tote along your high school transcript and copies of your AP
and Achievement Test score reports, if you have them; you may need
them in order to place out of various requirements. Since stationery
supplies are probably cheaper at home than near campus, throw in
notebooks along with your academic antiques if you'll be driving to
school; otherwise the money you spend on shipping might exceed the
money you save at the store.

In addition, unless you're Johnny Mnemonic you'll need some basic
reference books. Here's what's worked for us:

book of quotations
dictionary
foreign language dictionary (if you intend to continue study)
grammar guide (Strunk and White's *The Elements of Style* is succinct;
    Fowler's *Modern English Usage* is for the hard-core sentence
    diagrammer)
guide to writing research papers with rules for footnotes and
    bibliography (the Modern Language Association publishes a

small one; the *Chicago Manual of Style* is larger, and its system of documentation is also widely accepted)
The Real Freshman Handbook
thesaurus

Besides these, it may be in the interests of your wallet to bring along some of the books you studied in high school classes, even if they are a bit of a pain to lug. Who, after all, wants to pour more pennies into the coffers of the already flush Hemingway estate? One copy of *Great Expectations,* as far as we're concerned, is already one too many. For you slaves to distribution requirements, as well as prospective English majors, here's a list of some other academic relics you either can't or wouldn't want to own in duplicate:

Books you don't want to buy twice

Austen, *Pride and Prejudice*
The Bible
Brontë, *Jane Eyre*
Dreiser, *Sister Carrie*
Du Bois, *The Souls of Black Folk*
Eliot, George, *Middlemarch*
Eliot, T. S., *The Waste Land*
Emerson, *Essays*
Fitzgerald, *The Great Gatsby*
Foucault, everything
Gilman, *The Yellow Wallpaper*
Hawthorne, *The Scarlet Letter*
Homer, *Iliad* and *Odyssey*
Hurston, *Their Eyes Were Watching God*
James, Henry, *The Turn of the Screw, The Portrait of a Lady,* and *The Ambassadors*
James, William, *The Varieties of Religious Experience* and "The Will to Believe"

Kant, *A Critique of Pure Reason*
Kingsolver, *The Bean Trees*
Melville, *Moby-Dick* and *Billy Budd*
Milton, *Paradise Lost*
Morrison, *Beloved*
The Norton Anthology of . . . (anything)
Shakespeare, everything
Steinbeck, *The Grapes of Wrath*
Thoreau, *Walden* and "Civil Disobedience"
Tocqueville, *Democracy in America*
Twain, *Huckleberry Finn*
Washington, *Up from Slavery*
Whitman, *Leaves of Grass*
Woolf, "A Room of One's Own"
Wright, *Native Son*

For Your "Kitchen"

Some dorms actually have kitchens on every floor; if yours does, it's probably stocked with enough wares to at least make some ramen. If yours doesn't, you're going to have to be more creative.

Depending upon the strength of your ties with the culinary underworld, some of these items may be superfluous. Utensils and dishes can easily be smuggled from the cafeteria and returned for cleaning when crust makes fork indistinguishable from spoon. But if you're into clean living of all kinds, make like the Iron Chef and be equipped:

broom
coffee mug with lid
corkscrew, bottle opener, can opener (come with many Swiss Army knives)
dishes, cups, bowls, plates
dishwashing liquid
dustpan or Dustbuster
microwave
paper towels
refrigerator
shot glasses ("for paper clips")
sponge/scrub brush for washing dishes
tin foil
tub for dishes to dry in (can double as a serving bowl)
Tupperware
utensils—knife, fork, spoons
optional: coffee maker (doubles as a water heater), plug-in kettles and hotplates, blender

For the Bathroom

If you're like one of our freshman dormmates, you'll be adjourning to this little room for about one hour in every four, the exact timing of your visits vaguely related to the lunar schedule and/or the quality of Letterman's stupid pet tricks. And since, unfortunately for you, the demand for scientific study of shower duration is limited, you'll want to provide for your amusement as well as hygiene:

- aspirin or other painkiller
- Band-Aids
- cold medicine, if you use it
- contact lens or eyeglass cleaner, holder
- cotton balls/Q-tips
- cough drops
- cup for brushing teeth
- Gameboy
- hairdryer/curling iron (a "quiet" hairdryer is really nice for not waking up roommates)
- Kleenex
- knitting
- lotion
- magazine rack, subscriptions
- makeup
- mouthwash
- nail clipper, file
- personal flotation device
- plastic shower caddy or two; get one that you can hang if necessary
- razor
- roach motel
- shave cream
- shampoo/conditioner/gel/spray
- soap
- soap dish
- shower sandals
- tampons/pads
- terry cloth bathrobe and/or several *distinctive*-looking towels (you don't want someone to take yours by mistake and leave you in the buff); extra towels are nice to have around for guests
- Tums
- *TV Guide*
- tweezers

For Bedside

Sure, it's possible to walk across the room in the middle of the night to grab a missing essential, but if you're like us, getting out of bed once in twenty-four hours is hard enough. Here's what you'll need to equip yourself for a night of comfort and rest:

alarm clock
chamber pot
condoms
handcuffs
Kleenex/t.p.
light
lozenges
smokes
3D glasses

For Your Pocket

And they say you can't take it with you . . .

calling card
cash, traveler's checks
driver's license, social security card, etc.
key chain (one with a pouch for an ID card is especially nice)
watch

For Your Room/Life in General

We'll have more to say about furnishings in the chapter on room decorating, but keep these items in mind as you do your pre-departure shopping:

air mattress, if you don't happen to have one
bedding—in party-proof dark colors, and probably extra-long,
    depending on the size of your school's beds (check ahead); two
    sets of sheets is nice, and essential if you'll be using a linen
    service instead of doing your own laundry; also useful for guests

board games, videos, if you are so inclined

bulletin board

CD stands, tape racks

computer equipment (see chapter 4)

desk lamp

doormat (newspaper works)

halogen lamp (nicer to have than the average floor lamp because it has a dimmer switch and is also easily disassembled for storage)

iron, ironing board (see chapter 16)

mattress pad/cover (keeps fitted sheets from sliding off those vinyl mattresses and protects you from the aftereffects of 500 previous inhabitants)

pillows, including back pillows for sitting on the floor or on your bed (some dorms provide bed pillows; most don't)

posters

sleeping bag (in case you visit or have visitors)

stereo/boom box

TV/VCR/DVD player

vase

wastebasket

4
Word!
Computers

There are options. You can go to the computer lab, which is likely to have lots of machines, for all of your needs; you can buy a computer but use your school's printer (printing is free up to a certain number of pages per term at many schools); you can upgrade or use part of a configuration from home, if it's out-of-date; you can also look into renting or buying a used model from another student or a place like Computer Renaissance.

If there's a time to buy a new computer, however, it *is* the first year of college. It's extremely time-saving and fun, if not absolutely essential, to have your own set-up, and if you buy new now, it will probably stay current at least through the end of school. Some colleges "give" (as part of what tuition covers) computers to incoming students; most others have special technology loan programs over and above regular financial aid to help you buy. In making your decisions, consider . . .

What to Buy
The Great Computer Debate, Round One: *PC* vs. *Macintosh*

Design. PCs are undoubtedly more common, but if you have an eye for style, the iMac and its siblings can be tempting mistresses. The PCs, like Designer Impostors, keep imitating, but they never quite get it right.

Ease of Operation. Once again, Windows was modeled on the Macintosh operating system; Microsoft captured the look and feel, but Macs are still friendlier and are favored by people who work a lot with graphics, in particular.

Expense. Computers vary so much in capabilities that it's hard to generalize usefully, but PCs, simply because there's more competition within the group, tend to be a little cheaper. It is certainly possible to find reasonable Macs, however.

Compatibility. The biggie on the side of PCs. Since there are more PCs in the world than Macs, there's more software available, and it's easier to exchange files with friends, colleagues, etc. Having said that, most college computer labs have Macs, and many printers, Epson for example, are Mac- and PC-compatible. Sharing files is certainly not a frequent necessity, and translation programs are available.

The Great Computer Debate, Round Two: *Desktop* vs. *Portable*

In this contest, as was not the case in the last one, the differences are extremely obvious. The only thing laptops have going for them is portability, and from this great advantage stem all of their disadvantages. Portables are generally more expensive; more difficult to use (smaller screen, cramped keyboard); more vulnerable to destruction through dropping or beverage immersion (although some seem built to survive anything); and more expensive to maintain, unless you are always able to plug them in (some classrooms are modern; some have plugs only along the walls of rooms). Most important, portables are extremely vulnerable to theft, as the weekly reports of their disappearance from libraries, lobbies, and benches in our campus gazettes testify.

Whether the benefit outweighs the costs depends on the way you work. At this point it may be hard to judge which style will best suit your study habits and situation, but think about the way you studied in high school. If you take classes that demand a lot of writing, are easily distracted, and will be living in an environment full of distractions (i.e., any freshman dorm), a portable may be your savior. But if you work mainly at home and/or are clumsy, you may value the hardiness and expandability of desktops.

There is, of course, the PDA/folding keyboard option for those who don't want to invest in a laptop for the purposes, at least, of classroom note-taking (see "PDA, <u>Don't</u> Go Away," page 31).

And the Judges Say . . .

We've obviously, at great personal sacrifice, refrained from subliminal persuasion, despite our strong feelings/vested interests. And we'll continue to be unbiased; both bouts have well-matched opponents, and in the end the call you make depends more on personal preferences and priorities than on any inherent qualities of the machines. But whichever side you give the trophy (your money) to, keep in mind the following things that we average Joe users have found significant:

Memory. As trash-heaving capability is to a potential hubby, so is memory to a computer: the number-one item consumers should look for. Unless you'll be running *no* applications besides Hooked on Phonics, you're going to need all the memory you can get. Yes, it's possible to have memory added later—either by a professional or by a program —but such upgrades have their problems. One of our computers had a prolonged hospital stay following RAM doubling, and one of our friend's machines never recovered from a professional's insertion of an extra chip.

CD-R. Pretty standard on new computers; may well save you money in the long term.

DVD. Not exactly academic, but . . .

Ethernet card or modem. You'll need one of the two if you expect

Averting Catastrophe

There's nothing like stopping for a little drink while you rattle away, but down your brewskie or Minute Maid *away* from your computer. We're all for ergonomics, but orange pulp makes a poor lubricant.

Backup, backup, backup. Sure, it was just a joke when your friends were positioning you for a shot at the Grand Canyon, but a few broken bones shouldn't trash your trust for good. The power can go out, viruses can spread, files can be damaged for no reason, your computer can freeze temporarily or for days, hard drives can crash for good, so back yours up regularly. Floppies, zip disks, and e-mailing it to yourself all work.

to access the Internet from your room. Before you decide which one to buy, find out whether your school has in-room network or cable hookups. If it does, go for the Ethernet card (you can either buy a computer with one pre-installed, or buy the card separately); modems tie up the phone line. If you plan to be living off-campus freshman year or soon after, the Ethernet card may not be worth the investment unless you plan to be using a cable modem then.

Warranty. It's not a bad idea to buy coverage in addition to that coming automatically with your purchase: late nights of caffeinated beverages, dorm parties, and the accidents possible when carrying laptops around campus all make the risk of harm to your computer higher than it would otherwise be. Make sure the service plan is well-designed for where your college is located (if the coverage comes from somewhere out-of-town, make sure the company pays for shipping, etc.— see Where to Buy on next page).

Printer?

As mentioned above, laser printing in the lab is free on many campuses; it's at the very least available for a small fee for those important papers. You don't absolutely need a printer; it's more a matter of convenience in having one. Having one at home makes it easier to print drafts, receive faxes, and print off the Internet; it's especially useful for those late-night paper-writing sessions humanities majors are prone to.

If you're a science type and won't be doing much writing, your need will be less.

Laser vs. Ink Jet

Expense. Ink jets are cheaper (starting around $100), although lasers have come down to only several hundred. Ink-jet cartridges are relatively expensive (about $20 each, last 4–6 months with average use); toner for laser printers is more, but needs to be changed less frequently. There's evidence that laser printing per page over the life of the machine is not much more than that for ink-jet printing; it all depends on your time frame.

Quality. Ink-jet quality is certainly sufficient for the average paper; laser is necessary for term papers and important job applications. Ink-jet print has a tendency to bleed on exposure to water (you'll have to leave your papers behind when you go singing in the rain).

Speed. The slow speed of ink jets is probably unimportant for most students; if you'll be doing an absolute ton of writing and are a draft junkie, a laser may really save you some time.

Maintenance. Neither is terribly difficult, but lasers have a more complicated mechanism so are slightly more complicated to maintain.

Where to Buy

Your options may be limited by the location of your home and of your college, but there are six possible places or people from whom you can buy a computer. We list them, with pros of purchasing from each:

The manufacturer. If you know exactly what you want and if retailers aren't carrying it, this may be the way to go.

Online through a retailer. May be cheapest and may give you the option of mailing your computer in for maintenance, which can be an advantage if you'll be studying in a relatively rural area.

A retailer in your home city. If it's important to you to try out a computer before you buy it and/or your parents won't be accompanying you to school, this can work. There is the problem, however, of transportation if you'll be flying to school (see page 30).

A retailer in your college's town (assuming the town is large enough). Buying from a store close to your school means you avoid the expense of shipping, and the risk of damage in transit: UPS paid for a new monitor when it broke one of our roommate's, but it couldn't pay for the trouble it cost her. It also may be easier to get service through your warranty, although online and national retailers should give you the ability to get maintenance near your campus.

Your college. It's basically the same deal as buying from the CompUSA across town, except the maintenance facility is even closer, and the fabled student discounts may actually be for real.

Another student. If you don't insist on buying the newest model, or if you're cool with the possibility of being computerless for a few weeks, watch for signs around campus or postings online advertising sales of used models. They're always cheaper than new ones, but for good reason: the warranty has probably run out, and the hard drive may be, like James Dean in a red 'vette, spoiling for a crash.

How to Transport

Items like ink-jet printers, keyboards, and even the computer itself can sometimes be packed in luggage or carried with you on an airplane, and this method of transportation can save you money and time. But keep in mind that suitcases are often handled as roughly as boxes, and you'll have an easier time collecting for damages if you've shipped your machine insured.

To protect your computer, use the original boxes and packaging materials, if you have them. If you don't, you'll probably want to have a professional packager, such as Mail Boxes Etc., do the job. Make sure to insure your computer for its full value.

Troubleshooting

Hey, amigo, we've all been there. You've got a paper due tomorrow and your screen goes blank, Super Clock blares the hallelujah chorus every quarter hour even though you set it on Van Halen, your print monitor is giving you some weak line about "downloading font: Casablanca." You crack open your owner's manual only to discover you got the pig Latin version.

We'd love to give you the answers to all your woes, but unfortunately we don't know them; problems are too specific to given machines and conditions for us to offer any kind of comprehensive guide. What we can do, however, is pass along the general approaches to troubleshooting that have served us well:

If your computer hasn't totally crashed, you might try opening the "read me" file that came with your system's software. Sometimes there's info in there that doesn't appear in the owner's manual, and sometimes it's in English.

If the problem is with a specific program, you might try just re-installing it from the master disk.

If it's just a matter of slowness or the occasional freeze, memory problems may be the culprit. Try going through—either trashing or putting on disk—files and applications that you don't use much; this may do it.

If the problem is too serious for such puny measures to fix, your best bet is probably to pretend you're dealing with a corpse, i.e., don't touch anything and get help. In most dorms there is someone who knows his (or her) bytes. Luckily for the success of your all-nighter, this person is usually nocturnal; on the downside, he/she may be only slightly less reclusive than the average bat. Insider's locating technique: cut power to the dorm and see who's spoiling for some time in the straitjacket.

If your unpopularity or the fact that you're going to Oberlin prevents you from finding in-dorm aid, you may consider posting a request for help. There's a newsgroup for every breed of problem (printer screw-ups, Macintosh application failures, etc.), and it's important that you post your SOS on the right one or it will yield no helping hand. Surf around, especially on the waves made by big universities' computer societies, until you find the link-ups to the appropriate newsgroups.

But before you post, netiquette and your own self-interest dictate that you try to figure out exactly what the problem is. If you had a couple of applications running when the problem occurred, try running each of them separately. Try to remember what you were doing when things went wrong, whether you've made any changes in your computer usage recently, etc. Give the net-nurses as much relevant information as possible.

America's Online

Choosing an Internet Service Provider

Most colleges have Ethernet, free modem dial-in, or both, but some are imposing limits and/or charges on these as a result of music and software downloads, etc. overloading the network. Some colleges, for example, limit the number of hours a student can be online during peak hours, but provide access at other times completely free and without restrictions. Learn about your college's policies so you can adapt to them if necessary.

Even with restrictions, the college system is probably going to be the most economical. So far, the free ISPs have been a disappointment, plagued by poor service and irritating memory-consuming ads.

The Slings and Arrows of Outrageous E-mail

Before you send any remotely personal messages, check to make sure you have the correct address/spelling of your friends' names. The e-mail addresses "dschaeffer" and "dschaffer" differ by only one letter, but that one depression of the keyboard is the difference between a private communication and a more public proclamation of roommate problems. We've been on the receiving end of misdirected messages; don't be on the sending.

Don't send highly personal or highly gossipy e-mail messages at all. You really never know who's going to give you a friendly "guess who" in the computer lab, who's going to explore your files after you forget to log out, and which roommate of yours is going to crack into your account for a lark, the fun turning ugly when he finds you've written light verse comparing him to Little Nicky.

Change your passwords for e-mail, AOL, and important sites that have personal/credit information attached to them every 6 months to 1 year.

Don't use something completely obvious, like your initials, name, ID number, or telephone number.

If you receive a bizarre, shocking, or infuriating e-mail message, don't start whetting your knife; instead, try to find out whether it's a hoax. A girl at one of our schools received a message, supposedly from her roommate, saying that she was a lesbian and in love with her, and they needed to talk. Luckily for the "loved one," it turned out to be a practical joke, but it cost the two a lot of awkwardness to figure it out.

5
Planes, Trains, & Automobiles:
Transportation

If your college is in the neighborhood, you're in the clear—just put the saddlebags on Fido and giddyap. But if you got to make tracks a little farther, you're going to have to depend upon one of those newfangled motorized vehicles. It's likely that the car will be your engine of choice; not only is it cheaper (especially if the whole family's accompanying you), but you'll have less to worry about when it comes to getting your Lego collection settled in your new abode. If your college is far away, however, you may have to fly there, and fly home for some holidays. But before we give you the run-down on specific modes of transportation, here are some things to keep in mind no matter how you decide to travel:

If you are participating in a special orientation trip *before* move-in, consider having your parents come out at the *end* of your trip rather than at the beginning. Dorms will probably not be open a week before freshmen's official arrival date; your parents will be of more help to you during actual move-in, and this way by the time you really have to say goodbye to them and their credit cards, you'll have already bonded with your fellow crunchies over s'mores, porcupine sightings, Lyme disease, and more.

Provided you aren't opting for the former, plan to arrive in town the night before dorms open, if you and your family can afford to spend the night somewhere. Believe it or not, if the dorm opens at eight, it will be hopping by ten past, and the choice bedrooms/closets/desk locations will have been staked out by quarter after.

If your family plans to stay a few days to help you unpack, consider opting for accommodations a little ways from the campus. Motels in the immediate vicinity of colleges sometimes jack up the prices for high-traffic occasions, such as freshman move-in and parents' weekend.

Make your motel reservations *well* in advance, or other eager parents may crowd you out.

Them's the basics. Once you've chosen your mode of transportation, you'll be ready for the more specific advice we offer in the following sections, the first on plane travel and the second on road trips of all durations.

Travel by Plane

First they canceled our flight. Then they lost our luggage, putting us in mortal fear of having to sleep nude, unwashed, and *without our security corncob* our first night in the dorm! It turned out all right in the end, but it's our mission to see that you avoid our travails completely. If you've traveled a lot before, some of this will be old hat; but even if you've crossed the Atlantic more times than you have fingers, you're probably not used to having your life along with you. Here, then, are the basics, both for your initial trip and for subsequent ones:

Making Your Arrangements

Jimi the Volkswagen van is always rarin' to go, but jets require a little more notice. Make your reservations at least a few weeks ahead of time, even if you're not sure about the date you want for the return trip. For $50 to $75 you can always change your return reservation. Once you've picked your dates, you're ready to . . .

Work through a travel agent, if you and your parents aren't especially familiar with the online travel sites. The airline, not you, pays them, and they can save you hundreds of dollars by keeping an eye peeled for fare wars and special offers.

Check the Web. Individual airlines each have their own Web site showing schedules and fares, including special "cybersaver" and last-minute deals. Www.travelocity.com (also accessible through Yahoo! Travel) sorts through available flights for your destination and dates and ranks prices and airlines; www.expedia.com works similarly. Oddly enough, availability and prices sometimes differ significantly from those listed on the airlines' own individual Web sites. Www.priceline .com allows you to name your desired price and date of travel and see if airlines will match it; if they do, you may end up traveling any time between 6 A.M. and 10 P.M. and will not be able to cancel or change the ticket.

If possible, get on a morning or afternoon flight so if it's canceled, you'll be able to catch an alternate flight the same day.

If you're not concerned with earning frequent flier miles, look into charter flights. If you're willing to fly at slightly odd hours or into more distant airports/terminals of airports, you may be able to save yourself some money. Council Travel, STA, and CTS are among the services offering special tickets/packages for students, sometimes requiring the purchase (for a relatively low fee) of a membership card. These are particularly good, also, for vacation trips to hot college student destinations like Mexico and the Caribbean, and Europe in the summer.

Ask your travel agent about student discounts.

American Express offers credit and charge cards for students that give you special discounts on travel that are not always better than rates available elsewhere, but can be. See www.americanexpress.com/ homepage/personal.shtml.

When making reservations to come home for Thanksgiving or winter vacation, you may want to ignore your college's vacation dates. Consider coming home a day or two before your college officially goes into recess; professors sometimes cancel classes scheduled to meet immediately before vacation, and you may be able to get on less crowded, cheaper flights.

If you must travel on high-volume days, like the Wednesday before Thanksgiving, make it worth your while. A travel agent or an airline representative can tell you which flights are particularly popular, i.e., likely to be overbooked. If you're willing to let yourself be "bumped" and wait a few hours for another flight, you can earn anywhere from $100 to $1,000 worth of air travel.

Have a travel agent arrange your seat assignments when he/she makes your reservations. If you don't, you may not be able to sit with your family.

A little hamsicle is probably not what your nervous stomach will be crying out for at 30,000 feet—remember that when you make your reservation you can order special meals (the vegetarian offering is often a fruit plate) even if you don't actually have special dietary requirements.

If you are traveling alone, find out if your college offers a van service to and from the airport. If such arrangements are not available, or if your college is far from the town you will be flying into, ask your local alumni club for a list of incoming freshmen from your area. You may be able to get reservations on the same flight and share rides.

If your college's town is serviced only by a small airport with very few direct flights, consider renting a car at the nearest major airport and driving the distance rather than flying it. It may actually be cheaper and quicker, depending on how the connections work out, how large a plane serves the route, and how many family members are accompanying you.

Even if your college is in a major city, it may be worthwhile to rent a car. Not only will it allow you to stay in a more distant, cheaper motel, but it will be a great help with move-in. Not all colleges deliver shipped boxes to your dorm; you may have to transport them from a mail center several blocks away. Access to a car will also make it easier to get to discount or department stores, and to transport the lamps/rugs/furnishings you buy. As soon as you're finished acting as an unlicensed moving company, you can return the car at the rental company's midtown drop-off point, which may be nearer than the airport.

Transportation of Belongings

Most airlines only allow you to transport one to two carry-ons and two pieces of luggage to stow. The rule isn't always enforced strictly, and if your kid brother has a poker face, he can pretend that pair of 200-length skis are his. But unless your family tree, twigs and all, is accompanying you on the plane, you're not going to have enough relatives to claim and transport all of your belongings. You're going to have to ship the majority of your stuff.

Although your boxes will be leaving long before you do, it's a good idea to pack your suitcases first, without regard for placement of items, just to see how much they hold; that way you won't be left with a stack of Power Rangers towels and no spare duffels. When you've figured out how much you need to ship, you're ready for . . .

STEP 1. PACKING OF BOXES. Boxes that fold up are nice in some respects—you can stash them behind the bunk bed and reuse them come spring. But for transportation of anything heavier than clothes— books, stationery supplies, cosmetics—booze boxes are your best bet. Not only are they sturdy, but they tend to be a size that fits well in your arms or on a dolly. You can get them for free, but they're in demand; call the liquor store to see when the next shipment will arrive, and plan to get there a few hours later to give employees time to unload.

Line boxes holding delicate items like blouses or electronic equipment with plastic bags.

As you pack, keep a list of what's going in each box. Not only will this allow you to unpack your CD rack before your CDs, but it will help you assign a dollar value to the box when you ship them, and to file an insurance claim should it be lost.

Try to distribute heavy items, like books, among all of your boxes.

Don't ship all of your favorite tapes, sweaters, etc. in the same box.

Where possible, pack cosmetic products unopened. If you must transport partially used plastic bottles and tubes, loosen the lid before packing to squeeze out some of the air. The vacuum effect this creates will make leaks less likely.

Pack all cosmetic products—opened or unopened—in plastic bags, preferably in a different box from clothing. Stray suds wouldn't hurt those tube socks, sure, but how about a cashmere scarf?

STEP 2. SHIPPING. Your box number at school is not necessarily the address you should ship to, and forwarding may anger local mail carriers and delay the arrival of your possessions for as much as a week or two. Before sending that Jack Daniels box through the hands of hostile, thirsty postal workers, call your college to confirm you're shipping to the right place.

Write the mailing address in permanent marker on all of the box's surfaces. Tape over the main address label so it doesn't get ripped off. Write the address on a slip of paper and put it inside the box.

Some schools won't accept boxes until a certain day—so before you skip the fireworks to pack, find out what rules your college has laid down. Boxes shipped UPS ground rate take 5 to 7 business days to reach their destination; plan for your boxes to arrive a few days before you do, but probably no earlier. If your boxes are the first to arrive, they may well be at the back or bottom of the stack and difficult to reach.

"U-Hauling" your boxes to UPS is an option, but pickup is free. If you want to take advantage of the service, you'll need to make arrangements with UPS the day before you want pickup. Finish packing before you call, because the representative you speak with will want to know the dimensions, weight, value, and number of boxes you're shipping.

Insure all of your boxes, especially, but not only, the ones containing particularly expensive items. The $2 it cost one of our friends to insure her computer monitor saved her from a $600 loss when UPS broke it.

If you're shipping items like computers, televisions, or large stereos, consider having a company like Mail Boxes Etc. do it for you; they're professional and have all the plastic peanuts a chimp could ever dream of, plus you can insure yourself. It'll cost you and isn't worth it for the average box, but it's worth it for valuable items.

STEP 3. PACKING FOR PLANE TRAVEL. After putting your life in the hands of a UPS employee, you figure it couldn't get any riskier. Pardner, you just begun. In case you aren't a religious viewer of newsmagazines, we're here to inform you that your suitcases aren't only vulnerable to maiming by baggage handlers, but to theft. Here's what you can do to ensure your belongings' safe and timely arrival:

Pack everything that you will need the first few days of school — sheets, at least one towel, notes to review for placement tests, Kleenex, and enough toiletries to last a few days. No matter how carefully you plan, snafus can send the boxes you ship to Seattle on detours through the Everglades, and you don't want to be without essentials.

Pack irreplaceable items — letters, family jewelry, portraits of Butch as a young schnauzer — in your carry-on, if you must take them to college at all. Also carry on things you must have the first few days of school — key toiletries or medicines, information for registration — in case your luggage is lost temporarily.

Expensive jewelry of any kind should *not* be packed in luggage that's to be stowed. You are often *not* insured against its theft by airline employees, perhaps because its portability makes it so easy to steal.

Carry photographic equipment with you. Luggage that's going into the belly of the plane takes a trip through some powerful radiation that can damage film and even cameras themselves.

Try to use soft-sided luggage, if you can. Storing it generally takes up less space — which will likely be at a premium in your room. Also, expensive, sturdy luggage may protect your belongings, but it tells criminals that something inside is worth protecting.

Similarly, while luggage locks are useful for keeping your bag from popping open in transit, they also advertise that valuables are inside. Besides, if your snazzy suitcase meets a larcenous luggage handler, chances are he can pick the lock anyway.

Pack inexpensive items like underwear, socks, or cosmetic supplies on top—especially if you're using duffels or other bags that a thieving employee could easily unzip for a peek.

Make sure that your suitcases are clearly labeled with your name and address; not only will this help you confirm that you've taken the right bag off the conveyor belt, but it will become especially important if the airline loses your bags and has to run a search for them. If your luggage is especially ordinary looking, you may even consider affixing a more conspicuous sticker/tag/strap (available at travel stores).

Guarding of Belongings

Even if you get your stuff through the hungry jaws of airline staff, you may still face problems at the hands of roving criminals in the baggage claim. Do everything you can to avoid the situation our friend fell into, an hour off the plane and minus one third of his luggage:

Never leave your belongings unattended. Your Samsonite may be like a friend but, unlike some, he isn't voyeuristic; bring him in the handicapped stall with you if you're alone and need to use the bathroom.

If you don't see your luggage on the carousel, take a little walk around the claim area. Sometimes suitcases arrive on earlier flights and are lined up by the back wall or outside the office.

If you still don't see your little valise, you'll have to file a lost luggage claim. In the office behind the carousel, you'll have to present your claim ticket and fill out a form with a description of the item, your name, etc. If the loss was through no fault of your own (if you arrived well in advance of your flight, etc.), the airline's obligated to deliver your luggage to wherever you're staying.

Travel by Car

You thought something was funny when Dad donned his Oscar the Grouch suit and hopped in the trash can after the evening news, rope in hand. Things got even stranger when he strode in triumphantly at three A.M., shook the Hefty hanging at his side, whispered maniacally, "Old Dad trapped himself a coon!" and started to make a hat. But it wasn't until he stopped the first Native American and offered him a couple of beads in exchange for Montana that you realized the truth: Your road trip out to college had become *Lewis and Clark, Part Deux.*

You're sorely tempted to do a little bartering of your own—say, your father for a meal that hasn't been tenderized by tires—but before you decide to go it alone or go back for some friends, take pause. Pontiac pilgrimages, especially long ones, are tricky, and sometimes a couple of musket balls and some spare testosterone, no matter what pelts it's wearing, can put you at an advantage when Mr. Carjacker takes a shine to your vehicle. Whatever you decide, keep in mind the following as you plan your voyage:

With or Without You(r parents)

Join AAA if you haven't already. Membership guarantees you free towing anywhere in the country.

If you don't have a cell phone, consider borrowing/renting one (AAA or another auto club may have information) if your trip will be long.

Order Triptiks and maps from AAA's travel service. AAA can also discuss alternate routes with you, taking into consideration everything from your desire for autobahn-like roads to a hankering to see the eighth wonder of the agricultural world, the Corn Palace in Mitchell, South Dakota. They'll know, too, which roads are under construction and how to avoid them. Mapquest online is very convenient, but doesn't always give such detailed, up-to-date guidance.

If you'll be staying at motels along the way, reserve a room in advance. The last thing you'll want to do after a hard day's drive is scuttle around from Cheap-o-Lodge to Cheap-o-Lodge squinting at Vacancy signs. When you call, make sure to guarantee your room with a credit card, even if you think you'll arrive before six. Who knows what size balls of twine may stand between you and your destination? You wouldn't want to miss great photo ops just to get to the next Motel 6 before six.

If you have more luggage than can be stowed in the trunk, or if your car doesn't have a trunk, bring along a tarp. Don't advertise to vandals that you've got your life in the back seat, or you may find yourself, as one of us did, CD-less in Canada, and driving an Explorer-turned-convertible.

If it's been a while since you had a tune-up, make an appointment to have one. To ensure your safety on the road, you should ask your mechanic to do the following:

Pump your "gear shift."
Check the hoses and replace them if necessary.
Check fan belts for signs of fatigue, and replace if necessary.
Check the fluid level of brakes, battery, and back seat keg ("It's not an open *bottle*— ").
Check the distributor.
Check your oil and, if satisfactory, take ten for a full-body massage.
Check your wiring, and "adjust" in the back room as schedule permits.
Replace the fuel and air filters.
Check, and replace if necessary, the PCV valve.
Replace all spark plugs.
Wear a condom.

Under the stars. Chances are Mom, Dad, and the hamster are accompanying you on this jaunt, but if they're not, or if they're crunchy types, consider camping out along the way instead of staying at motels. Get a KOA guide and check out grounds along your route.

Carless in Colorado? If your family can't spare a car for the road trip but you still want to drive, look into borrowing one from a rental company. National chains are constantly needing people to drive their cars from one place to another; you generally won't get paid, but you'll get use of a vehicle.

Walden on wheels? Exciting as it sounds, it can be risky to road trip alone. If you'll only be on well-traveled interstates, traveling during daylight, and have a reasonably new car, you will probably be okay, but otherwise your nightmare may come true: Your car will come to a spluttering halt ten miles west of Wittenburg, Wisconsin, and the dog you brought along for company will nearly die of heat exhaustion as you wait two hours for AAA in 90-degree heat. It happened to one of us. Here's how we should have dealt with it, and how you should deal with it, whether you're by yourself or with others . . .

Trailers/Top Carriers

If you'll be driving a long distance and/or your parents won't be returning home with the car, your best rental bet will probably be U-Haul; they have pick-up and drop-off locations all over the place, and are pretty cheap (though you get what you pay for). Top carriers are getting harder and harder to find for rent; some cars aren't even compatible with the main ones out there. Trailers require a hitch on your car; these aren't too expensive and may not be a bad investment if you'll be moving long distances frequently, which you may be. Top carriers are also available for purchase at places like Target and on Yahoo! Shopping for $60–$120 (soft-sided ones tend to be cheaper).

If you're moving enough stuff (furniture) to require a truck, Ryder is also an option.

If you want to rent, call a good couple of weeks in advance of the move, especially if you're starting in a smaller city with fewer options. September is a big time for moving, and you may not find what you're looking for at the last minute. There's generally no penalty for canceling your reservation if you give the company a bit of notice.

How to Deal with a Breakdown

Get your car off the road, even if you have to put it in neutral and push.

If you don't know what the problem is, give the car ten minutes or so to cool off, and try starting it again. If it starts okay, run it a little and see if God has worked a miracle on your engine while you ate your taco.

When you've determined that the problem is not going to go away —either because you don't know what it is or because you don't know how to fix it—turn on your emergency lights so you don't get rear-ended by a drowsy truck driver (no, there's no such thing as a mirage in the shape of a Chevy).

If you have a cell phone and are a member of AAA, call them. The number is 1-800-AAA-HELP. Otherwise, call local information (1-area code-555-1212) to get the number of a towing service.

If you don't have a cell phone, put your hood up and sit tight. If you're on a fairly busy road, people will stop; you can afford to be choosy about whom you talk to. If you're a lone woman, especially, be wary of getting out of the car to talk to men or watch them tinker under the hood. Don't leave the key in the ignition under any circumstances. There's a chance your car isn't as immobile as it seems.

If you're alone, especially, don't let on that you're heading out to college. This admission will advertise your vulnerability, and the fact that all your possessions are in the trunk. Pick a town within fifty miles or so and say you're headed there to meet relatives, but they're not home so can't help out.

Don't let on that you're a woman alone, or two women alone. Say something like "My main squeeze, Fabian, went thataway for help, but could you call, too?" Weirded out as well as convinced of male proximity, he'll be less likely to start a rumble.

If the person who stops to help you can't fix your car, have him or her call for help (again, either AAA, a towing service, or the police as a last resort). *Do not get into a car with someone.* If they're going to drive you to a phone, it shouldn't be too much trouble for them to make the call themselves. Offer to pay them for their time and help.

If someone promises to call AAA for you but no tow truck appears, ask another person to call for you. There's a chance the first person bailed.

Depending on the snazziness of your coverage, AAA will tow you free, either anywhere within 3 miles or anywhere within 100 miles of the breakdown location. If you think there's something seriously wrong with your car, or if it's a foreign or unusual make, you may want to request towing to the largest city within that radius. Even if a nearby small town seems more convenient, the mechanics there may lack the parts or the know-how to fix your problem. Many mechanics not affiliated with gas stations are, also, closed on Sundays.

6

Transportation on Campus

You've arrived. With a little luck, your prized 8-track collection and any vehicle you drove out in remain intact. Now it's time to make some decisions: Keep the car, if it's yours? Get a bike or blades? A subway pass? Some good walking shoes? (Your grandma a.k.a mall walker knows the brands.) In planning your peregrinations, think about the following:

Bikes and Blades

If you live relatively far (more than ten minutes) from where classes and/or essential stores and employers are, walking is probably not going to cut it, although it will get you in surprisingly good shape. Biking and blading are also good for you; the downside is that they limit your fashion choices, can be messy, and don't work very well in the winter if ice is a factor where you are. Bikes, also, are quite prone to theft on college campuses (see chapter 11); neither works too well when you're carrying groceries and/or drinks, either, although such trips may be infrequent. If you like them for the sake of general fitness, however, they will save you time to the extent that you can and choose to use them.

Campus Shuttles

Many large campuses have shuttle systems that run until late at night connecting all parts of campus including dorms. These tend to be quite safe and free, if somewhat slow (they tend to make a lot of stops). Your college's Web site should have at the very least some general information and a phone number, if not actual schedules. Look carefully at times; some don't run much at all on weekends. That may not be a reason to bring your own car, but it's worth knowing. Some colleges also run shuttles to and from the airport at vacation times and to places like Wal-Mart at the beginning of the school year for students to stock up, either for free or for a nominal fee.

Public Transportation

To check out your college town or city's options for public transportation, do an Internet search with the name of your town/city and "public transit." You should get at the very least the options; you may get maps and schedules of routes. Again, pay attention to times and days of the week; public transportation is often *not* designed with student schedules in mind, but if you're relying on it mainly as a way to get off campus (to stores or jobs), that will be less of a factor.

Cost varies with the community, but if you'll be using it a lot (many or most days in a month), a pass will probably be worth your while.

Keep the climate in mind; if your town has buses but not subways and an intense summer or winter, public transit's going to be a lot less fun.

Taxis

It may sound like it applies only to urban campuses, but taxis can be a great complement to other transportation options—even if you have, say, a car. In student areas they often congregate in front of student centers and groceries; you may well not even have to call your own. If you have a group getting groceries or going out, taxis can be almost as cheap as buses and subways. They are, of course, the method of choice when no one wants to be designated driver; if you go out a lot, program a taxi number into your cell phone if you have one so you won't be searching for a yellow pages in a less than clear-headed state.

Cars

'Biles are, of course, the Mack Daddy of the American transportation scene, and many students choose to have them. Before you bring yours out, however, do consider the following:

* Are freshmen allowed to have cars (either by policy or in the sense that they're eligible for parking passes in campus lots)? On-street parking on some campuses and in some cities is virtually impossible.
* How much does parking cost, and where can you do it? If it takes more time to walk to the lot than it would to walk to the subway station, it may not be worth it. Parking in isolated or very urban areas may leave your car vulnerable to break-ins and theft. Your car may also be towed, without you noticing for many days, increasing your cost of getting it back. Northern cities often have snow removal ordinances that seriously limit street parking in the winter.
* How will you deal with requests to borrow your car? It may be your buddy who totaled your car, but you're still liable—just ask one of our friends. Are you willing and able either to accept the risks of lending, saying no, or compromising by acting as a chauffeur?

If you've decided to have a car, you have a potentially big job on your hands taking care of it, especially if you've never done so on your own before. If you're going to toodle around campus honking at friends you'd better be ready to get down and dirty once in a while and glance at the oil gauge. Here, then, is all the information you'll need to make it through a year's worth of disasters as well as . . .

Maintenance

Check-ups

Now that you're away, Dad the moonlight mechanic won't be around to check spark plugs and tire treads, so it's time you started training for

Stalling in a Winter Wonderland

"California: A nice place to visit, but you wouldn't want to live there," one of our parents told us. To which we retort, in the same spirit of random proclamation: "Snowy woods: Nice place to drive through, but you wouldn't want to die there."

The point of all this pedagogical paradox is: Be equipped. If you're driving long distances in truly polar environments, you'll want Sterno and matches as well as more basic provisions. If your alter ego is not Saint Nick, you can make do with flares, a blanket, a gas can, a flashlight, and loose change (in addition to the basic jumper cables, spare, and jack).

parenthood by babying your 'bile. You probably won't be putting a lot of mileage on, unless you live off campus, but try and keep up with the following maintenance schedule:

I'm a little teapot, short and . . . Check the radiator occasionally, especially during extreme weather, adding water or antifreeze as necessary, depending on the season. If you'll be going on a long road trip in the summer, carry some extra water with you in case you need to cool it down quickly.

Texas tea. The Clampetts appreciated its importance, and so should you. Change, or have someone change, your engine oil every 2,000 to 3,000 miles. The oil filter comes due for replacement about half as frequently. A professional oil change should run you $20–$30; don't believe everything the mechanic tells you about what your car is in dire need of.

What would the Dukes of Hazzard be without it? You can thank power steering for those funky impress-the-local-wildlife stunts you pull on the logging road outside of town; preserve it by checking the level of power steering fluid every time you change the oil. Top it off if it's low.

Scarlett O'Hara had an eighteen-inch waist. Okay, so your car's a little paunchier, and his rubber belts aren't so stylish. But they need attention nonetheless, every 3,000 miles.

Rubber's ready. Although you may find yourself fiddling with your

Goodyears somewhat more frequently (see the next two pages), they really only require rotation every 10,000 miles. Develop the habit of glancing at your tires before you get in the car; in cold winters, especially, tires can get low. You can fill up on air for little or no cost at most gas stations.

Cars run better without insects in the gas. Replace your fuel filter every 15,000 miles.

Baby, you turn me on! Yeah, so spark plugs only wear out every 30,000 miles, but maybe you were overdue already when you pulled out of your garage at home. Check it out.

Rattle, Rattle, Thunder Clatter . . .

Even if you're religious about maintenance, the car god can take revenge. A little rattling can give you a satisfying sense of martyrdom or provide a little rhythmic relief when your stereo's on the blink, and often it doesn't signal anything other than your car's age or mood. But some noises mean trouble. If any of these noises are loud or persistent, they may indicate the presence of problems that require servicing:

this noise...	might mean this...
under-hood squeaking	loose or glazed belts
clunking on accel-/deceleration	worn joints in the drive or axle shaft
underbody roaring	holes in muffler, broken joints in exhaust pipes
whining brakes	worn brake shoes
engine rattling	may be cured by higher octane fuel; if not, could signal ignition or exhaust valve problems
vibrating floor/seats	transmission problems
underbody whine	rear axle/front drive problems

Signs Your Mechanic Is Actually Elvis

Sure, every mechanic looks like the King, but only one actually is. Could it be yours? Watch for these tipoffs:

* Does pelvic thrust to raise himself from garage floor, then pulls switchblade when you crack joke about Michael & Lisa Marie.
* Wears jailbird stripes instead of usual Oshkosh B'gosh mechanic wear.
* Inadvertently addresses you as "hound dog" instead of the name on your credit card when he thanks you for your business.
* Displays that famously subtle, anagrammatic mind in signing his name "YELSERP SIVLE"; responds slowly when you call him that.
* Has the safe sex scene with Priscilla from *Naked Gun* on continuous play in the workshop.
* Clams up when you question him about pre–1971 automotive experiences.
* Comments favorably on your blue suede shoes.

Troubleshooting

Like we said, it'd be nice if there were a clean-cut, eligible mechanic at every turn. Unfortunately, however, you may find yourself with a problem and no one jumping in to help. You need to know . . .

How to Change a Tire

AAA, if you're a member, can do this for you, but it may be in the interest of efficiency or masculine pride to do it yourself. For things to go smoothly you'll need a jack, wrench, and a 2- to 3-foot-long pipe that fits over the end of your lug wrench. Your car should theoretically contain the necessary equipment in the pouch with your spare tire. Here's how to do it:

If the tire went flat while you were driving, find a safe, level place to park your car. Flick on the hazard lights, put the car in park, and empty it of people (if you have a stick shift, put it in reverse) and then turn off the ignition. Brace the wheel diagonally opposite to the flat with a good-sized rock.

Remove the wheel cover with the flat end of the wrench handle. Use the wrench to loosen the wheel nuts.

If you aren't on concrete, put the board under the jack so it sits flat and steady. Connect the jack to the car's jacking point (see your owner's manual—the point is somewhere on the fender), and pump until the wheel is 2 to 3 inches above the ground.

Remove the nuts and stash them in the wheel cover. Slide off the tire and replace it. Screw the nuts (hey, we all need a quickie now and then). Lower the car and remove the jack. Tighten the nuts with the wrench, tap the wheel cover back on, and remove the rock.

How to Jump-start a Car

You wanted a little extra light on the subject as you changed your tire, so you left your headlights on. After the job was done, you felt so good you thought you'd have a smoke, and then do it again. One thing leads to another, and pretty soon you've changed all your car's tires. You decide to see how your handiwork has paid off. That's when you remember that your headlights went out a long time ago. You turn the ignition key experimentally, but no luck—your car's dead. Here's how to rekindle the romance:

Put your hood up, look troubled, and wait for someone to stop.

When said driver has agreed to jump you, have him park so that his car's front end is facing that of yours, but not touching it. Open his hood.

Set both cars' emergency brakes, and put both cars in park or neutral. Turn off everything—including the ignitions—in both cars.

Using jumper cables, connect the positive terminal of one car's battery (it will be labeled either with a + sign or *pos*) to the positive terminal of the other car's. It doesn't matter what color the ends are that you use, but if you use red on one car's positive terminal, use red on the other's as well (unless you want to see some pre-Fourth fireworks). It also doesn't matter which connection you make first—to the dead car or the live one.

Connect the other ends of the jumper cables to the live car's negative terminal and to an unpainted bolt on the dead car's engine.

Car Insurance

. . . is going to be expensive, if your car has any value (or if you choose to insure its value). Ways to minimize cost:

* Insurers will often let you stay under your parents' policy while you're a student. You are separately covered and pay your own premiums, but they will often be lower than if you had a separate policy.
* Insure only against liability (if your car really isn't worth much).
* Challenge allegations of moving violations by going to court. You may still have to pay, but may be able to negotiate keeping the charge off your record.
* Some insurers give lower rates to students with good grades.

Start the live car first, and then the dead one. Leave both running, remove cables, and drive the formerly dead car for at least twenty or thirty minutes. Have the battery recharged/checked at a service station ASAP.

How to Open a Frozen Car Door

Some hardware stores sell special handheld, battery-powered tools that heat a strip of metal which can then be inserted into the lock. If you don't have one of these, or if it's in your glove compartment, you can heat your own key with a match or cigarette lighter. When the ice melts enough to allow you to open the door, push the lock lever/button up and down a few times; the friction will smooth away any remaining ice.

The ice may also be in the cracks between the door and the body of the car. Try running your key or an ice scraper around the door to clear it out.

Terminal (?) Illness

As a skinned knee is to full-body warts, so are the piddly maladies above to an actual *accident*. If you're a typical red-blooded American

Minimizing Tickets/Towing When On-street Parking

* Try to park on blocks that are obviously accepting of long-term parking (the ones that are pretty full). Many cities have rules about how long you can leave your car in any given place; these rules are usually not enforced, but can be if neighbors demand it. Such people's homes can also be egged if the situation demands it.
* If you're parked even on a block where you normally don't park, check your car every couple of days and consider moving it, even slightly. Police will often ticket before towing; moreover, the longer your car sits after being towed, the more you will have to pay to get it back.
* Check/use your car at least a couple of times a week regardless. Police sometimes post signs about street cleaning or snow removal a couple of days in advance of its occurring.
* If you receive a big snowfall, call the police department or look on the city's Web site to ask about snow emergencies. Cars on certain sides of the street may be towed as the city removes the snow.
* Pay parking tickets promptly—they're sometimes cheaper if you do.
* Consider challenging—either by going to court or just writing a protest letter—tickets that you think are unfair, excessive, or just don't want to pay. Sometimes making a stink will get you out of the ticket or at least keep the violation from going on your record, which might increase your insurance premiums.

youngster, you've got some accidents under your belt already. But in case you've somehow avoided learning accident etiquette (call it *luck*, bub, not skill) or if your parents dealt with everything the first few times, here's how to deal:

Obviously, don't go anywhere, even if you and your car are capable of doing so. Sure, the White Castle down the road is clamoring for its king—you—but a square burger isn't worth a day in court on hit-and-run charges.

Before the other driver gives in to the temptation you were man enough to resist, get his/her name and telephone number at the very least. Better, get an address; driver's license number and expiration

Getting a Guaranteed Parking Spot

There are two kinds of guaranteed spots: ones you can use 24 hours a day, 7 days a week, and ones you can only use during specified hours. The first kind may be available from your college; it is also available through renting from an individual either in his or her driveway (the driveway of an apartment building) or, if certain on-street parking requires a permit, through buying a permit from someone who lives on the street. Monthly fees range drastically; some college Web sites or town newspapers' Web sites have classified ads selling parking spaces. If it's on-street, it should go for a lot less than off-street, obviously; if your town gets snow in winter and requires people to move their cars off the street for plowing regularly, an on-street permit isn't worth much at all.

For guaranteed spots in campus lots, check the college Web site or call the parking office early; they may be first come first served or there may be a day early in the semester when everyone lines up to get passes.

date; license plate number; make, model, and year of the other car; and insurance policy name and number.

Contact your insurer to get the appropriate forms and, if necessary, appraisal of damages. If your state doesn't have no-fault insurance, you'll have to prove the accident was the other driver's fault in order to collect. Send your claim to his or her insurer. If your state has no-fault insurance, you'll file your claim with your own company regardless of whose fault the accident was. Before you file any sort of claim, you'll probably need a couple of estimates of damages to the car and, if appropriate, to you and any passengers, human or pigeon.

Especially if the accident was piddly and/or one of you has had some recent driving problems (accidents, tickets) you may decide to not file insurance claims and just settle between the two of you, if you can agree on an allocation of fault. This way the accident won't get reported, which would increase your insurance premiums.

7

Bonding to Blowouts: The Law of Roommates

Ah, friends. What would life, or for that matter syndication, be without them? Freshman year in college, perhaps to a greater extent than any other year of your life, will be about people. At orientation mixers, you'll meet Cranapple addicts, former Cambodian refugees, and future goldfish vendors; the group you introduce yourself to in the dining hall will be composed of a redhead from Massachusetts identifying herself as a witch, a preppie in an Exeter cap looking discombobulated, and a guy scribbling rap lyrics on a napkin. As the first weeks come to a close, you'll likely find yourself doing less random socializing and more bonding with the people in your hall and dorm. You'll laugh, you'll cry, you'll wrestle; you'll share *Fatal Attraction* stories and hair histories; you'll swap strategies for corn cultivation. By the end of it all, you'll be equipped for your life's work in reality TV and actually be sad to say goodbye for a summer to people who know you well enough to make a fortune should you ever run for public office.

Of all your social interactions, those with your roommate(s) are likely to be the most complex and potentially explosive. As you build your own relationships, you'll know best how to deal with specific situations. The beginning, however, is more of a blind walk, and as such there are certain precautions that are helpful to follow. We confine our advice, therefore, to issues arising in the early days, dealing with the three main stages—meeting, bonding, and conflict—(we hope) in their order of appearance. And since any dorm could clobber *Survivor* at the Emmys—college life differs from reality TV only in the fact that your sicko neighbor's cameras are *hidden*—we thought it would be appropriate to present our tips on roommate relations in the context of three all-new episodes from the acclaimed series *Little Sister*. As the drama unfolds, watch in trepidation as the characters' errors of thought and speech (italicized) foreshadow their tragic falls.

Episode One: Meeting

Jenny, whose slogan is "the early bird gets the worm," has arrived exactly one minute before the dorms are scheduled to open, at 7:59 A.M. Key in hand, she triumphantly sprints up the stairs, flings open the door of suite 301, and sees . . .

Gail: (rising from a futon) Hah . . . ?

Jenny: (setting down a suitcase) Hi, I'm Jenny. You must be . . .

Gail: Gail. But folks jus' as soon call me "Gal."

Jenny: (extending hand) Nice to meet you, er, Gal. So . . . (looking around suspiciously) have you been here a while?

Gail: Naw, not really. But mah mom called up an' see if ah couldn't get in here a night arly cause there weren't any fust-class seats leff comin' all the way from Cahpus Christi 'cept fer last night. Aw, you know how that goes, honey? (waving a hand at one of the bedrooms) Ah figgered since ah was all by my lonesome, I'd just stash my stuff in the single there. (aside) *Silly Yankee, I made up that story about no first-class seats, just as I'm faking this here drawl! Since sophomore year in high school I've been gathering knickknacks for my den of love, and nothing's going to stop me from having my single!!!*

Jenny: (aside) *Damn Confederate!!!* (aloud, as she enters the fully furnished, lived-in looking bedroom) Maybe I don't speak with cotton candy in my mouth, Miss Priss, but you're operating under a strange definition of the word "stash"!

Gail: Why, honey, don't get all het up bout a little thing like that thar! That ain't for keeps, ah just thought I'd set up and we's all can switch around once we get things worked out!

Jenny: We'll see, won't we (with a glint in her eye). Won't we . . .

Meanwhile, out in the hall, the third student assigned to this two-room triple, ALEX, has reached the third floor to find her future next-door neighbor, ALEX, struggling with his lock.

Alex (M): Geez Louise . . .

Alex (F): (sweetly) Something wrong with the door?

Alex (M): (turning in wonder) Yeah, the dumb thing . . .

Alex (F): (aside) *My, he's attractive. I haven't gotten a chance to know anyone else, but I'm pretty sure I want to marry him.* (aloud) Before I fix your door, I was wondering if you'd be interested in starting a relationship with me, infuriating all of our roommates by our incessant PDAs on the futon?

Alex (M): Sounds good. (stares at her for a while, the doorknob he has accidentally broken off falls to the floor)

Alex (F): (placing his hand on her butt) Come on, dear, let's meet my roommates.

* * *

If you value your relationship with roommates, don't claim a bedroom, especially a *single* bedroom, before other people have arrived. In fact, don't lay claim to any part of the room. If one desk locale, bedroom, or bed is clearly superior, you'll probably end up getting it for part of the year anyway. Even if you've scored a minor vic and end up getting to keep the bottom bunk, you've generated antagonism at the very time you should be trying to make a good impression. Not everyone forgives easily.

Leave reenacting the War Between the States to the Miss America Pageant. Our departed brethren returned a long time ago; under-the-breath murmurs about "secesh devils" and display of the Confederate flag tend to be counterproductive.

PDA, go away, come again some other decade. Aside from the wisdom of starting a relationship with the first person you spot (see chapter 21), it's not great policy to introduce your next-door-neighbor boyfriend to your roommates at the same time you introduce yourself, unless you're in the mood to bet on a wrestling match for who gets to not room with you.

Episode Two: Bonding

In a dramatic reenactment of the 1865 scene at Appomattox Courthouse, Jenny and Gal have staged a reconciliation, both expressing the tearful wish that it hadn't taken them so long to discover they were soul sisters. We rejoin their lives to witness a bonding scene worthy of Elmer's:

Gal: Where should we put our *joint purchases*—this supertelephone answering machine, this Franklin Mint collection of porcelain miniatures, this Ming dynasty tapestry, deluxe Barcalounger, and the Siamese kitty, Jenny dear?

Jenny: Wherever you want!

Gal: No! Wherever *you* want!

Jenny: (grinning wickedly) Wherever Alex doesn't want.

Gal: Hoho! You sly thing!

Jenny: You know what one of them said to the other? I can't really tell who's who now that she braided his ducktail with her teeth. They were making #%$%# wedding plans! They better not be planning to spend their honeymoon in the top bunk!

Gal: Don't worry. I know how to deal with her kind. (mysteriously) She's toast.

Jenny: Now who's the sly one?! (both laugh hysterically) You know, do you think before we pop her in our new, jointly purchased Toast-R-Oven, we all three should get together and make up some rules? You know? Because I'm sure we're all coming from different places.

Gal: Why honey, *that doesn't seem necessary. I don't think the little things matter a smidgen when you've got a friendship like ours!*

Jenny: Of course, you're right. After all, we do have so much in common! We both had high school boyfriends named John, both like Christina Aguilera better than Britney, and both use the same kind of contact lens solution! (enter Alex, timidly) Well, I don't know about you, Gal girl, but I'm ready for dinner.

Gal: (loudly) Yeah, I could eat a sheep! (glancing toward Alex) I've heard that sex diminishes appetite.

Jenny: Yeah, *let's just make it the two of us.* I'm sure we'll discover even more exact correspondences in our life stories. (linking arms and walking out the door) While we eat the same thing for dinner, why don't we talk about what extracurriculars we should both sign up for at the fair tomorrow.

Gal: Do you think they'll let us sign both of our names on the same line, so everyone knows we're best friends? You know, like we *named the cat Jengal?*

Jenny: We'll do it whether they ask or not. Gal, don't let me forget to *transfer into all of your classes.*

Gal: How could I let you forget? We're *one person!* (exiting joyously)

Alex looks at the floor and fingers her zircon engagement ring in silence.

* * *

Don't buy things jointly. This holds, in particular, for 1) expensive items, and 2) items that cannot be easily divided, such as domestic animals. For one thing, there'll be the hassle of reimbursement (you're not going to give the Tiffany's cashier two checks); more importantly, there's going to be the issue of dividing property if you go in different directions at year's end. If you split even earlier and more acrimoniously, you may lose, as one of us did, everything; after hightailing it across campus, the last thing we wanted to do was trek back and arrange a buyout of the microwave.

Be careful about gossiping. As a bonding mechanism it rivals Krazy Glue, but it can hurt you, as it has some of us, in the long run. Do you really want your friendships to be founded on backbiting? Do you want to close the door to any future friendship with the person you're talking about? Things you say "in confidence" get out; gossip may yield you more enemies than buds.

Do seriously consider talking over a few simple rules. It may seem as though you're all on the same wavelength, or that if minor differences exist, they don't matter. *They do.* Everyone has pet peeves—toothpaste stuck on the sink wall; people borrowing clothes without asking; Violent Femmes as wake-up music; windows left open at night—and if you keep getting your roommate's goat, it could strain the relationship. Better to air grievances before everyone's ready to climb the walls.

Don't become Siamese twins with your roommate. Or, for that matter, anyone you meet right away. For one thing, the friendship may not last; for another, constant companionship may breed rivalry; and

Speak the Speech

Sometimes a language barrier is a good thing, preventing one roommate from taking offense when cursed in Urdu. But when it prevents meaningful communication, it can be a real problem. To test your preparedness for rap sessions with "foreigners" like Gal and for the inevitable "what do you call a carbonated beverage" conversation, try this quizlet:

Your California roommate bursts through the door. After weeding through a field of "dudes," you catch an actual word. "Dude, I'm so stoked," she says breathlessly. She is

- a. pregnant
- b. coming off a breast implant operation
- c. psyched to the max, à la Jennifer Capriati
- d. constipated

That crazy Rhode Islander is wandering around your floor again. "Run, Bud! Run!" someone snickers—a joke that hits too close to home. He looks at you dolefully. "Excuse me, sir, can you tell me where the nearest bubbler is?" He

- a. is propositioning you
- b. wants some *agua*
- c. craves a snack of guppies, but wants to be subtle about it
- d. has the hots for the Doublemint twins, or anyone with their chewing habits

Your Minnesota friend's agricultural wisdom has brought the entire dorm to its knees. Suddenly she breaks off her narrative. "Jesus, I could use a pop," she says. Anxious to satisfy the desire so that the Socrates-like oration can continue, you

- a. reluctantly pass her your cap gun
- b. murmur some greeting card reassurances about the advantages of broken homes
- c. say suggestively, "My thoughts exactly," and open your fly
- d. grab a Sprite from the fridge

Answers: 1. c 2. b 3. d

finally, you might just get sick of each other. Even if none of these apparent undesirables comes to pass, you'll be shutting yourself out of opportunities to make other friends.

Don't name pets after the people in your roommate group. Just spells I-D-E-N-T-I-T-Y C-R-I-S-I-S for Mr. Hamster when you guys split up.

Episode Three: Conflict

Time has passed. Jenny and Gal's bonding, to all appearances, has continued unabated, as have Alex²'s public, private, and sonic (the walls are thin) displays of affection. But their life ain't as rosy as it seems . . .

Jenny: (sitting at computer, muttering to herself) Damn that Gal, she's gabbing again. Well, the least I can do is get a couple of laughs if I'm going to have to be distracted by this crap. (tuning in to the conversation, laughing wildly at Gal's synopsis of her love life, past and present) Well, that was funny, but I've thought of something better to do. *Gal's got some franks in the fridge. Gonna microwave me a couple of dogs and go visit that hot guy Gal was telling me about in 202.* (exits)

Gal: (still on phone, breathes sigh of relief) Thank God, she's gone. Girlfriend, what am I going to do about this pathetic roommate of mine? She can't get along with Alex, so she's always hanging around me, asking me who I've met, borrowing my boots, and now she just took my last box of weenies! Well, hon, I'd better go finish my problem set before the wench gets back or I'll never get it done. I'll keep you posted.

Jenny: (returning in excitement about an hour later) Gal! Guess what!

Gal: (making an effort at a smile) What?

Jenny: I just had the most amazing conversation with Jed, that guy you were telling me about? And guess what? We're going to continue it over coffee! I just came up here to get a jacket. (grabs one of Gal's off the coat tree)

Gal: (eyes narrowing into slits, hand staying Jenny's grabbing arm) Just a gol darn second. You stole my man, my dogs, and now you want to steal my jacket?

Jenny: (spluttering) *Your* man! *Your* dogs! As though he even liked you *or* them!

Don't Count on the Twinkie Defense:
How to Restrain Criminal Impulses

You've followed all of our well-meaning advice. You've bought one of the new straitjacket teddies to prevent yourself from acting out your recurring dreams of murder. But still, you find your hands creeping forward, ready to strangle, when the two of you are brushing your teeth, and you can't help thinking her Snapple is crying for a few dozen Valium. It's time to get it together before you find yourself an unwitting extra in the remake of *Jailhouse Rock*. Attributing violent episodes to a sugar high may work on television or in other fantasy worlds in the pocket of the Hostess corporation, but it ain't going to cut it in the freshman dean's office. Talking it out is the ideal solution, but if your roommate's idea of a couch session involves *Monday Night Football,* you may need to take a more indirect approach. Here's how:

Just kidding. Sometimes the best way to release hostility is to act it out, to engage in "joke" arguments with your would-be victim. Laughingly insult taste in boxers, music, women; "pretend" to be mad about his spilling Just for Men in your soap dish. Watch in wonder as bad habits/hair coloring jobs go bye-bye.

Get out. Freshman rooms tend to be indistinguishable from closets; sometimes all it takes to decrease tension is some space. Study in the library instead of the room; do your talking on the phone when your roommate's disappeared into the bathroom, *Playboy* in hand.

Gal: $%^$@#&*^*()*()*!
Jenny: Two can play at this game! &*(&&(##@@!@$^&76283!
All: %#@#@%%^())(*%##@#%$#&^*((*)(**(&^^$#@@#@@@%^%%^&^
&!!! (falling to the floor, wrestling)

* * *

If you have the gift of gab, be stingy with it, or at least exercise your generosity quietly. It sounds petty, but we know of roommate relations—especially early in freshman year when friendship bonds are weak—poisoned by conflict over phone use. Don't use it constantly, and when you do have a long conversation, take the phone into the hall or a room where no one is working.

Drop eavesdropping. We know of some families where it's cool to pick up the phone and listen in when TV doesn't satisfy your entertainment needs, but check it out with roommates before you continue the practice. Even if you can't help overhearing, preserve the illusion of deafness by not laughing at jokes or commenting on the conversation later. There's little enough privacy at college as it is.

Don't "borrow" food or clothing without asking. Most people don't have a problem lending, but they still like to be asked. Do watch, however, for body language; some people won't say no, but are still bothered by your dipping into their yogurt pretzel caches.

Don't go after the same person your roommate is after, unless you value the possibility of a relationship more than peace in your room. Competition over guys and dolls has strained or wrecked more roommate bonds than we can count.

A good cursing out may work wonders, as it did for one of us, but it's so much better to talk things out calmly. If you've let things come to a boil the way Gal and Jenny did, though, it's pretty hard to restrain yourself when the breaking point comes.

When to Move Out

"I should have moved out when my roommate called me 'nothing,'" one of our friends said. Unfortunately for her happiness, she waited until she'd been locked out of the room, doused with beer, and had her clothes borrowed and stretched to twice their size before she hit the road.

While it's possible to wait too long, it also can be bad to be hasty; almost everyone has moments when they'd like to have a different living situation, but the alternatives aren't always peachy either. There's a lot to be said for sticking it out and talking things through; serious discussion of problems, in some of our cases, turned hated bunkmates into friends.

If and when you decide your living situation is unbearable and improvement impossible, try to get out quickly. It's easier at some schools than at others—at one of ours the dean wouldn't let a girl out of a triple even though her two roommates were lovers—but if you make a big enough stink, *any* school will find some kind of new arrangement.

How to Make a Voodoo Doll

Generic ones are available in Haiti and in stores near many campuses, but for maximum effectiveness (ask one of our roommates) it's best to get personal. If your little sib isn't too observant, you might be able to snag a doll off her; otherwise you can throw one together with a couple of Styrofoam balls or Hackeysacks, and some napkins or stray tube socks.

If it's primarily physical pain you want to inflict, just murmur a few appropriate words and stick pins in vulnerable areas. In psychic torture, on the other hand, there's more room for creativity. As you work, punishments suited to your particular victim will occur to you. Here are a few suggestions:

heart	gets period during final exam
	power goes out during all-nighter
butt	*bad* mid-movie gas
	attack of 'rhoids strikes in midst of limbo contest
legs	rate of leg hair growth doubles in time for
	skinny-dipping party
armpits	even men's deodorant won't work

It's better not to bring your parents into it, but if the dean has a thick skin or secretary, you may need their help in harassing him into letting you transfer.

To Cell or not to Cell?

We consider this deep question in the context of roommate relations because it can influence them. It is, of course, partly a financial issue or may already be answered. If you already have one, the only question may be whether to get a new number if you're moving to a different city. If you're planning on using it primarily to talk to people in your old area code or will only be making outgoing calls and have free long distance, you may just want to keep your old number. If, however, you'll be using it as your primary line for calls around campus, you probably don't want people calling you to have to pay long distance.

If you don't yet have one, consider the following factors in deciding:

Pros

Money. If you will be doing a lot of long-distance calling to your girlfriend/boyfriend, friends, and family, the price per minute will probably be at least competitive with the cheapest long-distance plans and calling cards. In a dorm, you seldom can choose a long-distance carrier and the rates imposed on you are likely to be above-market. Calling cards require dialing lots of numbers; they can be stolen; and if they aren't prepaid, the rates can fluctuate unpredictably. There is, of course, the initial cost of the cell phone itself, although some are available now for as little as $20.

Convenience/mobility/modem. It's sure nice not to have your friends aware of what a nerd you are, on the Internet all the time. A cell phone preserves the illusion that you actually have a life and might be going somewhere.

Effect on roommate relations. Conflict over the phone can be a major source of friction among roommates. If your cell is your primary or even alternate point of access, you won't be dependent on roommates to take messages for you or to get off the phone when you need it. If you don't use the room line at all, you won't be obligated to answer and take messages for roommates, either.

Privacy. Having a cell phone allows you to make private calls where you otherwise would have few opportunities to. It's a great luxury to be able to be honest about your dormmates and general situation when talking to friends and family.

Safety. In cars, walking back from library, parties at night, etc.

Cons

Health effects? The jury seems to be still out, despite the best persuasive efforts of the cell phone industry. Everybody seems to know or know of someone who used one all the time and now has brain cancer; whether there's a connection is anyone's guess. Flip phones supposedly direct radiation away from your head more than other styles.

Obsolescence and long-term contracts. The time will no doubt come when particular phones aren't usable only on specific carriers, but it's not now. Prepaid systems like tracphone *can* present another option if you really only want the phone for emergencies and want flexibility for future purchases. See www.tracphone.com.

Limited coverage. If your college is in a rural area, coverage (at least by the major carriers) may not be good, and committing yourself to a local carrier may be more expensive long-term than you think. Even if the area's technically covered, service may be bad (too few lines, etc.)— if you don't have a cell phone yet, consider waiting till you get to campus to get the scoop.

8

Urban Sophisticate: Apartment Living

Let's face it, people who live off campus freshman year are different from other people. They have a certain *je ne sais quoi*, a certain comfort with the realities of life that their peers perhaps blissfully lack. It takes guts to live on your own at eighteen, especially in an unfamiliar city. But the rewards can be commensurate. Many of the facts of dorm life (see chapters 7 and 17) apply to apartment living as well, but see below for the practicalities:

On or Off?

At many schools, all freshmen live on campus whether they want to or not. If you have the choice, however, here are some considerations to keep in mind:

Living On Campus

Living on campus makes things logistically simpler but socially more complex. Your furniture, meals, utilities, and maintenance will be taken care of, and your expenses as a result will be quite predictable. You may find, as well, that your parents are more willing/able to help you foot the bill: dorm expenses come in chunks and aren't discre-

Doing the Math

Rents vary *extraordinarily* from city to city and to some extent within cities. In many, the hub around a college is particularly expensive and the apartments not particularly well-maintained: landlords know that many students lack cars or want to live near campus, so are a captive market. Among the advantages of these areas are leases geared toward the school year (May to May, September to September, for example), proximity to parties, campus, and business areas, and a certain casual attitude toward maintenance which may suit your lifestyle and abilities. You'll have to deal with subletting if you don't stay for the summer, but by the same token you can stay past finals or over vacations if you want to whereas dorms' schedules are rigid.

Start looking as soon as you know where you're going and have decided to live off campus (actually, it may be a good idea not to foreclose living on campus in case you're disappointed by apartment choices), early summer at the latest. Apartments in student areas often come available well in advance of move-in date.

---

tionary, so your parents won't worry that they're funding your pay-per-view (it's a "utility"). Your commute time to class will be on the order of minutes at most, probably obviating the need for a car if you don't have one or don't want to bring one. If you do, however, you may not be able to park it near your room or, at some schools, anywhere. You won't need to worry about summer subletting, and some schools allow you to store your belongings over the summer.

You will meet a lot of people, but you will also have very little privacy. You will almost certainly share a small bedroom with at least one other person, who may or may not be at all compatible with you—music-wise, schedule-wise, and in terms of nighttime frolicking.

Living Off Campus

College, particularly freshman year, can be a very intense experience, and the ability to truly get away from the scene may be of great value to you. If your family lives within easy driving distance, they may provide the necessary outlet (if they live close enough to allow you to commute to school, they may also save you a lot of money, effort in food preparation, and laundry costs). Getting an apartment fairly near campus can be a good option as well. You will almost certainly have significantly more room and privacy than you would on campus, as well as the chance—or burden—of improving your cooking and general "life" skills, which can be an enjoyable antidote for too much book learning. You will also not have to deal with either the noise of dorms or, on the other hand, the "policed" aspect of dorms with respect to drinking, smoking, etc.

Things to Consider When Looking for an Apartment

Once you've decided to live in an apartment (or decided to *consider* doing so, if you still have a chance to choose on campus), keep in mind the following factors in checking out the scene around town.

* Rent, obviously.
* Which utilities are included (gas, electricity, water).
* Whether it is air-conditioned.
* Age of the building (can give the apartment character, but may affect plumbing, insulation, etc. in ways that aren't visible).
* Provisions in the lease for early termination.
* Off-street and/or covered parking; if not, availability of places on street.
* Loudness of the neighborhood/street. This can be hard to detect if the windows are closed when you visit.
* Access to public transportation.
* Condition of windows. If there are no screens and/or the frames are cracked, you may have a lot more insects to deal with. If heat is your responsibility to pay for, your bills may also be significantly higher.
* Thinness of walls and ceilings.
* Who the other tenants are.
* Whether pets are allowed (for an extra fee?).
* Cost and availability of laundry machines in the building.
* Presence of dishwasher and microwave.
* Amount of storage space within the apartment or in the basement.

* Whether it is furnished.
* Whether mailboxes are *inside* the outside door (makes it much easier to receive packages and not worry about theft).
* Whether there is a doorbell or intercom.
* Whether smoking is allowed.
* Maximum number of people allowed to inhabit the apartment.

Landlord-Tenant Relations

You've decided to live off campus and have found a place; now your task is to make it as easy to live there as it would be to live in a dorm, so you'll have time to focus on the things that matter.

Unless you're in a large, expensive, very professionally run building with a reputation to uphold (probably not, as a student) or have an exceptional landlord, the landlord-tenant relationship can have its tense moments. Landlords know that students are sometimes low on financial, legal, and informational resources; they have been known to take advantage of that. On the other hand, students are not always the quietest, cleanest, or most reliably paying tenants. The details vary with state law, but here is, in general, what the two sides can expect from each other:

What You Can Expect from Your Landlord

* Notification of when he/she will be showing the apartment to possible new tenants.
* Courtesy notification of when he/she will be coming over for repairs/maintenance etc.
* A copy of your lease (consider making one yourself if you have the chance).
* Repairs of problems not caused by you (plumbing, roof, wall, door problems, locks, and insect problems).
* Maintenance of common areas (light bulbs, snow removal, etc.).
* Your security deposit returned to you in full, sometimes with interest, assuming your surreptitiously kept hedgehog, Max, hasn't done any lasting damage.

What You Owe Your Landlord

* As specified in the lease, notice of intent to vacate may be required. In many cases, there is also some sort of penalty if you vacate before the lease is expected to terminate.
* Payment of rent made promptly on the first of every month, or other day as arranged, whether or not you're in town or even living there. A lease is a binding contract.
* Repair or payment for repair (from your security deposit) of damages you, your guests, or your pets do to the apartment.

What to Do If You Have Problems with Your Landlord

* If it's a relatively minor repair, do it yourself or hire someone (a plumber, say) to do it for you. Deduct the cost from your next rent check and send the receipt to your landlord.
* Know your rights. Most cities have some sort of tenants' union; there are also provisions in the laws of your state dealing with landlord-tenant issues; look up "*your state* statute" on the Web and search the code by landlord, tenant, lease, etc. The state government or attorney general's Web site should also have such information linked.
* Under severe circumstances, you may break your lease, not be penalized, and get your security deposit back. Your landlord owes you a habitable apartment; if maintenance or insect problems render it otherwise, you may move out.
* If worse comes to worst, you can take your landlord to small claims court . . . or threaten to.

Keeping It Livable

Let's face it, few student apartments are camera-ready. But there's a big difference between a place that lacks the amenities and one that lacks good hygiene. At a very minimum, you're going to have to master a few techniques to tide you through your landlord's Mexican vacation and keep the inspectors and pests at bay. Remember the following . . .

In the Bathroom

PREVENTIVE MEDICINE

* Don't flush pads or tampons down the toilet.
* Don't use Kleenex in lieu of toilet paper. It is almost always thicker and dissolves less easily, contributing over time to buildup in the pipes even if the toilet appears to be working properly. For similar reasons, if your toilet is finicky you may want to use cheaper, thinner toilet paper.
* You know you want to finish that article anyway. With older toilets, using multiple flushes to diminish the load-per-flush can be the key to bathroom pleasure.

UNCLOGGING A TOILET

Sometimes they unclog by themselves, but not usually. If you've flushed twice and it's still not going anywhere, probably don't flush again: sometimes overloaded toilets will overflow if you flush too many times and the water has nowhere to go but up and out.

First, try a plunger. Fit the suction over the hole in the toilet, trying to leave no air around it. Pump hard, repeatedly. Try different angles and twists (this is where high school band baton skills finally hit pay dirt); sometimes straight down seems to work best, sometimes pumping in the direction of the hole works best. When you hear a noise that comes from deep inside the toilet, you'll know you've gotten somewhere; especially promising is a sudden draining of all the water left in the bowl after you release the suction. If you've worked a long time and notice neither of these, it's probably still worth a flush to see if anything's changed.

If not, try an auger. Augers are long, menacing-looking metal snakes with a loose coil on the end and a swivel handle. They are sold at hardware and general merchandise stores for under $10. Insert the coil into the toilet drain so that the coil just disappears from sight. Then slide the metal pipe down as far as it will go. Push the snake as far in as you can; then begin swiveling the handle. Again, you may need to try different angles. The snake may well not go all the way into the toilet; it does not necessarily need to. Get it in as far as it will go, then pull out and try flushing again.

In the Kitchen

See chapter 17, "Odors," "Pests," and "Damage Disguise."

Keeping It Tasty

Once your kitchen is in a sanitary state, it should be possible to enter it without fear. Cooking is one of the joys and motivations for apartment living. You ought to eat far better than your compatriots in the dorm, but many first-time apartment dwellers end up eating *worse* because of lack of confidence in their abilities, difficulties shopping for and maintaining a supply of groceries, or laziness. In default, there are always ramen noodles and mac and cheese. But you can do better, our friend.

It's all about equipment, ingredients, and the relationship therebetween. Start with the things you can buy (these come cheap from your parents, at secondhand stores, or, as a last resort, stores like Target and Bed Bath & Beyond):

The Most Basic Cookware

Measuring cup and spoons (teaspoon, tablespoon)
Saucepan (2 ½ qt or larger) with lid for boiling water, cooking rice and pasta, and warming soup and tomato sauce
Wide, shallow frying pan for pancakes, meat, vegetable stir-fries, eggs, and grilled cheese
Cookie sheet for baking meat and cookies
CorningWare-style baking casserole for heating and serving dips and cooking stews
2 mixing bowls for baking, storing fruit, serving chips and popcorn
hand-held electric mixer
rubber spatula—great for making batters
wooden spoon—useful especially for nonstick cookware
plastic spatula—useful for nonstick cookware
can opener
colander for washing fruit and vegetables and draining water from boiled pasta and vegetables
sharp knives

oven mitt

cutting board (wooden ones can't go in the dishwasher)

You'll need, similarly, the staples in the food department. The following will make little more than cookies on their own, but they are the building blocks of many great dishes:

salt
pepper
white flour
wheat flour
cane (white) sugar
brown sugar
baking powder
baking soda
vinegar
milk
vanilla extract
cooking oil
butter/margarine/shortening
eggs
spices
yeast

The above staples, with the exception of eggs and milk, last a long time. Not all food is so lucky. In shopping, consider the wildly varying shelf lives of other items. Here are some examples of common food items and how long they last.

Hours. Opened avocado, banana, peach, apple, and fresh cookies or cake

Days. Lettuce (head), celery, sprouts, strawberries, pineapple, grapes, cooked vegetables, peppers, bakery bread, broccoli, cold cuts, soft cheeses (like Brie), and raw meat

Weeks. Milk, cream cheese, chips (bag opened), raw meat (in freezer), yogurt, cottage cheese, carrots, assembly-line cookies and breads, eggs, butter (in refrigerator), Reddi-Whip, semi-soft cheese (like cheddar), jam (jar opened), and olives (jar opened)

Months. Peanut butter, mustard, ketchup, coffee, frozen vegetables, ice cream, juice, onions, potatoes, salad dressings, crackers, maple syrup, honey, butter (in freezer), yeast, chocolate sauce, nuts, and hard cheese (like Parmesan)

Years. Spices, candy, staples like tightly covered flour and sugar, dried beans, rice, dry pasta, canned goods (look at the label), hard liquor, wine in an unopened bottle, popcorn, and tea bags

Once you've shopped for equipment and food, all you really need are the basic techniques:

Boiling (tea, pasta, beans, rice, vegetables, and sauces). Unless it's just water for a drink (you can use the microwave), fill a pot no more than ¾ full with the liquid you want to boil. Cover it, turn it on medium high, and wait until bubbles cover the surface. If you want it to continue boiling for a while without boiling over, turn the heat down to medium/medium-low.

Stir-frying (pancakes, meat, and vegetables). Heat about a tablespoon of oil on medium-high for a minute or two. Throw a few drops of water in; if the oil hisses strongly, it's ready. Throw in whatever you want to stir fry (cut-up meat and vegetables take about five minutes; larger cuts of meat can take up to half an hour; pancakes take until bubbles come up and burst through the batter, then 30 seconds or so after you flip them).

Baking (meat, casseroles, cakes, cookies, pies, and pizza). 350 degrees is the default temp for meat; recipes for dessert-type items should give you a temperature. Most meat takes at least half an hour or so to roast; thicker cuts of beef, say, can take an hour and a half or more. Test meat by cutting in with a knife, making sure it cuts smoothly, and looking for red (unless you like rare). Bake pizza at 375–400 degrees until the cheese melts and/or looks a little golden. Cake is ready when a knife in the middle comes out clean; smaller items like cookies are done when slightly golden but not burnt on the edges.

Leftovers last, on average, a week in the 'fridge, so you could theoretically (and some of us have) do all your cooking for the week on the weekend. Things like cookies and cakes last for months in the freezer; cooked casseroles and pizzas vary, but it never hurts to try with your favorite recipe.

9
Martha Stewart
Meets the Barracks:
Room
Decorating

Unless prison life has accustomed you to Spartan accommodations, you'll probably want to institute some improvements upon the cell assigned you by the Dean of Housing (or the Fates of apartment-hunting). Some people we know turned theirs into a worthy study for *This Old House*; others followed the call of Martha Stewart all the way to Kmart. Whatever the character of your television education and pursuant ambitions, the following practical and aesthetic advice will get you well on your way to baring it all as an *Elle Decor* centerfold . . .

Cheapendale

Space permitting, you'll want some furniture beyond that provided by Ma Superintendent. Your local department store, however, is likely to be a little beyond your means—and even if it weren't, a college room is no place for quality furniture. Just because you treat the couch with care doesn't mean the dorm dog isn't going to see fit to crash there Friday nights. Stay away from very bulky items: you may well be moving every year in college and even if you don't want to keep them beyond the end of the year, you'll still have to get them out to the dumpster.

Here's where to find the goods capable of withstanding this and other trials:

Discount superstores—Kmart, Wal-Mart, etc. The quality won't be great, but you'll know what you're getting and you might be able to arrange delivery or shipment fairly cheaply. Pier One Imports and Jennifer Convertibles both have reasonable prices if you're looking for a new couch or bed.

Futon emporiums. Often found near college campuses, these offer a wide selection of futons (a must-have if you're going to be opening your doors to friends from faraway, pre-frosh, cheap relatives, etc.) and sometimes offer deals/special delivery rates for students. Futons run $100–$300 and quality isn't a bad thing; covers run $30 or so; fitted sheets also work and are easier to remove and clean.

Antique stores, Goodwill, garage sales. For the bargain hunter, these can really pay off, especially if you have a little time before classes start.

Peers. Student sales come more often at the end of the year than the beginning, but check for postings just in case. Even if you don't see any sales advertised, you can sometimes wangle a deal on your own initiative; if you're in a student room and see a couch you like, offer to buy it. The owner will be flattered at worst, receptive at best. College students get sick of their La-Z-Boys; you may get lucky.

But before you shake on the deal, or on a deal with any of the above, give the item a last once-over. There's a lot of bad stuff out there, as our roommate who bought a used "refrigerator" (basically, it functioned as a cupboard) found out. And even if the quality's okay, the goods may be unsuited to your living arrangements. As you shop, keep the following in mind.

What to look for in a . . .	*condition & styling*
table	folds up or disassembles easily for storage (screws not nails); has wheels to facilitate transportation to and from storage; if wooden, has a stain-resistant finish; if to be used as a computer console, rises to the height of your elbows while you're seated in your desk chair; if used (especially if a card

	table), has functional legs (try moving it back and forth and see if the feet fall off or legs wobble).
couch	dark-colored upholstery, preferably textured (to hide stains); has easily removable cushions; has removable cushion covers (makes cleaning easier); is long enough to be used as a bed in a pinch, but is not longer than the longest expanse of open wall/open space in your room; will fit through your door; has a frame lightweight enough to be easily moved; if used, has still-springy springs and no visible rips or beginnings of rips.
futon	as with couch, is of dark color with removable cover; is lightweight (frames vary); has a simple fold-up mechanism (ones involving more elements break easily)
rug	dark, patterned, or neutral-colored; tassel-free (makes vacuuming easier should you choose to go that route)
used electrical appliance (TV, fridge, etc.)	make sure it functions!!! do not buy without plugging it in and trying it out!

Now that you've taken care of the big-ticket items, it's time to turn to the smaller things—the little touches that will give you comfort and tell visitors "You'se in a home now, honey." We've included some of these items in the packing list in case you wanted to finish your shopping before leaving home, but since most people buy this stuff near campus to avoid the effort of shipping, we've waited until now to justify their purchase. Be at least aware of dorm (or apartment) rules on potential fire hazards (space heaters, hot plates, and candles are sometimes *verboten*, but if you are smart about using them and conceal them over vacations when inspections occur you should be okay). Consider getting:

Decorating with Duct Tape

A few sessions with an expensive designer or trips to Crate & Barrel can get you the fancy look alright, but all you really need to make your room a glittering upscale *salon* is a couple rolls of the old classic. All you need is a trip to the hardware store and a look-see at these ideas:

Rhododendron. Who's going to spend money on a nice plant only to have it croak over vacation? Instead, fold strips of the tape lengthwise to simulate the effect and texture of long leaves. "Plant" in dirt and place near window where light of sun can strike it, allowing your creation to double as a disco ball.

R.I.P. For a funky icebreaker that also functions as a threat, make the outline of your least favorite roommate in duct tape on the floor.

Who's the fairest of them all? Mirrors can distort; rely on duct tape for some straight answers. When makeshift-looking glass gets dull, use remnants for posh, silverlike picture frames.

Tarzan, Lord of the . . . No need for a ladder to your loft when a duct tape "vine" can get you where you need to go.

Hi-ho, Silver! For another use that will give your room a ritzy Hollywood feel, turn duct tape into a sticky lasso, perfect for snagging that pipe across the room when your paper's keeping you tied to your computer.

Worthy of Calder. Make duct tape the skeleton of your personal mobile, affixing to the hanging strands items that remind you of home — retainers, 'cuffs, dog droppings.

This room ain't big enough for the both of us. Before roommate relations turn your room into the OK corral, get things under control by dividing the space in two. Worked for our friends and can work for you.

Telephone and answering machine. If you're going to be sharing the line with more than two other people, you may consider buying a machine that has separate tapes to record messages for separate roommates. It's often hard for a roommate to judge which parts of a five-minute blather are important; better to hear your own messages for yourself. Voice mail can also be arranged to provide this separating service, the only disadvantage being that screening calls becomes impossible. Cordless phones are nice.

Microwave. Useful for heating popcorn, ramen, soups, leftovers, and a whole lineup of TV dinners, the ovens really are indispensable for the nocturnal or the picky eater. Resist the temptation, however, to view microwaves as replacements for all appliances; as one of our friends found out, Maytag still dries clothes better—or at least their warranty covers spontaneous combustion of socks.

Refrigerator. If you're going to be doing any cooking or even snacking in the room, a fridge is pretty much a necessity. Leftovers, milk for morning cereal, pizza, and alcohol all require or benefit from residence in the icebox. If your dorm has a kitchen—find out whether it does, obviously, before you buy—you're in the clear; otherwise you can get a small new fridge for under $100. The cube-style ones are smaller than they look; if more than one person will be using, you might go for a taller rectangular one.

TV/VCR/DVD, as large a screen as you can afford/transport. On Thursday nights, watch your room become the haven for *Friends* groupies; on weekends, the movie loft for dateless wonders.

Halogen lamp. If your parents have been saving a lava lamp for your illumination, don't disturb their dreams, but if you're not yet equipped, go for the halogen. Elegant yet fairly cheap (about $30), their capacity for dimming increases (entirely accounts for) the romantic possibilities of your bachelor(ette) pad. The bulbs, unfortunately, are a bit pricey at $10, but require changing only once per school year or so. College dorm rooms are almost always *extremely* poorly-lit.

Diskmeister. Floppies have a tendency to live up to their names, and if you don't watch out, that backup disk you're depending on might just flop right out the fourth-floor window. Store your life safely.

CD or tape rack. Unless you're majoring in surfing, there won't be much room on the bookshelf for your music collection. Try to find a rack that will somehow fit into a box or suitcase at the end of the year.

Desk light. Give it a little trial in the store before you buy—the one we sprang for ended up functioning as a better lighter than lamp, since it practically incinerated all nearby objects if left on longer than ten minutes.

Wall decor. There's always your childhood fingerwork, but you don't want to get pigeonholed right away as the next Picasso. Used and

How to Conceal a Pet

There's the easygoing super, the kind who gives you the inside dope on the profs' tastes in bribes ("Mr. Astrology, he like slippers. Snakeskin"). Then there's the Bob Barker wannabe with a sheephide toupee and a matching mission to help control the pet population.

Though the latter may seem more threatening as he brandishes his stun gun, the former as well may have alternate plans for your boa. It's a wild world, and precautions are going to be necessary if you're going to retain control of the menagerie. For help where help's needed, try the following tricks:

And lying in a manger. Wrap kitty in swaddling clothes and strap on like papoose when it's time for afternoon mouse hunt. On the way to cafeteria, acknowledge jeers directed at you for interrupting your studies to care for an oppressor's child with a simple flip of the bird.

Dyed-to-match. Trade the turquoise wonder in for one of the new bred-in-Laura-Ashley chameleons. Lizards can change their skin to accord with a variety of floral and gingham motifs.

Embalming. Douse bird—including beak and talons—with shellac or styling gel. Remove immobilized creature from cage and solicit super's admiration of home 'dermy job during inspection. If a senior, respond favorably to offers of purchase; otherwise hose down following departure.

If you don't believe me, feel free to . . . Claim that the haunting howling emanating from the bedroom where you've stashed the chihuahua is just the *Jazz Loon* CD your roommate and her boyfriend insist on listening to while, well, you know . . .

new bookstores and music stores near campuses are usually full of poster choices: the campus bookstore in particular can usually be counted on for the usual impressionist and Ansel Adams fare. If you have something very specific in mind, try posters.com (music, sports, etc.), www.barewalls.com (everything), or www.metmuseum.org/store/ and www.museumcompany.com (art).

Crates/Rubbermaid boxes. In a stack by your desk . . . under your bed . . . perched on your windowsill . . . these will be indispensable storage tools. The boxes you shipped things in will work just as well, provided they're not too deformed. Try covering one in a sheet to make a nightstand.

Cacti and other desert plants. Portable and able to live without water for even the longest (Thanksgiving to New Year's) winter vacations, these charming plants will brighten your windowsill, as well as provide a means of fulfillment for sadomasochistic impulses.

How to Build a Loft

Not satisfied with your room, a.k.a. cupboard? It's time to take matters into your own hands. But before you start hammering, find out your college's regulations; some only allow lofts in certain dorms. If yours isn't one of them, it's no reason to abandon construction plans, but you may have to build sober.

It's best to build right away, before you've settled all your stuff in.

If you aren't picky, you can probably buy a secondhand loft either from previous inhabitants or from another older student; watch for signs.

If you've got architectural vision, on the other hand, you can either get out the wrench yourself or contract out. Send word around that you'll pay for an afternoon of carpentry.

You, or whoever does the work for you, should use screws instead of nails; these will allow you to easily dismantle the structure for storage.

To ensure that Chicken Little's fear of the sky falling doesn't prove all too prophetic, brace your loft with supports. Use also for suspension of key bedside items (see chapter 3, "For Bedside"), hang-drying beef jerky, etc.

Even if the sky doesn't fall, you might—and who's to say which is worse from Joe bunkmate's point of view? Guarantee you both a good night's (day's?) sleep by building a 6–8-inch lip along the edge of the loft.

10
Cheapskating Your Way through College:
Finances

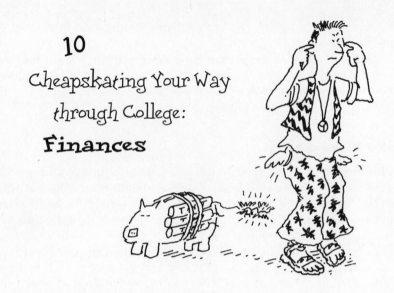

By the end of freshman year, most of our friends were about as broke as you can get without taking TNT to the piggy bank. It wasn't that they were spendthrifts; it's just that money, like dates and other forms of dried fruit, is scarce in the average college student's life, and you may not be accustomed to taking care of pleasure-free expenses like telephone bills and spiral notebooks.

The solution isn't doing magic tricks for your adoring little sib ("Gotta 'nother quarter, Ryan? Gonna have some fun, boy!"). It's rather checking out your sources of money, traditional and nontraditional, and being careful about the way you use it. We're not here to reproach you for splurging on that fancy-dancy pocket protector; whatever your spending habits are, the following chapter is intended only to guide you in indulging them.

Money: Requirements

If you're living in a dorm, most of your fixed expenses will be prepaid, either by your parents or your loans. This should make budgeting easier; in a pinch, you really won't need to spend much money at all. But to live normally, you can expect to spend somewhere in the neighborhood of the following amounts:

Entertainment. Snacks, movies, meals, and refreshments out. Roughly $30/wk.

Books. You can try relying on the library, but assigned books for large classes are in demand and in any case can't be written in. Used books can also be hard to get your hands on; get to the bookstore early if you want to find them. Expect to spend roughly $300/semester. (See below for info on getting books cheap.)

Transportation around campus and town. In many cases, nothing at all. If you live a ways away from campus, you may invest in a bus or subway pass (perhaps $30 a month) or spend about twice that on gas. If you'll be parking at meters or in pay lots around campus, the cost can add up quickly: at least several dollars a day. The cost of getting towed is easily more than $100.

Trips home. Anywhere from a $3 subway roundtrip to $350 coast to coast (assuming you get tickets far enough in advance). Expect two to three trips per school year if you live far away, five and up if you live in driving distance.

Stationery supplies, toiletries. Especially if you didn't come equipped with all of the items listed in chapter 3, you'll probably be spending $20 to $50 a semester on printer paper, ink cartridges, stamps, notebooks, pens, tape, etc. Depending upon your gender, expect to spend $50 to $200 a semester on toiletries, haircuts, makeup, etc.

Phone service. With features, perhaps $10–$15 a month per person if you're sharing a line and the fee isn't included in your bill for the dorm. You generally don't have a choice of long-distance service when you live in a dorm, and prepaid calling cards will generally be cheaper than the rate offered. Depending on your phone habits and where you are located in relation to friends and family, expect to spend from $5 to $80 a month on long distance (the latter figure arises from long-distance relationships).

Dorm decor. Expect a one-time (or at most once per move) expenditure of $150–$500 and up.

(see chapter 8 for additional off-campus living expenses)

Money: Getting It

Important as having a job is (see chapter 15!), the money you get from it is likely to be small potatoes; a lot of anchovies are going to hit the cheese before your salary for pizza-tossing makes a dent in tuition. Luckily, there are other sources of cash, and according to various reports, anywhere from 100 million to 7 billion dollars' worth of it goes unclaimed every year. Like the river of life, it flows from many sources . . .

Colleges and the Federal Government

The first step in the financial aid–seeking process, as you may know already, occurs around the time you apply for college: filling out a FAFSA form and sending it to the colleges you're applying to. The form requests detailed information on you and your parents' income, assets, debts, and expenditures (it's relevant, for example, whether or not you have siblings in college already). Colleges use the FAFSA form in calculating the financial aid package they offer you at the time they accept you or soon after.

This package will have three parts, normally: grants (basically outright gifts of money), loans, and work-study status. Grants are obviously the best; work-study status can enable you to get some plum (i.e. little work required) jobs, as many offices on campus can only hire students with work-study status. Loans are iffier: while interest will probably not begin to accrue until you graduate, this may limit your choices post-graduation, encouraging you to either continue school or prioritize salary over meaning in employment. Pay careful attention to the balance of grants, loans, and work-study money, not just to the overall amount; also keep in mind that you will have to reapply every year of college and may get a different-looking package another year.

Private (noncollege) Aid

To convince you that some of that free-floating cash has your name on it, we offer the following brief run-down of the possibilities:

Mega-achievement—in academics, sculpting, batting—still brings in the bucks. But you don't have to be a Hmong granddaughter of Einstein and Pablo Picasso to win scholarships; the bases for awards are much more diverse:

Quirks and past offenses. Ever done time for prostitution in the Pacific Northwest? Caddied in Jersey? Were you born June 17, 1979? Believe it or not, there is a scholarship waiting for you and people with other *specified occupational histories, birth dates, or criminal records.*

And you thought the collection plate went straight into the pastor's Florida Fund. There's also money available for members of various *religions/denominations*—common as well as more obscure ones.

Giddyap! If you're good enough at almost any sport, it can pay. Archery, badminton, fencing, and rodeo scholarships are all out there for those not too embarrassed to apply.

Dear Kellogg's, I've been eating your cereal all my life and would like something in return . . . The companies that employ your parents may have money earmarked for children of workers. It never hurts to ask.

Military Aid

If you're willing to spend your summers in boot camp, your mornings running around singing "Got a chicken, name of Lou / Bought a cock and made it two," and the years following graduation in the Philippines, you may just have your education paid for at the college of your choice. ROTC info is available from the following sources:

U.S. Air Force ROTC Recruiting Division
551 E. Maxwell Blvd
Maxwell Air Force Base, AL 36112–6106
http://www.afoats.af.mil (Air Force ROTC)

U.S. Army ROTC Commander
Fort Monroe, VA 23651
http://www.armyrotc.com (Army ROTC)

U.S. Marine Corps Headquarters
Washington, D.C. 20380
http://www.cnet.navy.mil/nrotc/nrotc.htm
    (Navy and Marines ROTC)

U.S. Navy Opportunity Information Center
P.O. Box 5000
Clifton, NJ 07012
http://www.cnet.navy.mil/nrotc/nrotc.htm
    (alternate address for Navy and Marines ROTC)

Resources

For the complete scoop on funds available, you'll need to check out a comprehensive guide—*College Financial Aid For Dummies* (Herm Davis, Joyce Lain Kennedy); *How to Go to College Almost for Free* (Benjamin R. Kaplan); *The Scholarship Book: the Complete Guide to Private-Sector Scholarships, Fellowships, Grants, and Loans for the Undergraduate* (Daniel J. Cassidy) to name just a few. There are also books tailored to specific kinds of students, for example: *The Black Student's Guide to Scholarships: 700+ Private Money Sources for Black and Minority Students* (Barry Beckham, Ed.); *A Parent and Student Athlete's Guide to Athletic Scholarships* (Dion Wheeler); *The Minority and Women's Complete Scholarship Book* (Student Services L.L.C.); *Making a Difference: Scholarships for a Better World* (Miriam Weinstein, Ed.).

There are also some great Web sites out there with up-to-date information. Take a look at:

http://scholarships.kachinatech.com/scholarships/scholars.html
    (college scholarships and graduate fellowships)
http://www.collegescholarships.com
http://www.scholarships.com
http://www.uncf.org (United Negro College Fund)
http://www.collegefund.org (American Indian College Fund)

For other Internet sources of general information, do a search under "scholarship search services."

All of the Web sites above provide information for free, but there are other sites and services that operate for a fee (sometimes refundable if they can't find you a certain amount of money). See http://www.collegefunds.net and http://www.4scholarship.com (try, once again, looking on the Web under "scholarship search"). We'd say try the free services first, though; they will probably be enough. Scholarship information is public, since people *want* to give the money away; with a little legwork on your part, it shouldn't be hard to track down.

Money: Handling It

Credit Cards

Unless you have a legitimate fear of going on a huge spending spree, get a credit card if you don't have one of your own already. It's never too soon to start developing a good credit history; getting cards with good rates and policies is easier as a college student than it will be later.

Having said that, we recommend against turning your wallet into a magnet, which would only result in an increased attraction to refrigerators. Too many credit cards not only means more problems if your wallet gets stolen, but it can lead to overspending and disorganization. Your college will forward mail over the summer, but to be safe you'll want to change your billing address with the credit card company; the more cards, the more calls you'll have to make. Also, paradoxically, having too many credit lines available to you, even if you don't use them, can impair your credit rating and make it harder to get the cards you actually want.

If you don't have a credit card yet, we recommend waiting until you arrive at school to get one. Your mailbox will be flooded with offers—often promising no annual fee for life—and banks won't expect you to show evidence of substantial assets or credit history. If, after several attempts, your application still hasn't been accepted, you may need to buttress your position by opening a checking account or having your parents cosign.

If you fly home for vacations fairly often, it may be worth your while to get a card that earns you frequent flier credits for charging. If you use the card enough, you can make up in mileage the annual fee such cards usually carry.

American Express offers a charge/credit card for students that entitles holders to a number of fixed-rate roundtrip fares, domestic and international, that sometimes are cheaper than the prevailing rates. See http://home4.americanexpress.com/blue/student/blue_student_home.asp

Ideally, you really should be paying your balance off in full every month, so interest rates shouldn't matter. But if that's somehow not re-alistic for you now, be selective about the cards you get and keep an eye on the fine print in the statements accompanying your bill; cards often change their rates. If you have the time, you can play the balance-shift-ing game to take advantage of better introductory rates on new cards.

Checking

If your college is in a city large enough for establishments to accept out-of-state checks, or if you don't mind paying the fee for ATM trans-actions with your home bank's card, you may not need a local check-ing account. But if you want the convenience of a nearby bank, here's how to approach setting up an account:

Consider ordering carbon checks, especially if this is your first ac-count or if you tend to be disorganized. Your irritation with the carbon copies will force you to balance your checkbook.

Shop around. You might expect that neighboring banks would offer similar packages, but that isn't always the case. Here's what to look for:

No monthly fee. You shouldn't have to pay just for the right to write checks or make ATM withdrawals from the bank's own machines. You may find that by opening a savings account, even one with a small amount of money, you can get free checking.

Many free ATM machines. The bigger (locally) the bank, the more machines they'll have around. You won't want to be keeping a lot of cash in your dorm room or backpack, so you'll probably be making fre-quent withdrawals.

Low minimum balance. Supporting yourself away from home is ex-pensive, and when times are tough—and reminiscent of the '70s—you may find yourself living from limbo victory to limbo victory. That $500 sitting in your account isn't going to do you much good when the barber's on the answering machine demanding you settle your debts; try to find an account that allows for maximum liquidity.

Interest-bearing checking accounts. If you're moving your savings from your home bank, or if you want an incentive to steer clear of bankruptcy, look for an account that will earn you money. To realize any profit—and often to open the account in the first place—you may need a minimum of $1,000 or so.

Saving Money on Books

Depending on the degree of your college's affinities with Scrooge, the prices at the campus bookstore may or may not be inflated. It may be worth your while, in any case, to explore alternative sources:

Local bookstores. If you still want to buy new, shop around at independent bookstores in the area. A different edition, say of a work of literature, is usually okay, but make sure the reason it's cheaper isn't that it lacks an introduction—since that may be the only part of the book you'll get to, and the only part you'll really need. If, however, it's a small class or seminar and you'll be expected to discuss the book in class, having the same page numbers as the professor may make buying the recommended edition worthwhile.

Used books. Take a stroll around campus/town before you buy new. You can often buy cheap, virgin (a good indication that the text is superfluous) books either from bookstore basements or from older students, who may advertise on the classroom door, on nearby carrels, or on bulletin boards in student centers. If it isn't the first assigned book of the semester, you'll have time to order, too, if you want. Amazon .com lists used books along with its new versions; try also http://www .half.com and http://www.thriftyscholar.com.

Library books. Consult the syllabus to see how many pages of each book are assigned, and consult your own motivation to see how much you'll realistically get to. If you won't be spending much time on a given text, or even if you will, a library copy may be enough. If you can't find one on the shelves, a reserve copy may serve your purposes.

Online. Public domain books (mostly written in the nineteenth century and earlier) are often available in their entirety online. Search under book title and author or a phrase from the book (put it in quotation marks) that would be unlikely to appear in another book or type in a mere quotation from the book you are searching for.

Money: Giving It Back (to Big Brother)

Provided you had enough income to require filing (or had enough of it withheld to merit a refund), this isn't a bad time to learn how to do taxes. Your finances are probably still quite simple, and you may find it empowering.

How to Trick Teller into Making "Bank Error in Your Favor"

Life isn't Monopoly—or is it? The teller, no doubt, got his early training somewhere between Baltic and Boardwalk, and with a little nudge from you he can revert to the world of his youth. To score yourself enough for a new vibrator, or at least some sweet corn, try the following stratagems:

Ask him if he wants to see a magic trick.

Walk confidently up to the window and say "I passed go."

Mutter numbers under your breath to confuse him as he counts out the bills.

Engage him in political talk by suggesting he run for public office. Steer the conversation around to president appearing on $100 bill and say "Now what did he look like, again?" Teller proudly displays c-note for your edification; as he waxes belligerent on the Fed, you pocket the demo.

If you had taxes withheld by an employer last year, they will send you a W-2 form. If you received income from other sources—on a one-time, contract basis, from a bank as interest on an account, from mutual fund distributions, etc.—you should receive a statement from the source of that income. If you worked on an informal basis—as a babysitter, handyman, etc.—you will probably not receive a statement of that amount, but you should report it anyway if it's significant and/or you plan to be nominated for Attorney General. Gifts from parents and money from loans do not count as income.

The main income tax form is the federal one, the IRS Form 1040. You may receive it in the mail; if you don't, it's available at public libraries and post offices or on the Internet (search for "federal tax form"). Check out the 1040-EZ first: it's a vastly simplified version, and it may well cover all your sources of income and deductions. State taxes are lower and use calculations and numbers from the federal form, so do your federal income taxes first. In general, you should file a tax return in every state in which you have income, but check the requirements: if your income is pretty low (which it probably will be), you may not have to file unless you are owed a refund. States also sometimes have reciprocal arrangements whereby you report all of your income as if it occurred in only one of them.

You will probably not be itemizing deductions, since those available to you are extremely unlikely to exceed the "standard," minimum deduction that everyone is entitled to without having to prove anything. There are a couple of important credits, however, available to either you or your parents depending on your status as a dependent. The Hope Scholarship can offer a couple of thousand dollars of tax relief for the first two years of college if you qualify (which isn't too difficult— based upon income and tuition costs). The Lifetime Learning Credit is available thereafter, and interest on student loans is often deductible. For more information, search the Internet for either term and you will get linked to IRS forms and explanations.

In lieu of filling out paper forms, you can also file electronically either with the revenue departments directly or via an accountant-type Web site. Quicken's Web site, for example, organizes your filing for free if your income is below a certain level, which it almost certainly will be. Filing electronically often results in faster refunds.

Keep copies of your tax returns in case they are lost in the mail or require fixing.

11

From Break-ins to Ben & Jerry's Bodyguards: Safety & Security

College campuses give space to a rogue's gallery larger than Dick Tracy's. Brownie bandits, laptop larcenists, backpack burglars, CD snatchers, jeep-jackers, and purse pilferers all frequent dorms, libraries, and town streets. Depending upon your college's location, more serious crime may also threaten you. Rape, mugging, and even murder can be very real dangers in urban environments.

In order to get an idea of your campus's crime level, don't just listen to the wind; one of us got nothing but the high sign from older students, only to read about two assaults the morning after we walked home alone. A better way of gauging the climate is to read the campus or town police reports, which are likely to be printed either in your community's or your college's official periodical. Look at the locations as well as the natures of the crimes so you can judge which areas to avoid. Another way of casing things out is to compare your campus's security with that of other schools you know of. If security is relatively high—if guards require, as they do at one of our schools, all dorm non-residents entering for even five minutes to submit picture IDs and sign passes, there's probably a pretty good reason.

Once you've taken stock of your environment, you'll be equipped to judge which of the following measures are necessary for you to em-

Special Precautions for Night

Take advantage of escort services if you'll be walking any distance. They're free, easily- and under-utilized, and can aid you in convincing gullible roommates that you have an active dating life. If you have a cell phone, program the escort service number into it even if you're not planning to use the service any time soon. At least it will be an option if you ever need to.

Should you contumaciously decide to walk alone instead of taking the above advice...

In keeping with your Hemingwayesque machismo, walk in clean, well-lighted places.

Avoid getting close to parked cars. For a while one of our campuses was haunted by a guy who would hide under the chassis and slash pedestrians' Achilles tendons.

Walk down the middles of streets, if they're not too busy. Criminals prefer to lurk behind trees, inside alleys, etc.

Try not to get too weighed down, especially with obviously expensive, easily grabbed items like laptops in special computer bags.

Consider carrying mace, pepper spray, or a rape whistle.

Don't use ATM machines unless they're in very bright places, and are ideally inside.

Stopping to give change, help, or anything else to an unknown homeless person is one thing during the day; it's less smart at night if you're alone or even in a small group.

Be aware of where campus emergency call boxes (often lit with blue or red lights) are.

If you have a cell phone, consider carrying it where you can reach it easily.

ploy. If you learned street smarts before or instead of your ABCs, you're set already for the hucksters outside your dorm. But you may be in the same boat as farm frosh like us when it comes to protecting your pint of Cherry Garcia from mooching roommates, or your notes from finals-period theft, or dealing with a rapidly spreading in-dorm blaze.

No matter how experienced you are in protecting yourself, unfamiliarity with your new surroundings can leave you vulnerable. To avoid returning from registration having gained a study card and lost a wallet —as one of our roommates did—and to ensure your continued protection, err on the side of safety at least until you've been on campus long enough to know that you really have found the autumnal Utopia of brochures. Take the following precautions:

In the 'Hood

The fewer valuables you keep on you, the better.

Don't carry money and credit/ATM/debit cards in the small exterior pocket of your backpack—in a crowd someone could open it without your noticing. Don't ever leave cards or much cash in your backpack if you often leave it outside a dining hall.

A front pocket of your clothes or an interior backpack pouch is the best place to carry any valuables. But if you must use a purse . . .

* Carry it across your body—with the strap resting on your right shoulder, for example, and the bag hanging on your left side.
* If you're walking along a busy street, carry it so that the bag is on the side away from the street; this will prevent cyclists and marathoners-turned-thieves from snatching it on the fly.
* Hold on to your purse. Don't hang it on behind-the-door hooks in public bathrooms or on the back of your chair while you eat. If you're at a restaurant or cafeteria, either set it on your lap or place it on the floor with the strap over one of your legs.

If you're in a high-crime area, conceal any expensive-looking jewelry. Slip necklaces under garments, turn rings so that the stone is on the palm-side of your hand, etc.

At the Bike Rack

Bikes are a lot like green card–seeking spouses: good for a brief ride and then gone. In the end, all you can do is take these basic precautions and send Santa some advance warning about how many speeds you'll be requesting on the new one come Christmas:

Get a really great, horseshoe-shaped lock.

In the Refrigerator

Slapping your John Hancock on a Ben & Jerry's isn't going to deter anyone. If you want to save that grub for yourself, you're going to have to take more drastic measures:

56 grams of fat per serving?! No one will notice the paste globs where you attach your table of fake nutrition information. If your roommates are proto-anorexics, exaggerate the fat content; if they're swimmers, shoot low.

Carbonated glass cleaner. Old Windex bottle + Mr. Yuck stickers = no more sleepless nights: the champagne's safe. Instead of questioning your choice of products, your roommates will marvel at society's technological advances, moving rapidly from bathroom cleansers to sliced bread to the female condom, the conversation ending as they disperse to try the last out.

What will those crazy Vermonters think of next? Your buddy's psyched to sample what looks like a new flavor of B & J ("Mmm, white chocolate chunks!"), until he takes a pre-gobble peek. Only then does he discover that it's not Toblerone; it's a tooth—yours—saved from a molar removal and positioned for dramatic effect in the carton.

Label it with the name of the grossest person in the dorm. Enough said.

Remove the front wheel if you're in a bad area or if you'll be leaving the bike for any length of time.

See if you can register your bike with the campus police.

Have your bike's serial number written down somewhere so that if by some miracle the police find it when it's stolen, you can identify it.

If you're indifferent to appearances, spray paint your bike a really obnoxious, distinctive color—so obnoxious that after a while you welcome its theft.

At the ATM Machine

Obviously, don't make a transaction if there are a lot of people around who aren't polite enough to keep their distance. Try not to be super-blatant about which numbers you're punching for your PIN.

Always take your receipt with you. If you leave it, thieves who snuck a peek at your PIN can use it to manufacture a duplicate of your card (if they don't have the receipt, it's much harder for them). Not only that, but if a crook observes that you've made a large withdrawal, he might decide to pursue you.

If something seems fishy, but you've already started your transaction, push "cancel" immediately, take your card, and make for terra firma.

Try to change your PIN every once in a while; at least make sure that it isn't the same as your password(s) on various Web sites. If one is stolen, you don't want all of them to be.

It goes without saying, but don't pick as a PIN something that would be completely obvious if someone stole your wallet, like the beginning or end of your social security number, student ID number, or even driver's license number.

In the Library

It sounds like something out of *Revenge of the Nerds: The Horror Movie*, but notes do get stolen on college campuses—some places, more often than money does.

Don't leave your backpack anywhere during reading or finals period. If you want to save your place in the library to go to the restroom or cafeteria, grab a stack of books off the shelves and strew them, opened, about your desk/carrel. Leave a pen and a blank notebook or blank sheets of paper to solidify your claim.

Clearly, don't leave your laptop unattended. There's less risk if it's inconspicuously tucked in your backpack, more if it's in a bag specially designed for computers. If you must bring your backpack to the cafeteria, keep it with you instead of leaving it outside the door.

You increase your chances not of theft but of an almost as irritating mix-up if you buy a very popular style backpack—say one with your college's name or logo. Guard against this and make a fashion statement by attaching some distinctive-looking item to your bag, or by affixing lettering spelling out your personal manifesto.

In the Dorm

Leave telling your life story to those pesky biographers, not your answering machine. Don't record your room number or especially your whereabouts or time of return ("We're all gone for the weekend! Please help yourself to milk, cookies, and the stereo system located conveniently near the door!"). Even your last names are probably unnecessary—how many Josés are there with phone numbers similar to yours?

One of us brought twenty movies to college and came back with twenty different ones. Label videos, CDs, reference books—cases and items themselves—with at least your initials.

Don't keep money or expensive jewelry in really obvious places, like on closet hooks, the tops of desks, or dresser drawers. Of course, the fewer valuables you have around at all, the better; but if you quit trusting banks in '29, stash stuff in the midst of your underwear, with the clothes that you've stored for next season, under your computer, etc. For a place *no one* will go snooping—and a sure-fire guard against workaholism—try hollowing out a textbook and using it as a safe.

It can be a good idea to get a spare room key made, but be careful what you do with it. Don't leave it somewhere obvious, like under your doormat or behind the friendly neighborhood fire extinguisher. Giving it to a friend is cool, but avoid entrusting it to compulsive "borrowers" (resident kleptos).

Carry your key to the bathroom. Your roommate may think you're gone and lock the door when he/she leaves. It sucks to be waiting for the police to let you in while you're wearing just a towel—we speak from experience. Bathrobes with pockets and shower caddies help.

No matter where you go to school, it's really best to lock the door to your room when you're not there. No matter what the cow concentration, no matter how rich the students, there are bound to be some bad 'uns.

If your room is in the basement or on the first floor, it's probably best to lock your windows if you'll be gone a while. Try, also, to place valuable items away from the windows, where they won't be a temptation to every passing lowlife with a penchant for Panasonic.

In the Bedroom

High school people, for all of their flaws, probably seemed pretty normal and incapable of the kinds of strange acts people in afterschool specials are prone to.

College is different. On their own, unencumbered (and unhelped) by families and rules, some people can get very strange. You don't want to believe that seemingly nice people, people who seem at first like you, can do bad things, but they can. This doesn't mean you have to be suspicious of everyone you meet, but you also shouldn't automatically trust them just because they go to your school or live in the dorm next door. Be aware of the following major problems on campuses:

Date Rape

Rape by a stranger is terrifying (see "Special Precautions for Night," page 95), but extremely uncommon; date rape, on the other hand, is all too prevalent on college campuses. It tends to happen under circumstances where you are not in complete control over your decision-making, company, or even consciousness, but to the extent that you can be rational, think about:

Not drinking until you pass out, especially if you're in unfamiliar surroundings or with people you don't know well and trust.

Not inviting people up to your room or going to theirs on an early date if you're not interested in sex. This is especially true if you think or know that none of your or your date's roommates will be there.

Stalking

The term sounds extreme, but even less-than-completely psychopathic behavior can qualify. If someone is calling, e-mailing, writing, or visiting you obsessively when you have made it clear you don't want them to, that's stalking and is a sign of problems the person is having that could escalate. It's unfortunate that some people fixate on others who don't share their feelings as a way of giving meaning to their lives, but it isn't your problem, you shouldn't try to help them with it, and if you do it will probably only make them fixate on you more.

Try reason. Tell the person to stop contacting you and that you are not interested and are not going to be.

Be consistent. Don't apologize, ask questions, do something to be nice like agree to go out to dinner, or get roped into explaining why you're not interested. Any signal that you are emotionally involved in any way will only encourage the person.

If the person persists in contacting you, especially by showing up where the person knows you will be, or says or does anything remotely threatening, if you're in a dorm, tell not only your resident advisor (R.A.) but also the campus police.

If none of this helps, go to the regular city police. They can guide you in getting a restraining order against the person preventing the stalker, as much as possible, from contacting you or coming near you.

If You Are Mugged

Your plan of action really depends more on the environment than on the kind of crime imminent: if you're in a crowded area, the best thing to do is go bananas, making clear that your fit has a cause other than epilepsy or proximate adults' refusal to buy you Raisinets. If you're alone or nearly alone, on the other hand, precisely the opposite approach is in order:

Make like the camel and keep cool—but not so cool that you haul out the *Seinfeld* impression, hoping to distract your adversary from the task at hand. Life's not *Naked Gun,* much as O. J. Simpson might wish it were. The thug's more likely to start shooting than slap his knees.

Comply with all requests. Don't try to bargain. Don't make sudden moves.

As you're handing over your dough, look him over. Is he taller than you? Heavier than you? By how much? What color eyes and hair does he have? Does he have any distinguishing features, tattoos, or tics? Does that beard look like a Halloween job? You'll be calling the police soon, and the more information you can provide, the better.

The most dangerous moment of the incident occurs right after you pay up. The thief will be using all his limited brain power wondering how he can ensure a clean getaway. If you muddy his efforts, he might lash out. Be and look passive, and make no movement or sound of any kind until he is *out of sight.*

If Your Wallet Is Stolen

With a bit of foresight, you have somewhere a photocopy of the fronts and backs of the cards in your wallet—which will not only tell you which cards to cancel, but will give you the phone and account numbers to do it. But if you don't, after notifying the police, use these tips to help you protect yourself:

Credit cards. You're only liable for a maximum of $50 charged on each stolen card, but that can add up to a lot if many cards were stolen, so speed in canceling is important. If you've saved your credit card's informational packet or receipts, or if you have an unpaid bill, the phone number should be there; if it's a card specific to one store, you can just call the store and they'll give you the bank's number.

Cash cards and checks. If you don't have your bank's number on a monthly statement, you can get it through local information. Do debit cards first—most have a higher liability limit than credit cards do; some don't have any at all.

Driver's license. Call the state department of motor vehicles.

Social security card. Call the Social Security Administration (there are local offices—get the number through information) or visit http://www.ssa.gov.

The number for information anywhere in the country is **1-area code-555-1212.** You can get the area code of the place you're trying to call by dialing local information (plug in the area code of the city or town you're in).

Fire Prevention

The odd oinker or klepto's an irritant, yes, but a greater danger to your entire store of possessions comes from fire. Sure, a little pyromania never hurt nobody, but what happens when a romantic desktop conflagration catches the Monet poster? Goodbye, *Waterlilies*—hello, *Backdraft!* Attracting the attention of the fire department does have its ups (why, it's Billy Baldwin!), but an inferno can have disastrous consequences for your lecture notes, Coors can collection, and other regrettably flammable valuables. Just ask the thirty residents who spent a month in temporary housing while their charred cooperative house was rebuilt, or the students in two other fires on the same campus in the same year who lost most of their clothes to smoke damage. Happily, their fate does not have to be yours. Take the following precautions to ensure you don't end up as a tragic example on a Smokey the Bear television special:

Don't burn candles late at night or when you're tired, intoxicated, etc. . . .

Don't position lit candles under your bed, no matter how delightful an Off!-and-Cub-Scouts aura it gives to your romantic encounters. The ensuing scene could end up resembling *Like Water for Chocolate* more than *Ernest Goes to Camp*.

If you're using a fireplace, make sure it has a screen.

Don't tamper with smoke detectors. It's better to brave the squirrels and light up outside than to endanger yourselves and the rest of your dormmates.

If you have a nonautomatic light in your closet, make sure to turn it off when you close the door. The heat from it could build up in a closed space, and clothing, especially if it's draped over the bulb, could easily catch fire.

When you leave the room, make sure to turn the fan off, especially if it's old.

Similarly, don't leave irons, hot rollers, coffee makers, hot plates, and space heaters plugged in and unattended.

If you're living in a dorm, it may disallow space heaters completely, but if you have one, be sure not to leave anything sitting on it—it can catch fire rather easily. Same goes for lamps, especially halogen ones.

Some campuses require students to use metal wastebaskets; even if yours doesn't, they're a good idea, especially if you smoke.

Be careful about using electric blankets, particularly old ones. Never leave one plugged in and unattended.

Know where the nearest fire extinguisher is.

It may seem that the only alternative to pushing your bunk bed up

Closet #2?

Tempting as it is to hang your tuxedo on that little hook made by the sprinkler spigot, resist the impulse. A freshman at one of our schools was responsible for $30,000 in water damage when the system turned on.

against the fire door is sleeping vertically, but try to find another way. Fires really do happen on college campuses—that series of sunrise false alarms notwithstanding—and it's worth the inconvenience to be prepared.

Don't Fight Fire with Fire, It's Too Much of a Good Thing

Depending upon the season and the degree of your rivalry with Eastern flameguzzlers, your initial response to flames may be either to enter them or eat them. Resist these natural impulses, for now; there'll be time to indulge them once you get the blaze under control.

If the fire is in your room. If it's just a small fire—confined to a wastebasket or stovetop, say—you can put it out with water, or, in the case of a grease fire, baking soda or salt.

If the inferno is more towering, call the fire department assuming the smoke detectors haven't gone off already. Then get out. You really shouldn't stop to take anything with you.

If the fire is in someone else's room. For once, the alarm is for real; you smell smoke.

Inspect your door to the hall before opening it. If it feels warm, or if there's smoke seeping in from under it, don't open it; exit via a window or your room's fire door (it functions as a means for your eavesdropping, yes, but this is what it really is for).

If the door feels cool, turn your face away, brace your foot against the door, and open it gingerly. If you're assaulted by heat or smoke, shut it immediately and find another way to leave.

12,
Don't Count on
the Premed:
Health &
Emergencies

Few things suck more than being sick at college, unless you count Dracula. You can call your parents, but unless they're nearby, the only chicken soup you're going to get is Campbell's; you can go to the so-called health services, but as likely as not they'll stick you with whatever hypodermic they have on hand (malaria vaccine, tranquilizer— too bad we're not kidding) and tell you to call them in the morning (if there is a morning for you, heh heh). Schools really do leave you pretty much on your own to deal with illness, so it's important that you know a bit about the diseases common among students: how to recognize them, how to deal with them, and how to avoid them. Once you've got some knowledge of your own, you'll know enough to question a prescription of Maalox for an eye infection (Say, isn't that "doctor" in your Chem for Poets section?) or bloodletting for strep.

In the interests of education, then, we offer authoritative information on a variety of medical conditions. For illnesses and stable conditions, we provide lists of characteristic symptoms; for emergencies like appendicitis attacks or losses of consciousness, we offer measures designed to prevent harm until you've contacted your resident advisor or sought professional help:

AIDS/HIV

See chapter 21.

Appendicitis

The appendix, like a small-scale AK-47, seems to exist only to kill people. Intact, it apparently does nothing; when it becomes infected, its subsequent rupture can have fatal consequences.

You'll recognize appendicitis by the extremely severe abdominal pain it causes victims, usually on their lower right-hand sides. This isn't just a bad case of cramps or a rancid meatball—victims are literally doubled over and immobilized by constant pain.

Other symptoms include stiffness in the lower right side of the abdomen, fever, loss of appetite, nausea, and high white blood cell count (which only lab tests can detect).

If you suspect appendicitis in yourself or a friend, get yourself/him/her to the hospital *immediately,* by ambulance if there's no car available or you don't know where the hospital is. Don't wait around to see if things get better, and above all don't resort to any kind of laxative in the hope that it's just constipation—this could stimulate rupture.

Athlete's Foot

Like us in so many things, fungi, too, prefer intimate attachments with the buff. But don't rush for the barbells—you too, inactive one, may be blessed by union with some microbes whose biological clocks are telling them to settle down.

Symptoms. You know it when you have athlete's foot. The skin of your feet, especially between your toes, is cracked, peeling, and blistered; it burns and itches.

Treatment. If your symptoms are mild, you can probably self-medicate. As Christ did, wash, rub away peeling skin, dry, and sprinkle with fungicidal foot powder or talcum powder. If, suspending judgment on your fungal companions, you've let it go a while, you may need to see a doctor.

Prevention. Wear flip-flops in the shower; shower after exercising; change socks regularly in hot weather.

Broken Bones

If the temptation to hurdle your way over to the stadium to run stairs strikes you, as it did one of us at midnight on the third day of college, think twice. A cast covering a broken wrist isn't exactly the ideal equipage for notetaking—and the broken rib another member of our climbing party sustained didn't make après-dinner tussling, his favorite form of male bonding, any easier. But we survived our injuries, and so can you. Here's how:

If you suspect a fracture—which you should, if pain from an impact or twisting doesn't fade within a half hour or so—seek medical attention. Move the injured area as little as possible to avoid worsening the damage.

If the suspected fracture is of the neck or spine, don't move the victim at all.

The suspected fracture may turn out to be just a sprain, in which case regular bathing of the area—twenty minutes of hot water followed by twenty minutes of cold water, three times daily—and gentle flexibility exercises should restore your ability to use the body part fairly quickly. But if you do end up in a cast for any length of time, keep these guidelines in mind:

Many colleges have escort services for disabled students; if your campus is large, you may want to use these to get to class.

If the cast you've been given makes it particularly difficult to write, ask your doctor if he can replace it with a more accommodating one.

Serious Illness at College

If you're seriously sick—say, with mono or pneumonia—you're not going to be attending too many lectures anyway; we recommend going home. One of us had to, and it was the right move; however kind and quiet your roommates promise to be, the college environment just is not conducive to R&R.

Before you leave, speak to your professors personally, making arrangements for missed work and giving them your home phone number. In addition, it's a good idea to have a dean send them a letter explaining your situation and justifying your request for extensions. Your instructors may be frustrated, but they'll almost always understand, sometimes to the point of excusing you altogether from writing a paper or two (it happened to us).

Our illnesses developed toward the end of second semester, and the dean recommended that we accept incompletes in several classes. We did, only to find out that our school doesn't grant financial aid to people who received incompletes. *Before you make the same mistakes we did,* find out your school's policy. Ask the financial aid office, not just your dean—ours, obviously, wasn't aware of the regulation.

If you can't write yourself, there is help available. Most colleges have disabilities personnel who can arrange for note-takers, audio recordings of classes, or special examinations to accommodate your temporary handicap.

Burns

Cold water immersion and a sterile bandage are usually enough to take care of minor burns, but more severe and extensive damage requires medical attention. Here's how to cope until help arrives:

Heat/Fire Burns

After cooling with water, elevate burned areas above the heart.

If burned fabric sticks to the wound, don't tug at it; simply cut away loose portions.

Remove all jewelry before swelling sets in.

Keep the patient warm, and have him/her sip warm water mixed with a little salt and baking soda.

If you need to wrap burns in order to transport the victim to the hospital, use sterile bandages or a clean sheet.

Chemical Burns

Chemical burns require immediate attention. If there are several of you with the victim, have someone call for help, but if you're the only one, flush the affected area for at least ten minutes before taking time out to phone the emergency room. Continue flushing for a total of forty-five minutes.

Electrical Burns

Before you touch the person who's been burned, disconnect the electrical source or you could be burned as well.

Heart and breathing problems often follow electrical burning; perform CPR (described later) if necessary.

Even if the victim's condition stabilizes quickly and burns appear minor, get expert attention. The skin's appearance is not a good measure of the severity of the burn; damage can be extensive beneath the surface.

Carpal Tunnel Syndrome (CTS)

While as a student you aren't in the high-risk group for CTS—unless you moonlight as a chicken picker or cow milker—improper typing can take its toll. Unfortunately, most college desks date from a pre-ergonomic era, and if your term-time job involves word processing you may find yourself riding a similar dinosaur. Activities like weight-lifting, racquetball, aerobics with hand weights, machine stairclimbing and biking, and playing musical instruments can add pressure on your wrists—leading, in the case of several of our classmates, to temporary immobilization of the hands. Luckily, carpal tunnel syndrome is fairly easy both to avoid and to treat if you know the right approaches.

Symptoms. If you experience any of the following symptoms persistently or intensely, see a doctor:

Pain—often at night, and intense enough to wake you up—in the
wrist, palm, thumb and first three fingers, and forearm
Burning, tingling, or numbness in the hand
Clumsiness of hand

Treatment. If the diagnosis is CTS (there's a series of tests the doctor
can perform), you'll probably be prescribed treatment involving warm-
water soaking, a splint, steroid injection, or, in advanced cases, surgery.
Prevention. To guard against recurrence of problems, you'll have to
avoid whatever repetitive motion irritated the nerve. In most cases, the
culprit will have been typing; to go easy on your wrists, use the following position when keyboarding: Bend your elbows, extend your hands
upward about thirty degrees from the horizontal line of your forearm,
and keep your fingers loosely curled.

If your problem is serious enough, you may decide to invest in an er-
gonomically designed keyboard for your computer or a special desk or
device to lower/raise the level of your keyboard. Less dramatically, a
wrist rest may help.

You also may consider avoiding laptop usage, since the slightly
stiffer and smaller keyboards can be tough on your hands.

The trackball or trackpad on laptops may also prove problematic; try
hooking up a regular mouse to your laptop when you're at home or in
the library.

Even use of a regular mouse—if it's dirty, tends to be rather unre-
sponsive, or is old—may irritate delicate wrists. If a cleaning and re-
configuration don't work wonders, you might want to check out the
mouse market. Evolution has been speedy when it comes to this
species of rodent; newer ones can be more comfortable to use.

Chlamydia

See chapter 21.

Choking

So, the clever plan you hatched up to give your friends a lesson in Neanderthal eating habits, a.k.a. family history, backfired? Well, you're in
good company—even the Flintstones had trouble swallowing the odd

vertebra. Here's how your tutees can get that baby out of your wind-pipe and back on your plate where it belongs:

Open the victim's mouth and try to snag the offending item.

If the item is too far down the throat to see or reach, try back blows. If the victim is standing or sitting, position yourself behind him/her, bend the torso forward, and hit the back hard four times just between the shoulder blades. If the victim is lying on the floor, move the body on its side, chest facing you, and perform the blows.

If hitting doesn't work, resort to the Heimlich. Stand behind the victim, folding your arms around his or her body. Make a fist with one hand, clasp it in the other hand, and position it, thumb inwards, slightly below the rib cage. Thrust inward and upward, alternating this procedure with back blows, until the object is expelled.

Seek medical attention.

Crabs/Lice

See chapter 21.

Depression

On the morning before the last final one winter, a neighbor of ours hanged himself. A few months later, one of our brothers withdrew from college, unable to make it to classes, to tests, or even out of bed. Even in less dramatic forms, depression is common on campus and can inhibit performance in school and stymie relationships. The first time one struggles with it, in particular, it is easy to blame the wrong things or people and seek to make external changes rather than internal ones. Depression isn't necessarily *un*related to external events, but it can be, and however it takes hold it can develop a life of its own unaffected by apparent improvements in one's situation.

If depression is sometimes difficult to recognize in oneself, it can be even harder to recognize in other people, especially new friends. Even if some change is obvious, the reasons may not be: maybe the person was just acting friendly at the beginning of the year and is now show-ing his or her true colors; maybe the person no longer wants to be your friend; maybe the person is simply stressed or tired, or dealing with a situation you don't know about. You are certainly not responsible for the mental state of someone you've known only briefly, but at the same time you may be in the best position to recognize a problem and at least let people better equipped to deal with it help.

Symptoms

In yourself or in others, look for the following symptoms:

Change in sleeping habits. Most depressives sleep more than is usual for them, or usual for people in general; some sleep much less. Some, too, operate almost nocturnally, or keep otherwise extremely irregular hours (even for a college student).

Change in eating habits. Most depressives eat less than they should and lose weight; appetites increase in a few.

Lack of affect; indifference. The word "depression" suggests a flattening out, and this is exactly what happens to many sufferers' personalities and even voices. Little excites them; little amuses them; little moves them except to sadness.

Irritability. Some people struggling with depression become oversensitive/humorless, particularly if an eating disorder has also entered the picture.

Withdrawal. Not only does the victim not enjoy social interaction, but after a while stops even going through the motions.

Lack of motivation. Even procrastination becomes arduous. Deadlines slip by, or are met only by all-nighters and a six-pack of Jolt; grades decline.

Great sadness. Depression is different from grief, grief being a more passionate, violent feeling that wears itself out. But some depressives find themselves not indifferent but incessantly, tearfully despairing.

Treatment

Depressives often lack the initiative to seek help themselves, but they tend to be tractable; if you recognize the symptoms and think the situation merits attention (it probably does, if it's acute enough for you and others to observe), you might want to tell the R.A. or a dean who can talk to the person and/or help get the person to a psychiatrist who can prescribe antidepressants if necessary. If the sufferer (you or someone else) doesn't want therapy or antidepressants, there are other things that can help, especially if it's a relatively mild case. The following suggestions may sound silly, but have worked for some of us:

Exercise, especially outside. The body is just happier when it's being used, and when the body's happier, the mind is too. Fresh air and sunlight, even on their own, help a lot as well.

UV light boxes. If winter is new to you, it may have a depressive effect. You can buy a box that simulates the effect of sunlight.

Fun. Let go of your troubles a bit and indulge in whatever makes you happy—ideally not illicit substances. If art—music, movies, museums—haven't been part of your life lately, bringing them back may help a lot.

On the opposite side of the coin, self-discipline may help. No, accomplishing that cover letter or paper won't directly solve your problems in life, but it will make you feel good about yourself. Same goes for social stuff—force yourself to keep up with the flow of get-togethers even if your heart's not in it. When you're feeling better about life, you want your friends to still be there.

Communication—with old friends, new friends, family members, teachers, and counselors. Sometimes just airing a situation makes it easier to deal with, even if the person you're talking to doesn't have any concrete advice. Then again, your listener may have more than you think; depression is a common affliction.

Drug Overdose

Seek professional help immediately, even if—especially if—the drug ingested was illegal. It is extremely unlikely that your college will punish the patient, you, or anyone else for involvement in such an emergency situation, and in any case your main concern is with preserving your friend's life, not the purity of your disciplinary record. Call a poison control center, hospital emergency room, doctor, or college infirmary. They'll want to know the amount and kind of drug taken, the time of ingestion, and the victim's condition, and they'll ask you to save the container, if you can find it, and the rest of its contents. While you're waiting for help to arrive, take the following steps:

If You Know That the Overdose Was by Swallowing

Call 911.

Check the breathing and pulse of the patient. If either is nonexistent or irregular, administer CPR (see "Loss of Consciousness," p. 119).

If the patient is conscious and the drug overdose has happened within the last thirty minutes, induce vomiting with ipecac (send a fast runner to the drugstore for some, and also powdered activated charcoal). If no vomiting occurs within fifteen or twenty minutes, give the patient another dose.

Make sure that the victim is facing down when throwing up begins, so that none of the vomit can enter his/her mouth or lungs.

After the patient has thrown up, make him/her drink 2–4 teaspoons of powdered activated charcoal mixed with water.

If the drug was a tranquilizer/sleeping pill, make sure the victim doesn't fall asleep.

If the Overdose Was by Injection

Call 911.

Administer CPR if victim has lost consciousness.

When the victim regains consciousness (or if he/she never lost it), get the person to the emergency room immediately; there isn't anything you can do by yourself.

Eating Disorders

Everyone responds differently to the stress, social and sexual pressures, and competition of college, and anorexia (starving yourself) and bulimia (binging on food and then purging it somehow) are among the most popular responses of many women, as well as some men. Unfortunately, as an observer of emaciation there's little you can do. Eating disorders are profoundly isolating illnesses; if sufferers were in touch with reality, they'd know enough to stop starving. Here's how to recognize problems in others, deal with them, and avoid developing them yourself:

Symptoms of Anorexia

Rabbitlike and obsessive eating habits: nibbling at or playing
    with food; attempting to make up for calories with spice ("like
    a hamburger without the calories," a friend of ours would say,
    dipping celery in ketchup); avoidance of all fat.

Dependence on diet sodas, black coffee, cigarettes.

Frequent discussion of/fantasizing about food (the majority of one anorexia study's subjects began contemplating culinary careers).

Thinness, sometimes to the point of emaciation. Depending upon the person's bone structure, she may retain the appearance of curves, but in areas like the face, neck, and waist, skin will be taut.

Swollen ankles (an effect which often scares sufferers into increased dieting).

Brittleness or thinness of hair.

Growth of fine hair (the body's attempt, in the absence of fat, to warm itself) all over arms, chest, back.

Coldness.

Stress, irritability, oversensitivity.

Humorlessness.

Across-the-board perfectionism.

Sluggishness of thought (more apparent to the sufferer than to anyone else).

Obsessive exercising.

Eventually, serious heart problems caused by electrolyte imbalances.

Symptoms of Bulimia

The diseases often go hand in hand; people who are classified as bulimics exhibit many of the above symptoms of anorexia, and vice versa. To the extent that bulimia is an independent disease, it involves periodic relaxations of the self-control that anorexics exert: sufferers, unable to keep starving themselves, will gorge themselves and then purge either by gagging themselves or taking laxatives. Repeated vomiting causes damage to the throat by stomach acid; overuse of laxatives and the general binge-purge cycle can cause, as in anorexia, serious heart and electrolyte abnormalities. Malnourished people are also vulnerable to a variety of other health problems, including stress bone fractures.

Treatment. Diagnosis of eating disorders is easy for people who live with sufferers; it's initiating treatment that's hard. It's made difficult not only by the victims' resistance to change, but by much of society's blindness to the diseases' prevalence. After all, many people in the middle stages of eating disorders look healthy—but it's just in these middle stages that treatment needs to intervene. The further the diseases progress, the more desperate and resolved the victims become, until they starve their bodies to death, as one of our neighbors did, or they collapse on the plane home, or have to withdraw from school for heart treatment, as our friends have.

As a roommate or friend the burden of reversing the disease is not yours, but it's worth doing what you can:

Some schools have eating disorder hotlines; if yours doesn't, a talk with the more general peer counseling group may give you some ideas.

Show the sufferer that you notice and are concerned. If you let the weight loss go unacknowledged, your friend may think it doesn't show, and redouble her efforts at starving.

If the situation persists or worsens, you may consider taking extreme measures—calling your friend's parents, for example, if you think they're not aware of the problem and should take action.

Prevention. Eating disorders are contagious: Sometimes without even realizing it, you may find your own ideal body image thinning as your friend or roommate does.

Don't abandon your friend at mealtimes, if she does indeed go to the cafeteria, but make sure she isn't the only one you're eating with, or pretty soon you won't be eating, either.

If it's your entire environment that's pressuring you to lose weight, try to regain some perspective—and we don't mean by reading *Vogue*. Get outside your campus, where you'll find that a waist larger than Scarlett O'Hara's is not a bar to happiness, marriage, or health.

Flu

Symptoms. Flu symptoms include weakness, stomach pain, lightheadedness, and respiratory congestion (or any combination thereof).

Treatment. Rest and time are the main treatments of the flu.

Prevention. If you aren't in the habit of doing so, start getting a flu shot in midfall when the vaccine becomes available. Dorm life in particular offers a multitude of chances for passing the bug.

Food Poisoning

A nasty bug in salad bar provisions sent a quarter of this year's fresh-man class at one of our schools to a pajama party in the infirmary. Luckily for them, the custodial staff, and you, food poisoning's usually gone within a day; but while it lasts there's not much you can do except sip water so you won't get dehydrated. Coke and similar beverages sometimes have a relaxing effect on the stomach, too, but abstain if your body tells you to. Don't phone out for an order of buffalo wings the minute you feel okay; relive your eating history by moving gradually from liquids to solids, with a pit stop in Gerberland for old times' sake.

Medical attention is only necessary if illness continues for more than two days, if diarrhea visits every fifteen minutes, if abdominal pain and/or fever are persistent and severe, or if you suspect . . .

Botulism

It's rare, but can be fatal.

Symptoms. Symptoms of poisoning by the bacteria include nausea, foggy vision, muscle weakness, dehydration, and problems speaking, breathing, and swallowing.

Treatment. The victim must be hospitalized immediately. Bring along a sample of the food you suspect is the culprit; it will probably smell terrible and contain gas bubbles.

Prevention. In addition to the smell and bubbles, botulism can be signaled from the outside of containers by bloating. Try shaking the container before opening it; if it practically explodes, get rid of it immediately.

Frostbite

Dixieland divas, take note: A winter jaunt to the drugstore for nail polish remover isn't going to result in a spontaneous experiment in cryogenics, but prolonged exposure to wind and/or temperatures below 20 degrees (usually quite a bit below) *can* be dangerous. The term for the whitening and profoundly numbing freezing of the skin that results is frostbite; if left untreated, it can result in permanent deadening of skin and body parts. Your best bet is to get the victim to a hospital immediately, but if this is impossible, find the warmest place you can and follow these measures while you arrange for expert help:

Resist the natural impulse to rub the frozen skin and immerse it in hot water. Instead, handle the frostbitten area delicately, treating it with only lukewarm water.

Do not allow the victim to smoke.

Once areas have thawed, dry them and cover them with sterile gauze. Don't coat them with oils, medications, or lotions.

Elevate thawed areas.

Gonorrhea

See chapter 21.

Hepatitis

See chapter 21.

Herpes

See chapter 21.

Iron Deficiency Anemia

Rather common among college-aged women, especially those who are dieting, iron deficiency anemia is usually a nonthreatening illness but nonetheless requires medical attention.

Symptoms. In its early stages, there are no apparent symptoms. In its advanced stages, however, symptoms such as fatigue, listlessness, pallor, inability to concentrate, irritability, and headache develop.

Treatment. It's not possible to catch up on iron just by slamming a couple cans of Lucky Dog. You'll need to change your diet for the long run to prevent recurrence, but in order to cure the anemia you'll require iron supplements available over the counter.

Prevention. You don't have to eat red meat to get iron; it's also found in poultry, fish, and whole or enriched grains. For milder iron deficiencies, such as those sometimes experienced during menstruation, taking iron supplements isn't a bad idea if dietary answers aren't within your control.

Loss of Consciousness

It may be just a faint, in which case the person should be laid on his or her back, legs elevated. If the victim doesn't revive in a few minutes, however, or if he or she is not breathing or lacks pulse, call 911, and administer CPR.

Cardiopulmonary Resuscitation (CPR)

Ideally, CPR should only be performed by someone trained and certified to do so, but if such a person is not available, don't waste time looking; immediate action is essential to preventing brain damage caused by loss of oxygen. If both breathing and pulse have stopped, have one person perform mouth-to-mouth while the other works on restoring circulation:

MOUTH-TO-MOUTH RESUSCITATION. Position the victim on a flat, hard surface, such as the floor or a table.

Tilt the victim's head backwards by placing one hand on the forehead and one on the chin.

Pinch the victim's nostrils closed.

Take a deep breath and make a seal with your mouth over the victim's. Exhale four times. Pause to inhale and repeat this process about once every five seconds until the victim begins breathing.

CARDIAC RESUSCITATION. Position one hand on the bottom of the breastbone (approximately in the center of the chest) and the other hand on top of and perpendicular to it. Your arms should be straight.

Press down, about 2 inches, once every second.

Lyme Disease

This inflammatory disease is most common in the Northeast, upper Midwest, and Pacific coast, but Mr. Deer Tick likes road trips just as much as you do, and you never know where you're going to meet him. His wanderlust isn't reason to cancel that back-of-the-bio-lab frolic, but you might take nudity off the list of planned festivities. The good news is that, while Lyme disease is debilitating in its advanced stages, if you catch it early, recovery is almost assured. Watch out for the following symptoms:

Symptoms. Chances to look at yourself naked are few and far between at college, but enjoy what moments you have and check yourself out for the classic signal of Lyme disease: a hot, itchy lesion surrounded by a ringlike rash, sometimes as large as 50 cm in diameter. Freedom from looking like a walking dartboard, however, doesn't guarantee you're healthy; the rash does not always appear. If you experience flulike symptoms—fatigue, chills, headache, fever, joint pain, and general malaise—at a time of year when the flu isn't at large (like April), you may consider having yourself tested. The longer you let the disease go, the more severe the symptoms become (heart or neural problems, arthritis), and the harder its progress is to reverse.

Treatment. You must see a doctor, who can prescribe antibiotics.

Prevention. Wear pants (ticks will show up better on white ones) and pull your socks up over the cuffs when walking in grassy or wooded areas. After you come in, check over your body, particularly the warm places where ticks like to snuggle up with a good Stephen King novel—between toes, on your scalp, behind your ears. If you live in an extremely tick-infested area and are in the woods a lot, consider getting vaccinated.

Meningitis

Symptoms. These include high fever, headache, stiff neck, nausea, vomiting, discomfort looking into bright lights, confusion, and sleepiness.

Treatment. For the less severe viral meningitis, often none. For bacterial, early treatment with antibiotics.

Complications if untreated: brain damage, hearing loss, or learning disability.

Prevention. As for flu, it's a good idea to get vaccinated if you are— or will be shortly—a college student. This sometimes-deadly, brain-swelling disease is transmissible in close quarters.

Hi, Gene!

Contagious illnesses spread fast in the close quarters of a dorm. Unless you're keen on becoming nocturnal (and even then . . .), there's only so much you can do, but give it a try:

Don't store your toothbrush in a cup with your roommates'. Germs can travel easily from bristle to bristle.

Wear flip-flops if you are using a common bathroom. Athlete's foot wants you even more than Uncle Sam does.

If you use a coffee mug, clean it often to prevent the growth of mold and bacteria. If you don't want to do it yourself, your cafeteria staff may be willing to run it through the dishwasher for you.

Don't share/borrow makeup, particularly lipstick, eyeshadow, and mascara.

Never share or borrow razor blades. No matter how sure you are that a friend/bathroommate is healthy, it is *never* worth the risk of mixing your blood with hers/his.

Even if you don't borrow other people's stuff, they may borrow yours. The only way to ensure that this doesn't happen is to carry your toiletries to and from the bathroom rather than leaving them there. It may seem inconvenient, but in the long run it's worth it.

Mononucleosis

Your big kisser used to mean party, party—lots o' women thirsty for your juicy lips, a satisfying brouhaha when you walked into Musicland humming "You can't always get what you wa-ant . . . ," and the like. But now the chickens have come back to roost . . .

Symptoms. Mono feels a little bit like the flu, except it doesn't go away. You're plagued by extreme weakness and exhaustion, severe sore throat, nausea and loss of appetite, headache and low-grade fever, enlarged lymph nodes, and enlarged liver and spleen.

Treatment. Pain reliever or antacid can relieve symptoms, but there's not much you can do to treat the disease, besides rest and rest until people start mistaking your chamber for a restroom and unzip their flies upon entering. Your doctor will also tell you to avoid vigorous exercise—it can lead to rupture of the spleen—and avoid Tylenol until you're sure the illness has passed.

Prevention. An innocent smooch (or other sexual contact) is a common means of infection, but even the casual contact you have with a sick roommate could do it. The disease is highly contagious.

Pinkeye (Conjunctivitis)

No, you haven't just been reading too much Kafka—if you see an insect when you look at yourself in the mirror, you may have pinkeye. Luckily, the condition is as treatable as it is contagious. Here's how to recognize it and avoid turning your hall into a large-scale bug box:

Symptoms. These include inflammation of eye, blurry vision, insectoid swelling of eyelids, and sticky, voluminous discharge.

Treatment. See a doctor if you suspect infection. He or she can prescribe drops or an ointment that will alleviate symptoms within two days.

Avoid touching either eye, but if you must, wash your hands thoroughly afterward.

Don't wear contacts.

Don't wear eye makeup.

Discharge may cause your eyelashes to stick together overnight. Hold a warm, wet washcloth over your eyes to soften the crustiness and lessen swelling.

Prevention. An infected person rubs his eye, grasps a doorknob; you touch it and then touch your eye. You've got pinkeye.

To prevent yourself from getting the infection: Avoid touching your eyes without using a tissue or washing your hands, especially if you hear that pinkeye's going around. Don't borrow makeup.

To prevent your healthy eye from being infected by your bad eye: If one eye shows signs of infection, make sure not to touch the healthy eye without first washing your hands. Obviously don't use makeup used on the bad eye on the healthy eye.

To prevent yourself from becoming reinfected:

Launder all towels and pillowcases that have had contact with your face.

Illness during Finals

It's like a nightmare, only your roommate's slapping you around a bit doesn't wake you up like Dad's used to do. You'll almost certainly be able to get an excused absence, but do you really want to postpone taking the test until the beginning of next semester, when makeups are often given?

If you think there's any way you can chug enough Nyquil to get you through studying and taking the exam, do it. You may not deliver a top performance, but a few months away from the material isn't going to do your grade any favors, either.

If you decide to take the exam, find some way to let your professor or T.A. know that you've been ill. A tearful trip during office hours with your face powdered ghastly white will probably advertise your acting ability more than your sincerity and sickness; a simple and brief note at the end of your exam is enough. Apologetic phrasing is effective; say you're sorry that you didn't do as well as you had wanted to because you were sick. You want your grader to give you a break, but if you ask for it directly he or she is less likely to give it.

If you have a short-lived illness that will prevent you from taking an exam at the scheduled time, but will allow you to recover quickly, consider checking into the infirmary. If the professor is certain enough that you haven't been able to pump your friends for test info, he or she may let you take the exam a day or so late, rather than making you wait five months.

If you do end up having to make up an exam the following semester, attend the course you've left incomplete if it's offered. Hearing the lectures or discussions again will jog your memory.

Throw away any eye makeup that you've used within the past few days.

To prevent yourself from infecting others: Don't touch your eyes, don't borrow washcloths or share makeup, and don't touch things like doorknobs and telephone receivers without being certain your hands are clean.

Pneumonia

Symptoms. If mono is the absence of feeling and energy, pneumonia is the presence of everything, in extreme form: extreme chills, fatigue, and sweating; extremely high fever, fast pulse and breathing; and extremely painful coughing of red-colored sputum.

Treatment. Pneumonia is a serious, sometimes fatal illness. You can't just let it run its course; you need medical attention, involving prescription of antibiotics and bed rest.

Prevention. The same old song deserves an encore: Avoid contact with diseased chums. And since poor nutrition, weakness, and exhaustion increase your risk of catching it, take pains to avoid these problems.

Seasonally Affected Depression (SAD)

See Depression, page 111.

Sexually Transmitted Diseases

See chapter 21.

Strep Throat

Symptoms. These include extreme, persistent sore throat, painful swallowing, fever, fatigue, chills, swollen lymph glands, and general malaise.

Treatment. A throat culture can tell you whether you've got it; if you do, antibiotics should do the trick.

Syphilis

See chapter 21.

Toxic Shock Syndrome (TSS)

Most commonly caused by use of super-absorbent tampons or prolonged usage of a regular tampon, TSS is a potentially fatal, rapidly progressing illness. You should see a doctor immediately if you experience the following symptoms:

Symptoms. These typically follow tampon use within a few days and include extremely high fever (over 102°), vomiting, diarrhea, headache, lightheadedness, and a red rash on palms and soles.

Treatment. Penicillin doesn't work in combating this disease; your doctor will prescribe other antibiotics.

Prevention. Either don't use tampons or use the minimum absorbency tampon necessary to deal with your menstrual flow. Make sure not to leave a tampon in longer than eight hours (boxes give instructions specific to the tampons inside), and make sure (it sounds stupid, but) to remove the tampon at the end of your period.

Ulcers

The stereotypical ulcer victim is middle-aged, male, and permanently stuck in the anal stage. But despite your superficial differences from this chap, you two could be siblings in stomach style; it's not so much the amount of stress as the way you hack it that counts.

Usually ulcers are more irritating than serious, but if you let them go, they can lead to dire consequences—in-stomach bleeding, anemia, even death. If you experience the following symptoms, see a doctor:

Symptoms. Not to be confused with pregnancy, an ulcer can make you feel hungry all the time—stomach growling and full of acid, even when you've eaten recently. Foods like coffee, chocolate, spices, fats, alcohol, and vegetables may be particularly irritating to your stomach.

Treatment. A pocketful of Pepto pills could keep you set for a while, but if pain persists, it's important to get more serious help. The doctor may administer the actual ulcer test—making you swallow radioactive chalk and then taking a picture of your stomach—but often you'll just get a prescription.

Most ulcers go away in a matter of weeks, with treatment. Stick to a pretty bland diet for at least a week after you've started the pills; after that, go with how you feel.

Prevention. Ulcers have a tendency to recur. Keeping them at bay isn't easy and may require a change in your lifestyle—fewer all-nighters, fewer stressful forays into the professor's office to steal future tests, more subliminal conveyances of the lyrics to "Don't Worry, Be Happy," etc.

Venereal Warts

See chapter 21.

Yeast Infection

See chapter 21.

13
B.S. & Friends:
Course
Survival

If you are going to "take a year off" academically, freshman year is the time to do it. Never again, probably, will you have so many good reasons to slack: tons of new people to meet, newfound independence to enjoy, and, if you are so fortunate as to attend a rural college, new fields of corn in which to frolic. Grad school admissions officers and future employers—perhaps through eyes clouded by nostalgia or hangover—tend to view the year as a kind of grace period; if your grades rise as you go on, you're in the clear.

Having said that, however, there are sound reasons for not letting the year go to the dogs. College courses are already, probably, significantly harder than your high school classes, so you may have to work harder just to do as well as you did in high school. Your transcript *can* matter in the short term, too; some summer programs, on-campus employers, and professors in charge of admitting people to seminars will be interested in your grades. And even if they don't actually ask to see your record, they may request letters of recommendation, which professors rarely write for students who blow off their classes. Perhaps even more importantly, habits formed freshman year die hard; if in first semester you get into the habit of doing all-nighters for every pa-

Pass/Fail

At some schools, all your first semester or freshman classes are pass/fail whether you like it or not; elsewhere, your pass/fail options are more limited first year than other years.

The first thing to do is find out when the last day you can elect to take a class pass/fail is. If the class is mandatory graded, this is effectively when you sign up for the course; sometimes it's within several weeks of registration; sometimes you can elect up to the time you take the exam. Pay attention to whether you can change back to graded if you want to.

Be sparing about taking classes pass/fail freshman year. It doesn't look good to have too many pass/fails on your transcript, and you may not be allowed to count those classes toward your major if you pass/fail them. A few less-than-great grades freshman year are par for the course, anyway, and graduate schools and employers will probably not hold them against you if your record improves.

Keep in mind, also, that most classes are graded on a curve. If it's hard for you, it may well be hard for everyone (this is less likely to be true if it's something you have comparatively little background in or is very far from an area you might major in), and if you're approximately in the middle of the pack you can expect some kind of B.

Having said that there is no shame in taking courses pass/fail. You get in over your head, you have a family or personal problem that cuts into your studies . . . don't think twice about pass/failing. It is far better to take one or even two classes in a semester pass/fail and get B+'s on the others than to spread yourself thin and get four C+'s.

Save a few pass/fails for last semester senior year.

per, you can look forward to seeing a lot more sunrises before four years are up; one woman we know remained trapped in the cycle throughout her first year as a law clerk as well. On the other hand, if you accustom yourself to doing well, you're likely to want to keep up a high GPA.

Only you can decide, of course, how significant grades are in your overall plan. Perhaps only those in classes related to your major will matter to you; perhaps, if you're an aspiring Ted Koppel, your work on the campus newspaper may be more important than any exam. If and when you decide scoring high is worthwhile, stop cherishing the hope that your 4.0's going to come via your roommate's death; the connection between morbidity and grades is mythic on every campus. Get your mind out of the graveyard and focus on the four main elements of academic performance: reading, writing, test-taking, and interaction with your professor and T.A.'s.

Power Reading

You're inclined to recycle or snack on the list of the Library of Congress's holdings your professor has inexplicably passed out, but to humor her you decide to skim it. That's when your doubts about the quality of the campus water, already quickened by the mysterious purpling of your hair, face, and teeth, begin to flower, for clearly she has gone insane: The document you hold is the course reading list. Before you issue a brisk warning to the health department, however, you glimpse the other syllabi you'd carelessly tossed inside your bag. Examining them for the first time, you murmur that if lunacy this be, it's collective: All of your courses assign at least a dozen texts.

Well, it is lunacy, in a certain sense, and it has less method in it than Hamlet's. Don't waste your time trying to psych it out, however; instead, use the following tips to save your energy and vision:

You don't have to do it all—in fact, you probably shouldn't even attempt to do it all. There have been semesters where some of us tried, and nearly succeeded, but only at the cost of our enjoyment of learning and social lives. If your and your professor's bullshit thresholds are high, you may need to do no more than 10 to 25 percent of it. But if you want to get something more than a passing grade out of the class, you'll want to approach the reading more carefully and thoroughly. There are three basic approaches to thoughtful, efficient reading:

Read it all, fast. This method is the exclusive property of speed-readers. If you weren't one at birth, however, don't despair; some colleges, or learning centers near colleges, offer courses.

Skim everything. Like the method above, this one—usually entailing reading the introduction, conclusion, and the first and last sentences of every paragraph—has the advantage of giving you a passing familiarity with all the material; you'll never find yourself totally blank in the face of a professor's question. But what you gain in breadth you lose in depth, and you may find yourself stranded in the shallows when the discussion gets intense or it comes time to write an analytical essay (see page 133). Such an approach, too, may end up functioning as a simple rehash of what the professor says in lecture; it may be that he has assigned the text for the nuances of argument hidden within the paragraphs.

Graze and chomp. For all its flaws, the skim approach does tend to work well for classes that emphasize examination over paper writing; the reverse is true of graze and chomp. This method involves an even lighter run-through than skimming, and diverts the time saved thereby to in-depth reading of a few well-chosen texts; you may not have heard of the Treaty of Guadalupe Hidalgo, but you're an expert on the Alamo siege of shortly before. This method tends not only to be more interesting than skimming, but, if you play your cards right, more helpful to your GPA. The skimmer may have only taken good lecture notes—but you, clearly, have read.

Do Grades Matter?

In a word . . . somewhat:

* If you know you want to go to graduate school, especially in medicine, law, or a particular field like history or economics, they matter a lot (though in all of these except maybe law, your grades in the classes related to your graduate school subject will matter a lot more than others). Of course, the more ambitious you are, the more your grades will matter . . . but it's better to leave the door open than close it, all other things being equal. Even at less competitive graduate schools, good grades from college can help you get scholarships.
* If you're going to business school, you'll be working for a number of years after college, and these will probably matter more than academics, although good grades never hurt (especially in business classes).
* If you wish to go for a competitive, analytical job after college—investment banking, management consulting, accounting—your grades will matter greatly.
* If you just wish to work your way casually up the ladder—starting with an administrative/legal/production/editorial assistant-type job, your grades may really not matter. We know people who got very interesting jobs after college without anyone ever asking for a GPA or transcript. This is particularly true for smaller employers and in medium-sized (not N.Y. or L.A.) cities.
* The last word is that they probably matter less than you think they do if you're used to working hard. Good ones never hurt and bad ones never help, but a lot of other things, even in the professional arena, matter more: connections, certain extracurricular experiences, summer and term-time jobs, life skills. And then there's your life . . .

The key decision, of course, is the choice of texts to focus upon. You may take your cue from the professor's preference, but if he doesn't display any, ask your friends who are reading more broadly which texts they recommend. If being up-to-date enough to participate in class dis-

Multiple Submissions

Faced with a deadline, particularly one in the near future, it's tempting to haul out papers on marginally related topics. If it's from high school, there's a good chance it's pretty unsophisticated; if it's from another college course, you could find yourself in the doghouse if anyone finds out. Unless your two professors are bitter enemies (i.e., one "capitalize God" and one "lowercase him"), it's better not to take the risk that they might talk.

If it's a matter of writing one paper to satisfy two assignments rather than simply recycling, you may be able to arrange something. If, say, you're reading *Confessions of Saint Augustine* in one class and *Sheaves of Corn* in another, and would like to compare them, bring your proposal to the two professors; they may allow you to write a single, longer paper.

cussion isn't important to you, you have the option of waiting until you receive the paper assignment, if there is one.

Writing

After four years of polishing, you had the five-paragraph essay down. Everything was there: the first paragraph, the second paragraph, the third paragraph, the fourth paragraph, the fifth paragraph, and the full-color "about the author" section. But now, suddenly, you're being asked to expand your thoughts. "But wait," you protest. "I only have five fingers! How am I supposed to—" Hush, my child, help's on the way—not in the form of a hand-dividing operation, but in the form of advice. For though the college essay is a more complex proposition than the high school essay, it too has a form that can be mastered.

You'll encounter four major varieties of assignments in your first years of college: the short reaction paper, the lab report, the research paper, and the analytical essay. The most commonly assigned of these, and for most students the most difficult to get the hang of, is the analytical essay. And since the other three are essentially just variations of it—they, too, are asking for an argument, though of a less formal, shorter, or less original form—the advice we offer on handling the analytical essay applies to all forms of college writing.

The Analytical Essay

This assignment is the most difficult and the most frequently assigned for the same reason: It demands the presentation of original thought in formally organized, polished prose. More than that, it often requires you to create, in effect, your own assignment—to read a text or series of texts, and while doing so find something interesting to say. Perhaps because this type of assignment asks so much, professors sometimes try to soften the blow by presenting it under a pseudonym. But don't be lulled into a false sense of security: Whether the assignment reads "explicate," "discuss," "analyze," or "argue," you're being asked to produce an essay focused around an explicitly articulated, specific thesis.

We'll deal with the problems such a task presents in the order in which they usually arise: 1) development and crystallization of your ideas for the essay's topic; 2) formulation of your actual thesis statement; 3) arrangement of main ideas; 4) approaches to introduction and conclusion; 5) mechanics and style; and 6) citation.

1. DEVELOPMENT OF YOUR IDEAS. Some assignments are as broad as the Jersey turnpike; others are as long as I-95. But whatever the highway it's your fate to travel, you'll first need to start your vehicle. Before you flip to the car care section (we are in the realm of metaphor now, my friend), consider these words from us road-weary trippers as you prepare to turn the ignition key of life . . .

If the assignment is fairly specific—asking you to take a side on a particular issue, like affirmative action, or asking you to explore a somewhat limited topic, like Frank Lloyd Wright's use of space in the Guggenheim—you're pretty much in the clear when it comes to idea development.

When an assignment is slim pickings, however, you're casting into a different bowl of fish. In these cases it usually does little good to approach the professor for clarification; there's a good chance he or she is being deliberately vague, asking you to develop your own questions about the topic. Rather than turning ornery and demanding a share of your professor's salary for doing a share of the work, try some of the following nonviolent approaches to getting started:

Follow your instincts. Sometime while you're alone and away from the material—taking a walk, cleaning restrooms for dorm crew, going to sleep—allow its topic to enter your mind. What is your immediate, unreflecting response? Admiration for the author's language in a certain section? Disagreement with a certain conclusion? Concern about the implications of the author's argument if applied to other issues and situations? Recognition of inconsistencies in the argument? In short, *what* about the material arouses your attention and interest? At this point, don't concern yourself with what exactly you're going to argue; the idea is just to discover what, in the most general sense, you would enjoy writing about.

Refresher course. The above exercise doesn't depend on the text's freshness in your mind—quite the contrary, it depends on its being sufficiently old so you can think about it as an abstract whole—but if actual botulism has set in, or if you don't experience any gut reaction besides hurling, then you may need to turn back (or turn for the first time) to the material. Did you underline any sections or write any comments in the margins? Are there any chapters or sections that might stimulate you if you reread them?

Bored. If neither of the above approaches works—you just couldn't give a flying bagel about the topic—you'll need to take a more scientific approach to generating ideas. Try one of the following:

"Dear Fred, I read the most fascinating book . . . " Pretend (this will take quite a stretch of the imagination, we know) that you're writing a letter about the text/topic to a friend or teacher—someone you'd like to instruct and impress. You may just begin writing and see what comes into your head, or you may structure your "letter" around such elements as explanation of topic or plot, short character descriptions, or theme. Try to avoid the thumbs up/thumbs down approach; go beyond mere likes and dislikes; try to justify your opinions. If you find yourself trying to persuade your reader of something, you may be on the road to a thesis.

Secondary source. Find books related to your topic. If it's "The Rime of the Ancient Mariner," do a keyword search for "Coleridge"; if it's the Battle of the Bulge, run up a list, ignoring diet books. You won't

Avoiding Plagiarism

In looking through secondary sources, there's always a danger that you'll somehow "absorb"—consciously or unconsciously—the author's ideas, and then present them as your own. If you do this, of course, you're guilty of plagiarism, a very serious offense on most campuses. To guard against it, try not to skim so many books that you're unsure where what ideas came from; if you take notes as you read, make sure to indicate on the sheet of paper that they're reading notes, not the products of a brainstorm. If you don't trust yourself to take these precautions or to keep possession of ideas straight, you may need to steer clear of secondary sources altogether.

have to read any books you find; the point is just to find some statement that you can use as a jumping-off point for your essay. Suppose Roy Rogers, Ph.D., claims that "Rime" is an atheistic poem. Do you agree? If not, you can write a paper presenting Rogers's opinion and explaining why you oppose it. If you do agree, is it for the reasons Rogers presents? Perhaps you can express agreement with his basic argument, but support yourself with different evidence.

2. THESIS FORMULATION. The object of the above exercises was to get your mind running; now it's time to concentrate on your form. You know the general area you want to write about; your job now is to refine your ideas into a thesis.

Usually appearing at the end of the essay's first paragraph, the thesis's job is to tell the reader, and yourself, what you're going to argue. As such, it must be a clear, specific, succinct, strongly worded statement of an interesting and/or controversial idea: clear because the job of writing is to bring order to thought; specific because generalities are usually boring and difficult to prove; succinct (never more than two sentences and usually just one) because it needs to be short enough for the reader to keep in mind as he or she proceeds; strongly worded because theses are supposed to answer questions, not ask them; thought-provoking because otherwise there is no point to your writing.

Not a Thesis	Thesis
"*The Scarlet Letter* is a book about evil."	"*The Scarlet Letter* concludes that Hester's act of adultery was not actually a sin."
"Is the death penalty constitutional?" *or* "The death penalty may be constitutional."	"The death penalty is unconstitutional because it inflicts cruel and unusual punishment, which the framers forbade."
"The South lost the Civil War."	"The South lost the Civil War because of Lee's poor tactics at Gettysburg, the loss there leading to a decline in morale."

3. ORGANIZATION. In some cases, your thesis dictates your organization. To prove the last thesis above, for example, you'll need to first prove that Lee's tactics at Gettysburg were poor, then that they led to a decline in enthusiasm, then that this decline in support for the war led to the South's defeat.

In other cases, you've got slightly more latitude. In compare/contrast essays, for example, you've got two choices: Either you can divide your paper down the middle, devoting the first half to one character/ novel/philosophical system and the second to the other, or you can talk about the two at once, discussing the plots of each, for example, in one paragraph, and the use of dialogue in each in the next. This second method tends to produce more sophisticated and interesting papers, but is sometimes more difficult to produce; if time is extremely short, you might opt for the first.

In still other types of papers, it will almost seem not to matter what order your points go in. If you're proving that Keats's poetry displays his preference for dreams over reality, for example, there are a number of possible ways you could organize your evidence. You could focus upon a particular poem and analyze it line by line; you could divide your evidence by type, starting with imagery and moving to poetic form. The important thing isn't so much which scheme you use as that you choose some scheme and stick to it. Confident presentation takes you far.

Creativity and thoughtfulness in arranging your evidence are, of course, ideal. But if you're unable to find a more interesting style of organization, try the old standby of arranging your paragraphs/points by importance. Put the least controversial, most basic paragraph first; the most interesting, sophisticated point last; the weaker paragraphs in the middle, where readers are most forgiving.

4. INTRODUCTION AND CONCLUSION. Once you've decided how you're going to arrange your ideas, you're ready to start writing. You'll begin, of course, with the introduction, but since conclusions have a lot in common with introductions, we thought we'd talk about them now, too.

The purpose of both is to jolt the reader—in the case of the intro, into curiosity about your ideas; in the case of the conclusion, into acceptance of them. In both, as well, you have more latitude than in the body of your paper; if your subject is Kant, for example, the beginning and the end are the times to place him in a larger context, or to make connections with literature or other disciplines. Both, too, are the places where it is most important to establish your presence as the writer—sometimes through personal anecdote, more often through the confidence and clarity with which you guide the reader.

It's no surprise, then, that introductions and conclusions are often the most difficult parts of the paper to write. But the work you put in will pay off; first and final impressions count. To make sure that yours are positive, be creative—and avoid the following problems plaguing the intros and conclusions of the college students we've tutored:

Overgenerality. You've probably all seen the hourglass model for the essay, which dictates that the opening and closing be broad, the main part of the paper specific. But that doesn't mean you have to wax cosmic about the origins of the English language or compare history to the Yangtze or any other river. The language may be eloquent, but it could precede any paper on the history of anything; you want to write an introduction in which each step leads closer and closer to your topic and your topic only, finally narrowing into a thesis.

Irrelevance. So irrelevance usually follows generality—but it can also accompany specificity. A common introductory technique is to tell an interesting, funny, or surprising anecdote relating to the author/subject/issue under examination. But while this can be attention-getting, it can also be off-putting for the reader if you don't establish why you have brought in the particular story. If you're writing about the poet Coleridge, for example, it isn't enough to regale your readers with the story of his opium addiction, and then move on to a thesis about the language in "Frost at Midnight." If you're bringing up his drug habit, it should be because it relates somehow to your argument —as an explanation of the hallucinatory quality of his imagery, for example, or the depression apparent in his ode on dejection.

Boredom. After all this, you may be tempted just to steer clear of anything fancy and take the Dragnet approach. But while there's a lot to be said for simplicity, if you simply state your thesis as an introduction and reiterate it as a conclusion, you're missing the chance to give your argument a wider significance.

5. MECHANICS AND STYLE. It seems old hat—every subject needs a verb, every sentence needs a period, every corncob needs a pat o' butter. But if a thoughtful, well-organized argument is the difference between a barely passing grade and a robust one, mechanics and style are the difference between a B+ and an A. "You've got the words, but where's the music?" a professor said to one of us, referring to a recently written essay. The missing tune, of course, was not a matter of quarter notes and horns, but of words and feeling, and the kind of rhythms made by well-placed commas, properly used prepositions, and accurate spelling. We won't trouble you with a guide to mechanics—it would take up too much space, and books like Fowler's *Modern English Usage* and Strunk and White's *Elements of Style* are so comprehensive—but before we send you to your Macintosh, a few guesses about what is at the heart of the more elusive form of lyricism:

Careful choice of words. Pretend you're writing fiction. Would you use the same word six times within a single paragraph? Would you use the word "flower" if you were talking about snapdragons? Would you use the word "section" when you meant "stanza"? The desire to get finished with an essay often impels people to jump at the first word that comes to mind—often a rather dull, general one. Don't assume that the reader will "know what you mean"; choose language that is precise, that conveys exactly the ideas you want to convey and leaves no room for ambiguity.

Humor. Many students, as soon as they open Microsoft Word, regress into a kind of R2D2 mode, thinking that because the topic of

Extensions (without surgery!)

The longer it takes for you to realize that most professors and T.A.'s give extensions on demand, the better—that's why we've incorporated a special time-release amnesia serum into the ink on this page! You avert your eyes quickly . . . but in vain, my friend. We dare you to keep in mind that turning in papers late gets to be a nasty habit very, very easily—and before you know it, it's the last day of the semester and you're having to FedEx fifteen papers, change the diapers of teaching assistants' foster children, hand wash their one pair of jeans (all a grad student needs), and—oh, what was that other bothersome task? How odd—we seem . . . to be . . . forgetting . . .

the paper is academic or dry, their writing needs to be. In fact, the opposite is true: The more desiccated the subject, the more lively—not to say moist—your voice needs to be. Such humor needn't entail, of course, random insertion of jokes borrowed from Letterman or marginal caricatures of your liberal prof's nemesis, Tom DeLay; it's more a matter of appreciating the wit of the text you're writing about, or of games with language.

6. CITATION. The proper form for citations is a matter of hot debate among grammarhounds with nothing better to do. Some insist that information appear in footnotes; others prefer endnotes; others like parenthetical citation; a select few demand illustrative cartoons. There's disagreement, too, about the positioning of colons and commas in the reference itself; ask your professor what he or she prefers. If you saw the professor escorting the T.A. home and don't want to disturb, however, or if you're reluctant to advertise that you're still working on the paper at five A.M., simply choose one method or another and be consistent.

How to cite is the annoying part; *when* to cite, the tricky. You don't have to provide reference information for facts that are generally agreed upon, or ideas that appear in many texts you encounter. But if something seems original or controversial, you need to indicate its source. Be on the safe side; if you're in doubt, give the reference.

Execution

After imbibing the previous information like a swig of fermented Mott's, you know how to write a paper. Unfortunately, you have yet to display your knowledge. The paper's due tomorrow. Kid, you gonna see the sunrise.

All-nighters work best, and are most enjoyable, when you approach them with a sense of adventure. Begin talking about projected all-nighters the afternoon before, when, if you were a more strait-laced type, you'd be formulating your introduction. Dinner table state-ments/exaggerations like "Christ, I think it's going to be a long one," or "I've got a thirty-page paper due tomorrow!" will serve the triplicate function of attracting sympathy, justifying your having fifths on congo bars, and giving you delusions of safaridom. By the time the computer strikes eight or nine, you'll be pumped for a night of kick-haunch writ-ing, if not actual cow tipping!

To maintain your excitement/sugar high—and to guarantee that you won't chicken out when the conjunctions start roughing you up—lay in these supplies:

binoculars
change of clothes
battery-powered alarm clock/watch
gorp
somebody's PowerBook
disks for backup
flares
a style manual for help with citations
all the books you could conceivably need to refer to
journal
dictionary and thesaurus, unless your word processing program has
   them
high-carbo snacks, especially Pixy Stix, popcorn
caffeinated, sucrose-heavy drinks—Mountain Dew, Jolt, anything
   nondiet
Walkman
rifle

Rough Drafts and Rewrites

If you're together enough to get a rough draft in, either to your T.A. or prof or to the campus writing center, more power to you. Each source of help has its advantages: Graders will be impressed that you're on the ball and interested in their comments; peer tutors may have the inside scoop on what particular instructors want to hear, and may also give comments more generously—not having to worry, as some professors seem to, that they're giving you an unfair advantage.

But often the only time you're going to have a rough draft is if you use sandpaper by mistake. After you turn the paper in, however, is not too late to improve your work. Even if professors don't offer rewrites, try going in after class and asking for one anyway. It worked for us; we came out with not only a higher grade, but a higher position in the T.A.'s estimation.

In keeping with your spirit of conquest—and your desire not to fall asleep—find a place other than a bedroom in which to set yourself up. Study lounges, if your dorm has them, work well; shun comfortable couches or chairs and set yourself up near a window, where in a few hours the rising sun will scare you into composition.

There's a certain Walden-like serenity to an all-nighter done alone, but the presence of friends may induce a helpful atmosphere of competition/commiseration. Try the computer lab, for instance, even if you have your own machine; your arrival there could trigger a veritable brainstorm.

Presentation

"Damn, this is good," you say to yourself as you roll into your final paragraph. "Brilliant, yet clear; complex, yet not discombobulating." You snag a bite of sweet corn, grunt loudly in pleasure, and type the final words to the rhythm of Beethoven's "Ode to Joy," which you have turned on in disregard of your sleeping roommates. You scroll to the top of the paper, delighting in the unbroken flow of words.

It's only when you've initiated the printing process that you notice the length of your effusion. You quickly cancel printing and scramble to find the assignment sheet. "Write a seven-page paper..." Seven pages! Your paper is five pages too long/short! Oh, woe!

Not to worry, pretty mama. Length, as men have tried to persuade some of us, is but an artificial construct with no basis in reality. And just to prove how right we are, we're going to show you the same paper, in the same size type, presented two different ways. The first, for the writer's purposes, was far too short; observe, on the following page, the changes we have made, nearly doubling the "length"—if you still have faith in that term—of the introduction. Windbags, simply follow these procedures in reverse.

From the days of Pocahontas to the modern-day pig feeds of Kansas, Americans have been obsessed by corn. But until recently its uses have been primarily pragmatic: as a tasty accompaniment to baked fowl, as the basis of Orville Redenbacher's fame, and as a homey decoration for doors when the chill winds of November make you want to burst out with a big "Welcome, friends! Our outhouse is your outhouse now that winter's a-comin'!" And corn still does do its duty in these capacities, as well as serving as good old-fashioned grub. But thanks to retired farmer-prophets like Bertha Stuttgart and Ole Ivarsson, corn has finally received its due as muse as well as crop in their joint volume of poetry, *Sheaves of Corn*. Ignoring the collection's literary merits, many reviewers have focused upon its slightly plagiaristic title. The poetry deserves better criticism than this. Harboring lyricism of great beauty, it presents corn as the uniquely patriotic crop that it is.

The poets' almost agroerotic intimacy with their subject is evident from the first lines: "I celebrate cobs, and sing cobs/And what I irrigate you shall cultivate/And what I put forth you shall eat, and all Americans/with me, all husking, all buttering, all spurning the hungry hogs that dance at our feet/like Communists, like goddamned flag burners" (1–5). Without waxing unduly admiring, I would like to...

↑

Same size type as next version, but much shorter!

no title page, so vital info
takes up more space
in the paper proper

Angus P. Johnson
paper #1
March 17, 2002
Tues. 9 a.m. section
T.A.: Johnny "Shakespeare" Kazmerski

the two-part title:
sophisticated,
space-filling

flattery
never
hurts

CORN AND COURAGE:
The Romance of America's Heartland Poets

good place for marginally relevant epigraph,
which we actually don't have room *for!*

From the days of Pocahontas to the modern-day pig feeds of Kansas, Americans have been obsessed by corn. But until recently its uses have been primarily pragmatic: as a tasty accompaniment to baked fowl, as the basis of Orville Redenbacher's fame, and as a homey decoration for doors when the chill winds of November make you want to burst out with a big "Welcome, friends! Our outhouse is your outhouse now that winter's a-comin'!" And corn still does do its duty in these capacities, as well as serving as good old-fashioned grub. But thanks to retired farmer-prophets like Bertha Stuttgart and Ole Ivarsson, corn has finally received its due as muse as well as crop in their joint volume of poetry, *Sheaves of Corn.* Ignoring the collection's literary merits, many reviewers have focused upon its slightly plagiaristic title. The poetry deserves better criticism than this. Harboring lyricism of great beauty, it presents corn as the uniquely patriotic crop that it is.

The poets' almost agroerotic intimacy with their subject is evident from the first lines:

if room, add
marginally
relevant
graphic

block quotation
= aesthetic
appeal plus 6
lines down the
drain

> I celebrate cobs, and sing cobs
> And what I irrigate you shall cultivate
> And what I put forth you shall eat, and all Americans
> with me, all husking, all buttering, all spurning
>   the hungry hogs that dance at our feet
> like Communists, like goddamned flag burners[1]

Without waxing unduly admiring, I would like to...

[1] Ivarsson, Ole, and Stuttgart, Bertha. *Sheaves of Corn.* Leech Lake, Minnesota: Pig Press, 1996.

footnotes take up more room than parenthetical citations

Academic Trouble

Most students frolic pretty close to the whirlpool. But there's a big difference between having your head barely above water and involuntary dunking, and once you start sinking it's hard to surface again. There's a temptation to deny your situation, or not to go to class for fear of being taken to task. The longer you let it go, of course, the worse it gets.

Deal with the situation as soon as possible. Talk to your resident or academic advisor about what's going on; if you're depressed or having any kind of emotional/mental trouble, make an appointment at the health service; try to find yourself a tutor, either informally or through the campus clearing-house.

Talk to your professors. If there's a good reason (basically, being a college-aged person) why you're having trouble, and if you seem committed to solving the problem, you'll probably find a lot of sympathy. Most professors worthy of the title have no desire to give failing grades, and they probably have a pretty good idea of your situation. Unfortunately, you're not the first student to have missed midterms or lectures. You're probably not going to come from behind to get an A, but with help you should be able to salvage your performance enough so you don't have to fail or drop. If not, you will have the option of taking the class over.

Test-taking

Writing is a science; taking exams is a crapshoot. In gambling as in any other activity, however, there are tricks of the trade, and we offer the following tips, from our roulette table to yours, in the hope that they may help you cash in:

Of course it's better to start studying a good couple of months before a midterm or exam; fortunately there are other things in life. But even if you don't haul out the flashcards more than a few hours in advance, do take the initiative to check out last year's tests. Some colleges bind and make them available for photocopying, and some leave it to the student network, but any effort you expend in the search will pay off. You want to spend your time cramming, not trying to psych out the format or style.

Go to review sessions. A lot of people don't, and many professors reward those who do by giving away answers.

Pulling an all-nighter to get a paper finished is one thing, but burning the midnight oil the day before an exam benefits only OPEC. Exam-taking requires efficiency, confidence, and mental agility, all of which are impaired by fatigue. What's more, studies have shown that several hours of sleep can have a fixative effect on material learned before going to bed—without which facts crammed in are likely to slip your mind at a crucial time.

Overstudying is an uncommon problem at most colleges we know—nevertheless it can get you. Trying to learn everything is bound to be futile, and is therefore going to lead to a sense of failure even before the test begins. Having confidence is more important than knowing the date of Hildegaard von Bingen's birth.

The idea of spending an hour or two snuffling may carry unpleasant associations to *Sesame Street* characters, but resist the temptation to take Nyquil right before an exam. Cold medicines slow down your thinking.

By the same token, avoid taking aspirin, Sudafed, or other patent medicines in the hours immediately preceding a test, unless the discomfort is so bad as to be distracting. Such medicines can whack your brain up.

Try dressing up for big tests. If your campus's style is casual, you may feel like a bit of a fool, but you may also feel more awake and confident.

If your school's a bit slow about sending out grades, you may want to slip a self-addressed, stamped postcard into your bluebook. Your professor or T.A. can fill it out and get your grades to you faster than the registrar's office can.

It's easy to second-guess yourself until the cows come home, but try to stop yourself sometime before you hear that distinctive moo: Your initial gut impulse is often correct.

If there's no time to finish the last essay, scribble down an outline in your bluebook to show that you're in command of key facts and ideas. You'll almost certainly get partial credit.

Similarly, if you don't have time to do a problem out, or are just shaky, write down what you can—formulas, equations, however much of the set-up you can do.

Averting the Freak-Out

Whether studying for a test or writing a paper, it's happened to all of us: You're up late, maybe alone, and you realize you have no idea what you're doing. Your paper doesn't seem to make any sense; you don't have a grasp of the material for a test tomorrow; you're missing two weeks' worth of notes and you have no clue where to find them.

It's going to be okay. That's the first thing to think, and it's true. The absolute worst case scenario, provided you don't sink to plagiarism or another form of cheating, is that you'll turn in the paper or take the test and do badly and the professor won't let you do it over, in which case you'll have to work extra hard the rest of the semester to get your grade up, take the class pass/fail, drop it, or face a bad grade on your transcript, which is far from the end of the world.

The worst-case scenario doesn't have to happen, however. Even this late in the game, there's a lot you can do not only for your mental health but for your actual performance.

Take concrete steps. Make a list of what you can do, if necessary: baby steps to restore your confidence. If you are missing notes or lacking in understanding, call people who are likely to be up or even ones who aren't; send out an e-mail either to the class e-mail list or a wider one. You're probably not the only one up. Do mechanical things like spellchecking, proofreading, formatting, or making flashcards. Reread the essay question; do your bibliography.

Figure out what you do know or have done well. If you've been reading and/or going to class, you probably are more ready for an exam than you think. Even if your paper has gone astray, there are probably parts of it you can feel good about. Go back to them and start over from there.

Set realistic goals for yourself. Okay, so maybe it won't be your best score or essay, but it doesn't have to be your worst, either. Given time and energy constraints, what should you really shoot for—mastering most of the sections and leaving a few thorny areas for another time? Fleshing out one idea about a book rather than bringing in a second to make things more interesting/complicated? Don't sell yourself short, but a clearly, confidently written essay will probably score better than an ambitious but muddy one. There'll be other chances.

Don't overdose on caffeine. It is indeed a miraculous substance, but there comes a time when it does more harm than good, blitzing you out rather than giving you that mental kick. Illicit drugs are, obviously, an even worse idea.

Relax. Make a phone call, get online, listen to some music, take a walk, and remember that life does go on in a pretty good way regardless of how well you do. No one's going to die or lose their shirt as a result of your grade, including yourself.

Professor-Student Interaction

Your tests may be graded by a computer, your nine o'clock may have more people in it than your high school, and exam attendance slips may ask for your ID number rather than your name, but—like it or not—you will find that there is still a significant subjective element in grading. This may creep into evaluation of the elements discussed previously, however objective professors claim to be in their standards for evaluating writing. But the places it enters most invasively are the professor's or T.A.'s classroom and office, in your contact—unmediated by well-worded thesis statements and swanky fonts—with your instructor. Here's how to cultivate a good relationship, and how to use it to get the most out of a class:

Show the professor that you care about the material and your performance. Come to class on time, or, at the least, come to class.

Show that you've thought about the material. A thoughtful question now, after class or during office hours, could make up for a sloppy assignment later.

Instructor-student relationships tend to be more formal in college than they were in high school, but they don't have to be. Having a friendly relationship can not only help your GPA (by motivating you as well as flattering instructors), but can be handy when you need recs, advice on career paths, or connections. Most professors and T.A.'s, even at large universities, are more accessible than they seem, if your interest is sincere and you're willing to make an effort. Go to office hours, get a group of friends together and ask your prof out for coffee, etc.

Don't judge the little guy only in relation to Letterman; he's only a

Ph.D., not a weatherman turned comic, and his jokes should be judged accordingly. Chuckle, wink, give him the high sign, bang on your desk.

Nominate the professor/T.A. for a teaching award, and don't check the "anonymous" box on the form. One of our friends, after putting his T.A. up for an award, actually got an A even though he'd bombed the term paper and gotten B's on the midterm. Registrar's error? We think not.

Choosing a Major

At most colleges, you won't confront an actual decision on this until sophomore year, and it's a good idea to take classes from a wide variety of departments in your early college years. At some colleges, however, freshman spring is the time to decide, and practicality may be at the forefront of your mind even if it isn't. Consider, therefore, the following factors in choosing a major:

The Course Experience Itself

Especially if you're planning to go to graduate school in something like law or medicine, your undergraduate major need only be so practical. You're really free to study what you like; so try to discern what you like. It's spoiling: you will probably never again in your life have the chance to just indulge your academic interests, and if you do a good job of it you will be an interesting person for the rest of your life.

Practicality

For many students, this is really where it's at. Some majors are just undoubtedly more practical, in the sense of directed toward a specific career, than others, and some colleges offer more of these than others do. If you major in accounting, you will have a pretty good shot at passing the CPA exam your second or third time and getting a solid-paying job as an accountant. If you major in business or economics, you will have a better shot than your classmates at lucrative jobs in management consulting and investment banking after graduation. But every major has its uses in the job market . . .

Biology, Chemistry. Pharmaceuticals; medicine; work in agribusiness or food science

Computer Science. Programming; business; patent law; Web site administration

Engineering. LOTS of job opportunities, since a B.A. in engineering is as marketable as a master's in a lot of other fields. If you don't like actually being an engineer, you can go to law school and become, if you want, a patent lawyer, which can be extremely lucrative

English or Literature. Administrative assistant; work for book publisher, newspaper, or magazine; copy editor; columnist; speechwriter; correspondence writer for a politician; public relations; marketing or advertising; law; literary agent; television writer; book reviewer; novelist; poet; teacher; Web site content producer

Environmental Studies. Nonprofit think tank or advocacy group; environmental education work in schools or camps; land conservation and restoration; park service work; law

Fine Arts or Art History. Graphic design; sculpture, painting, drawing; magazine or newspaper photography; photography for advertising; architecture; museum or gallery work; retail; art agent; Web site designer

Foreign Language Study. Diplomacy; translator; researcher or writer in international relations

Geology. Work in the oil, minerals, and water exploration/exploitation industry; lobbying on behalf of the industry; research; earthquake and volcanic eruption prediction

History. Writing; research for academia or for television and movies; museum work; law; politics; teaching

Music. Performance; law; music reviewer; composition; record label work; historian; work for a collector of traditional music such as the Smithsonian; teacher

Political Science/Government. Work for a political campaign in a research, writing, organizing, or door-to-door capacity; work in the legislative, executive/administrative branches as a researcher, assistant, speechwriter, mailroom clerk, page, etc.; law; lobbying; work for partisan think tank

Psychology. Social work; medicine/psychiatry; counseling

Sociology, Statistics. Political polling; census; journalism; nonprofit think-tank work; market research; consulting

Studying Abroad

Traditionally, this is done junior year, but some schools offer it as early as first semester of freshman year, and in any case, there's no reason you can't arrange it for yourself whenever it suits your schedule, including summers. Here's what to think about:

Timing. If a college requires you to take the first semester abroad before starting, don't dismiss the idea and choose another school. One of us spent first semester freshman year in London, making friends, getting used to college classes, and going to the theater. She came back second semester with a tight group of friends from her school.

Program. Most schools allow you to participate in either their own programs or those of other schools (see how to get credit, below). Going with your own school will be less socially challenging, but may be less rewarding and limit your choice of program.

Credit. Some schools require that your studies abroad have some relation to your major back home. If going abroad and getting credit for it is very important to you, you may want to choose your major accordingly. Many subject areas beyond foreign language and international studies can work if you make your focus within them culturally or regionally specific: history, anthropology, political science, biology, or geology.

Well in advance of getting on the plane—sometimes even during the application process—you will need to take steps to ensure you will get credit for studies abroad, if you want it. If you're going through a program sponsored by your school or, to a lesser degree, another American college, this should be relatively easy. Inquire. If you aren't able to get credit, it still may be worth it to go abroad either in the summer or term-time; graduating a semester or more late is not the end of the world. It's better to enjoy yourself and be refreshed than slog through.

Funding. Especially in the case of not-for-credit summer travel, fellowship money may be available to fund academic or experiential research. Planning, presentation, and timing are important in receiving aid; be sure to have an itinerary and goals determined and check into application deadlines early in the semester before you want to go.

Semesters abroad tend to be less academically rigorous. Plan to travel and spend money and time enjoying where you are.

GEOLOGY SECTION

ROMANCE LANGUAGE SECTION

AMERICAN HISTORY SECTION

14

Research & Romance:

The Library

You've humiliated yourself before the WB world on *Blind Date*. You even tried a surfboard for two on the Web until you got a shock from the computer screen trying to consummate with cyberchic #2's Web page. You've just about thrown in the towel when it comes to broads, until one night you remember you've got reserve reading for Shakespeare. Little do you suspect that what's in store for you is nothing less than the big kahuna of scamfests, the bookcased brothel, and the speakeasy of the stacks—in plain terms, the *library* . . .

Of course, there are about a hundred thousand other reasons—wearing chaste leather covers, not bustiers—to go to the old book bin. You'll likely need legitimate excuses for making the foray, and you won't have any lack of them. If you're a humanities major, in particular, you'll have research papers, and even if professors don't demand a three-page bibliography, consultation of sources outside the course material is usually impressive. But those graveyards for trees can be intimidating places, and not only for the ripe sapling out front. To guide you in your explorations, textual and sexual, we offer the following thoughts:

How to Approach Research

Books

Your first step, usually, is the online catalog. Unless your professor has already helped you out with some book titles, you'll probably want to do a wide search, just to see what the possibilities are. Many colleges use the Library of Congress subject headings system; if yours does, you'll want to look up your topic—*fin-de-siècle* France, the Human Genome Project—to see the precise wording LC uses. You can then use this to do a subject search on the computer. Keyword searches work well for more specific searches.

Another, sometimes less dizzying way to get a handle on your subject's parameters is to get hold of a comprehensive bibliography. Such guides, often available on surprisingly obscure topics, organize and present by subcategory relevant texts on, say, South Carolina history. In such a bibliography, for example, you'd find a chapter listing and perhaps briefly synopsizing books on the Colonial period, the Revolutionary period, and John Calhoun and the nullification crisis. To find one, search using an LC subject heading as above and the word "bibliography."

Once you've spent a little time with one or both of these resources and are armed with a few call numbers, your best bet is to just go to the stacks. You'll be able to take in the available books more quickly (the relevant sources will probably be confined to a couple of areas), and you may find sources whose title alone never would have caught your eye on the computer screen.

To narrow your search, and your topic, to something manageable, skim through the material, setting aside books that deal with your subject, even if their treatment of it isn't particularly stimulating. Once you've decided what your paper or presentation is going to focus on, use the bibliographies and especially the footnotes or endnotes in these books to find the names of sources the authors drew upon.

Armed with these titles, go back to the library catalog. If they're listed but checked out, you have the option of filing a request form. No matter who the borrower is, he or she needs to return the book so that it gets to you within a week or so or face heavy fines.

In the case of common pieces of writing, especially classics no longer copyrighted, you may be able to find the entire text on the Web —not a great way to read it, but an excellent way to search for a particular quotation or part if that's all you need.

If your catalog doesn't list the book at all (try both an author search and a title search—sometimes one works where the other doesn't), and you really want the book, ask the reference librarian about nearby colleges' resources. If you have a car or other means of transportation, you may be able to go and check the book out yourself; otherwise, the book may be sent via interlibrary loan.

Articles

Depending upon how current your subject is, periodicals could be your best resource. If you're lucky enough to be relying on a popular magazine, it may archive articles on its own Web site; try there first. More likely, you'll be using the library collections.

If your college maintains its ties to the dark ages, the blue-covered *Readers' Guide to Periodical Literature* may still be available; otherwise you'll probably have to go online. The periodicals index may be separate from the main one; check it out before you conclude in despair that your library stopped acquiring shortly after the Kennedy assassination.

> ## Library Cards: Not Just Razors
>
> That slim piece of plastic can get you not just "close as a blade or your money back," but some smooth entertainment! At many schools, you can check out movies, CDs, tapes, and driver's ed–caliber videos.

Periodicals are sometimes bound in noncirculative volumes, but they are often available, along with government documents, only on microfiche.

Microfiche/Microfilm

Nobody disputes that it's easier to snag a book from the shelf than to wrestle with film rolls and big gray machines, but in some ways the inconvenience of microfiche/microfilm is the main reason for using it. Because most students are unwilling to go to the trouble, you'll be able to distinguish your paper with ideas that other students didn't bother accessing. Not only that, but if you can find some sly way to indicate that your sources were microdocuments (like in the citation), your grader will probably be impressed by your effort.

Nausea and fun rarely walk hand in hand, but for the hour one of us spent spinning through editions of *Ladies' Home Journal* from 1900, the two made an extended PDA. We could have avoided the necessity of bringing along a PanAm barf bag, however, if we'd realized that once you've *found* the article you want, it's much easier to read a hard copy. Not all of the reading machines may be hooked up to a printer, so look for one that is.

Leaving ten pages of writing for the night before is one thing, but don't plan for last-minute microfiche reading. The hours of the areas offering it are sometimes different from those of the rest of the library.

Reference Books

One of libraries' great underutilized resources, the reference section can help you not just in your formal research ventures, but in your day-to-day studying. These dandies are just a sample of what you'll find:

Dictionary of American Biography. Does your history professor assume, incorrectly, that you're familiar with Aaron Burr's birthplace, political career, and position in the "tastes great/less filling" debate? Turn to the D.A.B. for a concise run-down before the midterm.

Bartlett's *Familiar Quotations.* Indexed by subject as well as author, these pithy phrases can sound just the right note of false erudition, or add just the right quantity of cheddar to your concluding paragraph. Professors will be as mice in your trap.

Contemporary literary criticism. Need a jumping-off point for an English paper? See what wacky new terms professors' toddlers have invented and have no trouble finding a statement that you can totally disagree with as a basis for your essay.

Master Plots. A legend in its own time—'nuff said.

Online

You don't need to be in the libe to use a computer, of course, but it never hurts to get some facetime (see below). Online research is most useful for current events, sociology, business, and science research, but it can also be useful for more past-oriented fields like English and history. For just a flavoring of the Web's offerings, we offer the following examples of its usefulness in . . .

English. Many works of literature exist online. If you want to know the source or location within a source of a quotation or name you remember, type in a few of the salient words. The Oxford English Dictionary is searchable for a fee online at www.oed.com; the site also offers a free word of the day, complete with its history.

Science. Www.ncbi.nlm.nih.gov/PubMed offers free access to thousands of medical journal articles; these can provide jumping-off points for research projects, essential materials for literature reviews, or ideas for interesting introductions.

Under Cover

Come-hither glances and offers to share encyclopedias work their magic in due time, of course, but if you want action fast, you're going to have to send signals another way: through the books you read. Classics like *No Charge for Looking* and *Come Love a Stranger* attract a variety of classy potential suitors sneaking a peek at the title of your book, but other texts are less universal in their appeal. So before you pick up that volume, consider the message you're sending about your taste in spouses:

You read:	You get:
Women Who Love Men Who Kill	human version of Max, your aging pit bull
Polo in the Rough	Izod God, but with a crunchy side evident in five o'clock shadow
Kill as Few Patients as Possible	idealistic premed
What Am I? Looking at Shapes through Apples and Grapes	angst-ridden, what-is-the-meaning-of-life type from a banana republic
Looking for Mr. Goodbar	Hershey heiress
I Can Be an Animal Doctor	canine-featured hypochondriac

Law and Government. Www.findlaw.com is an encyclopedic resource for law of all kinds; current information on legislation is available on http://thomas.loc.gov. The ability to do a full-text search of the Jefferson presidential materials, for example, is at http://memory.loc.gov/ammem/mtjhtml/mtjhome.html (Library of Congress, manuscript division).

Archaeology. Http://archnet.asu.edu is a portal site for archaeological information online; the Perseus Project, at http://www.perseus.tufts.edu/art&arch.html, offers an image and text database for art objects, sites, etc.

Business. Www.forbes.com, the Web site for *Forbes* magazine, posts and archives tons of articles at no charge to readers; the Securities and Exchange Commission's mammoth compilation of company information is at http://www.sec.gov/edgar.shtml.

The Internet can be an alternative as well as a supplement to traditional library research (again, at some cost to your vision and/or love life). Professors sometimes post reserve or supplementary readings on their personal or course Web sites; sites like www.questia.com provide a subscription-based online library. If you're looking to lighten your backpack as well as wallet, sites like www.ebookhome.com and www .ebookmall.com can help you out.

Check-Out

Reference books, of course, stay in the library. But when closing time comes on a Friday night, you're going to want to have something to show for your evening out. For the most part, borrowing is a simple procedure, but here are a couple of tips to keep in mind:

Reserve materials generally circulate for only two to three hours at a time, but sometimes can be borrowed overnight. Most libraries have a fixed time (not necessarily closing time; at one of ours, it's eight P.M.) after which borrowers don't have to return books until the next morning. But before you jump on it, make sure you're willing to be at the returns desk when it opens or accept the heavy fines.

It's easy to let books go overdue, especially when you're doing research and have checked out many with different due dates. Fines for nonreserve materials aren't too heavy, but do watch yourself; if you're a persistently delinquent borrower, you may have borrowing privileges suspended.

If you have privileges suspended or aren't equipped with a dolly to carry all the books you need home, create your own reserves section by stashing the books you need in a little-perused section of the shelves — say, "Biography, Liberace." When you've finished with them, do everyone a favor and leave them out somewhere so they can be reshelved properly.

The scanners you have to walk through as you leave the library can sometimes damage computer disks. Interrupt the checker's crossword puzzle and ask him whether the ones at your school are okay.

Be careful and keep track of whom you loan library books to. Don't count on them to return the books on time, or at all. Plato can get lost in someone else's pit, or your own; before you casually give it up for lost, keep in mind that charges for lost books are *heavy,* far in excess of the book's actual value. One of us got charged $75 (on top of a month's late fees) for a collection of political writings that looked like it had spent most of its life in a dog's mouth.

15
Get a Job

If you want to live it up, you're either going to have to memorize the contents of chapter 10 or get a job (even for us, that's an easy choice). The financial status of you and your family, or your lack of bankable athletic talent, too, may force you to put your nose to the grindstone. In either of these cases, salary may be your number-one concern.

If you're not in dire financial straits, we recommend waiting until second semester of freshman year to start working. Unless you've got presidential ambitions, as some of our hallmates have, there's no need to start building your résumé just yet, and you'll find that adjustment to classes and the new social scene takes most of your time. Not plunging in—literally—to a high-paying job like student janitor will also give you more time to look into the possibilities and determine your priorities.

Whether you're starting a week before school with fall dorm cleanup or not until after finals, take at least a little time to consider the following:

How many hours you want/need to work. College jobs tend to be pretty flexible about hours. The average job asks for a commitment of five to ten hours a week, but many employers demand fewer. If you don't want to make any kind of commitment, there's always temp work. If you're work-study, you may not have a choice.

Which hours you want to work. Many offices are only open Monday through Friday, nine to five; if you'd prefer to work evenings and weekends, you'll have to do some looking. Libraries, cafeterias, gyms, dorms, and computer labs all need employees during nonbusiness hours. For maximum flexibility, go for either temp work or—sometimes even better—a job that pays by the task and lets you do it on your own time. One of us was a member of a staff whose members each got paid $70 per week for a writing job that took no one more than two hours (it was supposed to take ten); one of our roommates went nuts with the mop and accomplished her custodial work in half the allotted time, at no sacrifice to Mr. Clean's standards. There is a reason why college is expensive; once they get the money, they're not particularly tight with it.

Whether you prefer to work alone or with coworkers. If your job is temporary or done on your own time, you'll likely be doing the solitary thing. But jobs can act as a dating service, too, particularly if they unite people with similar interests/bodies (*Baywatch* meets U. Pool).

Whether you're willing to work off campus. You'll meet fewer campus *confrères* and may have to pay for transportation to and from work, but maybe a little getaway is what you need. (It may be that you have to try it, if campus employers favor work-study students and you don't qualify.) Baby-sitting, retail, and restaurant work all offer some perks; if you have a weekday, or several blocks of time per week without classes you may be able to get an office job doing clerical work, reception, research, etc. Check out newspaper ads for part-time employees or get in touch with temporary or regular employment agencies. Noncampus office jobs (in "the real world") will also make you stand out from your peers and looks more professional; everyone knows that campus jobs are fairly cake.

Whether you're willing to accept a low salary for some excellent experience. Maybe your career path, and long-term financial interests, will be better furthered by a great internship with a local magazine than a lucrative but dull stint on first boat in the dorm crew.

Once you've decided your priorities, your first step is the student employment office. It will usually have separate categories of jobs for on-campus/off-campus, work-study and non-work-study (work-study are generally the choicest). If you are work-study, make sure to mention this in applying even for jobs that aren't limited to work-study students; it may make you a more attractive applicant since your salary will be subsidized or covered by some other source than the department hiring you.

If the office of career services doesn't yield anything, check out campus and local newspaper listings, the college's careers Web site, and kiosks around campus and town. Ask people you know what they're doing, and get the lowdown from your R.A. Check out bulletin boards in offices, particularly those of foreign language departments. (One of our friends, using this approach, landed a job earning him $10 an hour merely for conversing in Spanish with a woman preparing to go abroad.) Another place to look is online; even if you aren't looking for a computer-related job, you may find listings.

Temp Options

If you're not ready to commit to any particular schedule or type of job, you're primed for temp work, and there's plenty out there. Here, only a few examples:

Baby-sitting. It may seem like a thirteen-year-old's job, but it gives you freedom to catch up on work and may pay better than you think. Near campuses, wages tend to be comparable with those for work-study jobs, since parents know they have to compete. Many colleges make lists of willing students available to neighborhood families; consider adopting an alias beginning with A to place yourself at the head of the list, from which most prospective employers draw.

Psychology experiments. If your school has a graduate program in psychology, or even a strong undergraduate department, it may pay students $7–$12 per hour to act as subjects. Click a mouse in response to beeps, try to remember the dates of Washington's presidency, drink a milk shake, and collect. Look for ads in the psych department or student newspaper.

Snow shoveling. And they say money doesn't fall from the sky. Start counting flakes, man, because the more that fall, the more you can make.

Weird Science: The Lab Job

Yes, freshman year is early to begin looking ahead to med school. But chances are that many of your fellow rodents in the rat race that is the application process have their beady little eyes trained on the finish line, and if you make too many pit stops for Cheez-its, they may crowd you out.

Besides being an important—in some ways essential—step in bolstering your candidacy, a lab job can also provide you with the opportunity to *make* discoveries in addition to hearing about them, and give you material for a senior thesis. Here's how to go about getting one:

If you attend a university with a graduate program in the sciences and/or a medical school, there should be no shortage of professors who need assistance. Before you call up and ask, however, find out either from a premed advisor or from journal articles (search the periodicals index or online for professors' names) what exactly the lab is studying. Not only will this tell you in advance whether it's a lab you're interested in, but you'll come across as more curious and clear about your interests.

If your campus doesn't have a lot of lab openings, look into nearby universities and hospitals. If you're still foiled, you may have to wait until the summer, when you can relocate to an area with a more promising job market. In the meantime, you may be able to get hired as a lab leader/assistant in an introductory chem or bio course you've taken. You're not doing research, probably, but you're making connections and getting experience in the lab.

Tutoring. Many campuses have clearing-houses through which students in need of help get hooked up with peer tutors. Did you make it through a particularly difficult math class first semester? Do you speak enough German to help an ESL student with her language study? Put your name in as a prospective tutor; when a given call comes, you can decide whether you have time to take the job.

Proctoring and aiding with registration. The demands on department personnel are particularly heavy at the beginnings of semesters, just when your workload is the lightest. Such jobs aren't usually advertised, but ask around; one of us made enough for a nice pair of socks just for carrying a stack of bubble sheets across campus.

Bartending and aid at reunions, receptions. Again, such temporary positions may not be advertised, but the tips you'll collect from deep-pocketed alums will be well worth the trouble it takes to seek these jobs out. Once you get on the list of people to call, you'll be in the black for the rest of your years.

The Summer Job Search

Your natural impulse when it comes to the summer job search, we know, is to turn tail and run for the corn fields. But while it's true there isn't anything quite like a long June night under the stars—just you, the corn, and the weevils—there are also advantages to more urban occupational environments.

Unless you're planning to stick with a current job, return to your high school summer job, or simply take a lap around the mall scanning for Help Wanted signs when finals are over, you'll want to start looking in January or February. Such an early start will allow you to jump on any winter deadlines and to have yourself together by the time the job hunt heats up in the spring.

There are five main stages to the quest for employment: 1) deciding what kind of job you want and where; 2) seeking out names and contact info for employers; 3) preparing your application or résumé and cover letter, and soliciting references or recommendations, if necessary; 4) interviewing, by phone or in person; 5) accepting an offer. We'll deal with each one in turn:

What Kind of Job Is for You?

It depends what your goals are. If money is a priority, you'll want to steer clear of camp counseling positions and opt for something like caddying, waitressing, clerical work, or work in computer science (if you've got the guts to take the courses, you'll be set for salary). If you just want to experience a new part of the country or world, look into nanny positions or employment in national parks, or wait till you get there and check out the retail scene. If you like independence and flexibility, consider starting your own business, as one of our roommates did. Using her connections from high school baby-sitting, she made a mint running a week-by-week daycare camp for neighborhood children.

And then again, you may want something preprofessional, something related to your prospective career. Are you thinking of med school? Labs hire qualified freshmen. Are you interested in history? Many National Historic Landmarks, such as Thomas Jefferson's home near Charlottesville, Virginia, or Andrew Jackson's in Nashville, offer summer employment for college students. Journalism? Newspapers, in both small towns and large cities, often take on students for the summer in either volunteer or paid positions. The most prestigious, big-city papers can have deadlines in December and may not hire freshmen; call early. Economics? Investment banks in large cities hire summer help, and merchant banks in smaller communities often hire students as tellers. Politics? Members of Congress often take on students for the summer; if it's an election year, campaigns (municipal, state-level, national) will certainly need people.

If you are willing to work for free, almost any kind of organization can fit you in at least for part of the summer or part of the week. The term "internship" is sometimes used to describe paid positions, but more often to describe volunteer work, either full- or part-time. What unites internships is their goal to give students not just a salary but an education through practical experience. Sometimes, in fact, an internship is the *only* way to get to know a particular profession as a young student: Christie's auction house or the publisher Houghton Mifflin just can't afford to entrust a temporary, untrained employee with real responsibilities and a salary but may feel comfortable offering you a post-graduation job if you prove yourself while in college.

Finding and applying for internships sometimes is no different from the process for normal jobs (see below). If, however, you're applying somewhere that hasn't advertised for interns and hasn't taken many before, you may have to do some persuading. Think through and convey exactly what you want to get out of the experience (time observing how a biologist interacts with dolphins? A couple of published columns for your clippings file?). Organizations may have trouble imagining what to do with you on a daily basis if you don't give them an idea of what you want. Prove that you can be independent in setting goals and achieving them.

Places to Look

Once you've chosen the general areas you want to explore, you're ready for more detailed charting of possibilities. Unless you've got a username for the old-boy network or a close relationship with a professor, nothing's going to fall into your lap. So instead of looking at the sky, Chicken Little, look at . . .

College Office of Career Services. The first place to go is usually your college's office of career services or career library. They're likely to have guides with names and telephone numbers as well as actual job advertisements sent in by nearby businesses and programs.

Financial Aid Office. On some campuses, summer (and term-time) work-study jobs are listed here.

Newspapers. If you're looking for a job in a city other than the one your college is in, you may find it useful to look at the Web site of a local paper. Even if you don't see actual ads for summer jobs, it will give you a sense of what employers to contact or what kinds of jobs are generally available so you can apply close to the time you'll be ready to start work.

The alumni network. Depending upon your college's incestuousness/spirit, previous grads may or may not be falling over backwards to help you find a job. But it's usually worth a try. Write letters. Make phone calls. Help Mr./Ms. CEO home from the alumni picnic/rave.

The Yellow Pages. If you're interested in, say, environmental work, you might consider just going down the list and calling all the organizations. It sounds a little random, but this approach scored one of us a job offer in under half an hour of telephoning.

Web sites devoted to particular cities or types of jobs. The federal government, as well as many counties, cities, and states, have online job banks and application forms. There are also Web sites with national or local listings of jobs in entertainment, nonprofit work, etc.

Web sites of individual employers. Most large companies and nonprofit institutions have sections on their Web sites displaying current job openings.

Books. Publications like the *Job Banks* series (published by Adams Media Corp.) give you a general sense of the opportunities available in particular large cities; there are also books revised yearly (*Peterson's*

Guide to Internships, for example) that actually list specific internship and job programs.

How to Apply

Once you've collected ten to twenty possibilities (many won't pan out), you're ready to start the actual application process. If you think or know that any of the jobs you're interested in have prepared information or applications (government jobs, large retail chains), you'll want to call and have it sent to you or get the site to download it from or fill it out online. Even if you're pretty sure all they require is a résumé and cover letter, you may want to call and talk to someone about the job. You'll get a better idea of whether the job's right for you and how you can tailor the way you'll present yourself to impress the employer. Calling is also a way to find out if a particular organization is hiring at all or would accept interns, if you aren't responding to an ad.

Special essays, recommendations, or exercises may be required; at the very minimum you'll send a résumé and cover letter.

RÉSUMÉ. Tailor it to the specific employer. If it's a camp counseling job you want, expand the description of your daycare center experience. If you're after a job as an editorial assistant at a magazine, you may want to strike off your teenage movie theater job, thereby emphasizing your sustained, single-minded interest in literature and journalism. Showing early work experience in menial/mindless jobs can be good, though, even if it doesn't relate to the job you're applying for, because it shows you have a strong work ethic and won't think you're "too good for" certain tasks.

Include extracurricular and volunteer as well as paid positions (in high school as well as college). "Manager, radio station" is an impressive title, even if the station did broadcast out of the band room.

Make it short (one page) and visually appealing. There are a number of possible organizational schemes; software is available that can arrange your pieces of information in everything from the classic, spare list to various funky, rodentesque shapes. We recommend a straightforward presentation of education (first, since that's what your main activity is now), experience (title, employer, short description, dates of work), honors (if any), and computer experience (only if more extensive than Word and Netscape/Internet Explorer), along with your postal and e-mail addresses, and telephone number at the top. A phrase or two, at most, is sufficient to explain each item; you'll have more space in the cover letter to highlight important items and follow the common thread among them.

COVER LETTER. The relationship between your résumé and your cover letter is like that between a newspaper article and an accompanying graphic; both elements communicate the same message, but in different ways.

Don't be afraid to repeat things in your cover letter that your résumé illustrates. Employers often read applications as though with a borrowed pair of glasses, and it can take a couple of repetitions to guarantee passage through the blur.

Don't simply repeat, however; where the résumé is by definition a collection of fragments, the cover letter is, ideally, a complete picture. Show your audience your progression of experience and skill-gaining from an internship at an emergency room to a counseling position at a camp for children with cerebral palsy; show how the job you're applying for is a logical next step in this progression.

Having said that, make sure the picture isn't so complete that it becomes a mural; a cover letter should not be more than one page. If you think you have so many stellar qualifications that you absolutely cannot squeeze your discussion of them onto a normal page, you are wrong. For one thing, you're probably under twenty; for another, an interview is the time to elaborate.

Finally, try to write in your own voice. It's a formal letter, yes, but that doesn't mean you can't display enthusiasm or a sense of humor about yourself, especially if these qualities are demanded by the job.

RECOMMENDATIONS. It's best to ask for recommendations as you go, propositioning your profs right after they hand you that A+ final exam. Faculty tend to skip town a lot—tenured ones to do "research" (yeah, in Daytona?), and untenured to wander the highways and byways of the Midwest carrying Will Lecture for Food signs. But a general rec from last semester may not suffice; some applications demand that letters address your candidacy for their particular job. Even if they don't, there are advantages to offering something more tailored than the multipurpose recommendation you've got sitting in your file. Your professor may be able to revise the old recommendation just slightly to make it more appropriate; if you think it would help, see if he or she is willing.

It's good, obviously, to get recommendations from teachers who have given you top grades, but it's more important that the professor knows you than that you aced the class. If the employer just wanted to know how you did, he or she would ask for your transcript alone. Find a professor who can describe what kind of a person you are.

As you're deciding whom to ask for recs, think about the way your professors/teaching fellows write—both in their comments on your essays and in any published material you've come across. If they're stingy with praise (some young faculty, in particular, can be), look elsewhere. The typical rec is effusive, and employers allow for exaggeration when they're deciding how stupendous a human being you really are; if your rec isn't luminous, it's going to look darn fishy.

Along those same lines, don't select a professor whom you know to be disorganized. Sure, the absent-minded professor can be cool ("I can't seem to find my grade book. Er, can you young 'uns handle the honor system?"), but the fun turns to infuriation when your request form asphyxiates under his bong.

At the same time that you ask for the specific rec, have your professor send a copy to be kept in your file. If he or she's a real anti-government, anti-regulation, flag-burning type, you might consider retaining your rights of viewing, otherwise, you'll probably either have to or want to waive them.

Once you have your application materials together, you can mail, fax, or e-mail them in to the employer. Mail is the default, tried-and-true way; use an 8 ½" x 11" envelope if you're sending more than a few sheets (say, a requested writing sample or other sample of your work). Laser print if at all possible; run the envelope through a printer if you want to look extra professional/computer-savvy.

Especially if you weren't able to laser print to begin with and are sending from a fax machine yourself, faxing can sometimes produce a poor quality product, especially if there is also an older machine on the other end. The quality deteriorates further when employers photocopy it to give to interviewers.

E-mailing works well, but clear it with the recipient before you do it, especially if it's a big file. People are justifiably wary of opening attachments from people whose names they don't recognize.

How to Approach the Interview

More than any other part of the job application process, the interview is kind of a crapshoot. If you're doing it in person (which is a good idea, if it's possible for you to arrange), you may be confronted with two or three greenhorns trying to prove to each other that they know which end is up even though they've only been on the job for two paychecks; you may find yourself on the phone with a touchy-feely bloke whose idea of safe sex is anything with people in his employ. Basically all we can say is be ready for anything, but be especially ready . . .

To make furious eye contact, to smile until your Chapstick fails you and your lips start bleeding, to deliver a firm handshake.

To ask several *informed* questions about the job, not just "You musta made a lot of dough to buy that suit, huh?" Ideally, you actually *are* curious about the job and want to know more about responsibilities, a typical day, the sort of work the organization as a whole does, what the employer is looking for in a candidate, etc. If you are somewhat confident you will have choices, feel free to ask more probing questions: whether the job provides a good entry level to the company/industry, what your chances are of doing particular things you'd like to, how much supervision/mentoring there is. Hold off questions about salary until you have an offer, unless the interviewer broaches the topic.

You will probably be asked to "tell a little bit about yourself." The interviewer doesn't want funny prom stories or a list of your hobbies; this is your chance to tell, as you did in your cover letter, résumé, and/or application, why you're qualified for the job. Yes, he or she also wants a sense of you as a person, but you don't have to disrobe to convey it; the way in which you talk about your accomplishments will reveal as much as you need to. Your personal qualities are more or less relevant depending upon the job. Every employer wants professional, responsible, courteous people, but most jobs are about employers getting work out of you and giving you money in return. One of employers' biggest peeves about college students is that they expect people to hire them out of a personal interest in their development. You may have some right to expect this in unpaid internships or if the employer sees you as a recruit for after graduation, but most of the time, they want your labor.

Say that you want the job and why you want it. It seems obvious, but enthusiasm is rarer than you might think. If you don't feel much of it, consider looking for a different job.

Wear what is appropriate for the job you're interviewing for, and err heavily on the side of formality. The worst you can possibly do is show up in a suit at a casual workplace and have them think you look well-dressed and eager.

If you are interviewing for a job in business/investment banking, be prepared for some rather technical questions. You may be asked, for example, to figure out how many plumbers there are in Kansas City. To solve, you'll have to do some creative estimation. This is actually a simple one: Guess at how many plumbers are in your town, what the population of your town is, and what the population of Kansas City is, set up the proportions, and you've got it:

$$\frac{16 \; plumbers}{12{,}000 \; people} = \frac{x \; plumbers}{500{,}000 \; people}$$

You may even be asked to analyze a business case, although this sort of question is more likely to appear in interviews for employment post-graduation. If you are interviewing for this type of job, ask your office of career services for help; they may have a list of sample questions or someone they can refer you to.

After the interview is over, it's appropriate to send a short, typed, straightforward note thanking the interviewer for the opportunity to learn more about the job. Then it's just sit tight until you get . . .

Job Offers

Wouldn't it be neat if employers, like colleges, notified everyone at the same time and gave you a couple of weeks to decide? Unfortunately, floating your boat isn't what employers are about. Your offers will probably be staggered over a couple of weeks or months, and deadlines for accepting come before you've heard about all the positions you applied for. Here's how to deal with an early offer from an employer who is not your first choice:

The employer will want you to decide quickly, but don't let yourself be rushed. Get as much time as you can without irritating the person (a week is pretty standard).

Try calling the other employers who have your applications on file. Say you've got to respond to an offer, and you'd like an assessment of your chances. All they can do is say they're way too busy to deal with special requests from plebes like you. They may, on the other hand, offer you an interview in person or by phone or be able to give you an answer one way or the other. Your professional approach and interest in their job may actually tip the scales in your favor.

If you decided that you basically don't want the job and have a good shot at a more desirable one, don't accept the offer just so you can feel secure.

It's when the offer appeals to you but you think you might get something better that you have a dilemma. It's unkind to back out once you've agreed to take a job (they've sent the rejection letters out, they've stopped worrying about who's going to make the Sanka), and it's also bad business; the world is small, and word might get around that your word is unreliable. You might even later decide you want to work for the employer you rejected. But on the other hand, it sucks to be in the mailroom when you could be doing research; maybe your résumé and your summer experience are more important than some administrator's mental well-being.

16

The Tide of Love:
Laundry

We didn't hear any water pouring in, but we assumed that the "silent" washing machine must just be yet another of the inventions that somehow hadn't made it to Minnesota yet. "Jiminy!" we exclaimed quietly. "Well, soon's they get that stagecoach line from Chicago run through, them'll be fat times. Until then, guess if I ain't got something to write home about."

It was only after half an hour that our dreams of high-speed transportation and flooding technology were marred by suspicion, concern, and finally the dawning realization that we had put our clothes and a heaping cup of Tide in the *dryer*. Removal of the clothes was easy, since the heating action of the dryer had turned the detergent into a top-notch adhesive. For only the second time in our lives, we mourned our lack of Siamese siblings; the stuck-together shirts could have clothed a litterful.

"Well, thanks for wasting my time with that story," you say, "but I think I can tell the difference between a washer and a dryer. Got a head on these shoulders." Well, privileged Easterner, our blessings. But looky here, identification isn't everything; the ability to distinguish doesn't guarantee you a clean load. We mastered the art of laundry the hard way, as you might imagine. Now you can learn it the easy way:

Don't Blame Maytag

Many items of clothing, seemingly designed more for mannequins' use than ours, aren't supposed to be machine washed. So before you undress directly into the washing machine, check out the following:

Follow the care instructions on the label at the top of the garment or inside on the seam. It basically boils down to these precepts:

Cotton can almost always be machine washed and dried, but beware shrinkage and wrinkling (see sections on washing, drying, and ironing).

Cotton dress blouses and button-down shirts can be cared for as above, but if you're not a whiz with the iron, consider taking them in to a laundry (often at same location as dry cleaner) to have them washed, ironed, and starched, especially for special occasions. The cost is $1–$2 per shirt. You can, of course, have them dry cleaned, but that's more expensive and offers the accompanying delightful carcinogenic smell.

Formal or informal garments made of the following fabrics should almost always be dry cleaned rather than machine laundered: rayon, silk, acetate, and velvet.

Linen can be machine or hand washed, but it is an ironing nightmare. Consider dry cleaning it or having a laundry wash and press it for you.

Pantyhose is too delicate to be thrown directly in the washer. Either hand wash it in the sink, or place it in a special mesh bag (available in department stores and drugstores) or a pillowcase with a rubber band on it before throwing in the washer.

> ## Your Very Own Maid
>
> Many campuses have services that will do your laundry for you. The fee varies, and is certainly much higher than that of doing it yourself with coins, but if you're particularly rich, busy, or inept, it's an option.

Lace lingerie survives the spin cycle better than hosiery, but it, too, is better off protected in a bag or in a pillowcase tied shut.

Wool sweaters, especially hand-knit ones, aren't meant to be machine washed, and in fact don't need any kind of frequent washing. A simple brush-down is usually enough to remove dust and rejuvenate the knit; if they're stinky from smoke or wet, an airing does the trick. But if an intimate encounter with a cup of coffee does make cleansing a necessity, hand wash with Woolite in the sink or bathtub or machine wash if necessary. Dry flat on a towel.

Machine Washing and Drying (in that order)

Pacifists' Guide to Laundry: Stop the Bleeding

Wash light and dark colors separately, unless you like the idea of a wardrobe full of Barbie Mobile–style pastels.

Wash and dry your towels and terry cloth bathrobes separately from the rest of the wash, at least for the first several cleanings. Not only do they often bleed, but lintlike bits sometimes separate from them and attach to other items of clothing.

If you're unsure whether something will bleed or not (some brands do more than others) or lack confidence in your laundering abilities, go for cold water. It cleans almost as well as warm, and prevents bleeding. If your machine's settings are labeled by color rather than temperature, "bright colors" = cold water.

Be especially careful with clothing that's designed to "weather" quickly or is advertised as already weathered; often this just means that the manufacturer has used cheap dyes that bleed readily.

If color blindness struck in the middle of your sorting, wash the clothing that's been bled on immediately in color-safe bleach.

If the bloodshed is caused by factors outside your control—a green rugby bleeds onto its own white collar, for example—demand your money back, even if it's obviously worn. There is some minimal guarantee of quality even cheap stores want to uphold.

Powdered, color-safe bleaches are idiotproof, and as idiots, we recommend them. Although it is better to add them after the washing machine has filled with water, it generally works to dump them in along with the detergent and clothes. Bleach is most important for whites, but also brightens colors.

Your Dog Has Enough Hand-me-downs: Drying without Shrinkage

Bleeding is the major danger posed by washing, shrinkage the one posed by drying. Unless you're in a rush, have a very full load, or have resolved to shed several pounds in the course of the dryer cycle, "warm" is usually the best setting. Hot settings—often indicated by the label "permanent press" or "sturdy"—are more appropriate for sheets and towels.

The only way to truly guard against shrinkage, however, is to hang dry. Inexpensive elastic clotheslines designed for stringing in the shower or your room are available in luggage departments or other places selling travel items; try also folding drying racks available at places like Target. Before hanging up garments, either stretch out the wrinkles by hand or tumble clothes dry for fifteen to twenty minutes.

Dry all sweaters flat, even if the label says otherwise. Machine and line drying can cause them to stretch out and lose their shape.

Ironing

Sometimes you can get wrinkles out simply by hanging garments in the bathroom during a few hot showers, or by removing them from the dryer while still a bit damp, and then hanging. But for truly stubborn wrinkles, shun BoTox and look for . . .

An iron. Before you hustle off to the store to buy one, check around your dorm. Your resident advisor may have one; there may be one lying around your laundry room, or that chap who wears jodhpurs and cuff links to class might be willing to rent you his, unless he's using it.

An ironing board isn't absolutely necessary; if you can't find one the same place you found the iron, any flat surface should do. Make sure, however, that it isn't made of or coated with plastic, or you could find yourself with a slicker where you once had a blazer. The tabletop-sized ones work well for dorms, if you're buying.

Plastic melts; so do synthetic fabrics. Your iron should indicate which setting to use for which fabrics, but if there's ambiguity, use the lowest setting for materials like rayon and polyester, the highest for linen and cotton.

Give the iron five or ten minutes to heat up and cool down. You can test it by pressing it on a slightly wet surface and seeing if it hisses.

If it's cotton or linen you're ironing, sprinkle the garment with water, roll up for a few minutes so the moisture can spread out, and unroll just before ironing (or use a steam iron for best results).

Never leave the iron pressed down in one position for longer than four to five seconds. Instead, keep it moving in small circles, using moderate pressure to smooth out the fabric.

If you haven't ironed much, you might want to iron the garment inside out. An inside job produces almost as good results, and guarantees that any scorch marks will be invisible except to you and the guy who watches you undress from the neighboring dorm.

Stain Removal

You think you're pretty stylin' in that pink pleather skirt—until a bottle of ketchup in your lap makes for Valentine's Day attire, a little out of season. A few minutes later, the holiday fun is interrupted by the landing of some off-color relish. Pretty soon, you're wearing enough food to feed your dorm hamster and all other local pets.

A speedy application of a stain stick/treatment (after which in some cases you can wait up to a week to actually wash) is usually enough to combat the average stain, but when the situation's a bit more serious, as it is now, drastic measures are in order:

Beer—Treat stain with small squirts of liquid detergent and white vinegar mixed with two cups lukewarm water. Launder as usual.

Camouflage

Some stains, like a hibernating groundhog, just won't come out. If the stained item is just a pair of jeans, you might consider ignoring the stain or covering it with a patch. But our limited military experience has taught us that if you can't beat 'em, join 'em. A water stain on a taffeta? Dunk the entire dress. Turtleneck gone slightly pink from a colored load's crimson tide? Send it on a few more trips with your Valentine's Day apparel. Beer-battered T-shirt? Start moonlighting at the brewery.

Bleach—Went Clorox-happy? Mix liquid detergent and lukewarm water and rub into stain.

Blood—Apply meat tenderizer to area. Add cold water and mix to make paste. Sponge off with cold water after fifteen to thirty minutes. If you aren't equipped with condiments, hydrogen peroxide may also work, but be careful using this on colored fabrics.

Chocolate—Submerge article in cold water for half an hour. Rub detergent (or bleach, if the fabric is colorfast) into stain and launder as usual.

Coffee—Whip together liquid detergent, white vinegar, and any volatile solvent. Treat stain and launder.

Deodorant—Try one of the following methods:

Rub stain with ammonia (diluted if you're dealing with delicate fabric), and launder as usual.

Rub stain with white vinegar; if this fails, soak garment in rubbing alcohol for half an hour, rinse with cool water and launder in hot.

Dirt/dorm socks—After washing, boil socks in a hot pot for half an hour with a few lemon slices filched from the coffee tray. Drain (lemonade!) and launder as usual.

Fruit/fruit juice/punch—Try one of the following methods:

Hold stained section taut over a bowl and pour boiling water on affected area from a few feet above it, if possible.

Rub stain with H_2O_2 (flatter your premed roommate by asking for help with that one). When it stops foaming, rinse article with cool water. Repeat process until stain vanishes, then launder as usual.

Rub stain with lemon juice (available in cafeteria), rinsing every fifteen minutes until stain disappears. Launder as usual.

Grass—More multiple-choice:

Submerge garment in cold water for half an hour. Rinse, rub detergent into stained area, wash in hot water with bleach.

If the fabric is silk or wool, soak the stained section in a mixture of two cups water and one cup rubbing alcohol. Rinse and launder as usual.

Grease—Rub stain with detergent, scrub with warm water, rinse, and launder as usual.

Put talcum powder on stain. After ten or fifteen minutes, brush off. Rub a little shampoo into stain, wash in hot water.

Gum—Wrap gummy article in plastic and put in freezer (or out the window, if it's cold enough). Scrape off frozen gum, and use as Silly Putty for cheap fun.

Ink—Cover stained area with hairspray or nail polish remover, then rub dry with towel.

Lipstick—Rub Vaseline into stain, hand wash in warm water, rinse, and launder as usual. Paint remover also works, but be careful.

Makeup other than lipstick (mascara, eyeshadow, blush, powder, foundation)—Rub detergent or bar soap into stain, rinse with cool water, and launder as usual.

Mud—After mud has dried, rub off with a brush. Rub stain with cool water. As a final resort, try rubbing alcohol. Launder as usual.

Nail polish—Treat with volatile solvent and launder.

Pencil—If an eraser doesn't work, rub detergent into the stain and rinse. As a last resort, try ammonia; after rinsing, launder as usual.

Soda—Immediately rub stain with a mixture of rubbing alcohol and water. Rinse and launder as usual.

Sweat—Let article sit in warm water with a little vinegar.

Vomit—Mix water, white vinegar, and a little warm detergent (let your bottle sit on the dryer or on the windowsill in the sun), and treat stain. Launder as usual.

Wine—Combine liquid detergent, ammonia, white vinegar, and water. Treat and launder.

Dryerside's the right place for love, but it serves equally well as a place for some well-planned revenge. The public nature of the laundry room guarantees that your roommate/ex-girlfriend will never blame you for her misfortune; the blind trust with which people empty their lives

Laundry Room Come-ons

The dryer is lowing like a well-fed cow, the washing machine is sloshing like a tall glass of Lowenbrau, and the folding table's whispering your name. She senses it, too, her murmur about the "protein power of Era" obviously a tribute to your virility. Everything's perfect. All you need is the right line:

"Hey baby, what's your setting?"

"Make like a Maytag, baby, and spin me."

"Are you feeling dizzy? Cause you been tumbling through my head all day."

"Say, it must be raining cats and dogs out there. Need a tumble dry?"

"The clothes are still damp. Do you think it's time to move up to *permanent press?*"

"Let the protein power of *Erik* do the talking!"

"Nice load."

"Can you make me Cuddle Soft–fresh?"

into a Maytag makes your sabotage all the easier. Here, some tactics:

Alternative garbage can. Leftovers been in the fridge a couple of months too long? Dump them overboard while washing machine is on spin cycle.

Switcheroo. Switch victim's load with Pigpen's halfway through, so that her brassieres get a bath in his gross water. Stay and watch as he handles her laundry until the "mix-up" is discovered.

O Canada . . . Replace all the quarters in her not-so-well-hidden change pot with Canadian ones. Watch from behind a dryer as the diversity cheerleader curses "Canucks." Emerge to expose her as a criminal when she tries to throw her detergent-soaked clothes in someone else's machine.

Mmm, a new scent. While she's sneaking a glance at herself in the dryer window, quickly replace her liquid Tide with Cranapple.

1-900- . . . Take intimate apparel out of dryer before the load's scheduled to be finished (undies always dry first). Label every pair with her phone number in permanent marker and arrange on folding table with Take One sign.

17
Room or Ruins?
Simple Dorm
Maintenance

The football team beer and prunes reception was fun, but the after-math left your toilet as clogged as sinuses in goldenrod season. You call the dorm superintendent, but two hours later you glimpse the hunched form of someone doing Jell-O shots in the bushes, finally disappearing with a muffled cry. It's the super. You start doing the bathroom dance that made you famous in preschool, but it doesn't bring the chicks bearing plungers like it used to.

Alas, you are not alone in your melancholy ballet, or in your frustration with Facilities Maintenance. College life is a story of foggy mirrors, empty bottles of Drano, and broken promises to remove the petri dishes from the shower floor. In the absence of proper maintenance, one alternative is to hire your own domestic, as one of our friends did. But even if you've got the dough and the desire to hire out, there are problems you're going to have to solve on your own. To keep your bachelor(ette) pad in shape, or at least trim enough to pass inspections, use the following tips:

Odors

Just some stale Brut? Think again. Your own dog wouldn't accept a bottle of that stuff. Face it, the chamber of love has become a chamber pot. To reverse the degeneration, sniff out the source and take these steps:

Cigarette odors. In extreme cases, you might need to break out the air purifier or open the windows, but first try burning some candles or setting out a dish of vinegar or ammonia. The former's available at the salad bar; you might need to mooch some of the latter off dorm crew. They're not using it themselves, so they shouldn't mind.

Mildew. The water moccasins make nice jump ropes, but living in a swamp has its disadvantages. That musty smell is from a fungus that can wreck books and clothes and even hurt your lungs if you let it go. Brushing with a little talcum powder or dousing with bleach usually does the trick; to prevent its renaissance, leave a few boxes of baking soda in various places—closets, shelves—where you won't be too tempted to snack on it, and keep windows open on muggy days.

Bathroom odors. In coed bathrooms, especially, it's a good idea to bring a matchbook to the bathroom when you've got big plans. Strike a match to celebrate your carrying them out.

Drain odors. Clogged drains can get stinky in a snap. If yours looks like it's got a Barbie Doll stuffed down it, get rid of the hair by sloshing with boiling water and baking soda. Chemical cleaners like Drano work as a last resort; they're extremely toxic and damaging to skin, however, and they cost more than Arm & Hammer.

If you don't think that over-the-sink Mohawk job had anything to do with it, simpler solutions may work. Try tossing in some baking soda and rinsing with hot tap water, or pouring in a cup of vinegar and letting that smell overwhelm all others. After half an hour or so, rinse.

Pests

Unless you count that prepubescent prodigy next door, the main pests threatening your peace of mind are roaches, ants, and mice. If you're careful about crumbs, you may well avoid problems completely. But if you do notice your cupboard becoming as a trough for small-scale live-stock, stem the epidemic before it reaches *Arachnophobia*-like proportions:

Roaches. Turn your room into the Holiday Inn of roach motels not by instituting a turndown service, but by serving your patrons the following savory hors d'oeuvres:

Minor Repairs with Corn

Expensive spackle, plungers, and light bulbs are okay for some spend-thrifts, but if your last name ain't Rockefeller you may not have bills to burn on such luxuries. Instead, simply cut a stalk of corn from your windowsill row and you're in business:

Knock, knock...Doorknob fall out last time roommate tried to lock her boyfriend out when he took an untimely bathroom break? No need to interrupt the super, simply insert half an ear of corn. When in need of prelecture snack, simply hold lighter under cob, ready salt shaker, and open your kisser.

Hammerhead. A fist or bottle can do the job, but for a professional nail insertion, turn to the cob.

Drain stopper. Chances are, your prepubescent predecessors ripped off the stopper for use as a pacifier; before your contact goes down the open drain, equip sink with a slice of corncob. Porous enough to allow water through, the snug fitting will yet hinder passage of rubber ducky/pet fish into underworld.

Never say "clogged." Just to show you how many hats corn can wear, the same cob that plugged the sink drain can be used to *un*plug the toilet. If you're man enough to get down and dirty, a few well-directed thrusts should have the problem cleared up; if you insist on impaling the cob on a mechanical pencil to score yourself a handle, your plumbing job will be longer but mess-free.

¼ cup margarine
⅛ cup sugar
8 oz. powdered boric acid (chem lab?)
½ cup flour
½ small onion
water as needed

Mix, moistening to form a dough, and form balls. Scatter throughout the room as though they were potpourri. Inform your human guests that they're not cookie dough.

Ants. Show a similar form of hospitality to ants and you'll be blissfully out of business in no time. A cup of molasses, 2 packs of dry yeast, and a half cup of sugar mixed together and applied to small cardboard squares gonna shut those suckers down.

Mice. Unless you want to share your Cheez-its with rodents as well as the wildlife specimens parading as your roommates, mice are a problem. To forestall their arrival, keep food in sealed containers. If they come anyway, try traps. To lull them into a false sense of hospitality, put tasty morsels on traps without setting them for a few days. Then set the traps and let the soothing rhythm of snapping springs put you to sleep.

Damage Disguise

No matter how careful you are with the plutonium, chances are your room's going to take a bit of a beating. And even if you somehow avoid inflicting damage, there's a strong possibility that some scars remain from previous inhabitation—scars that the administration preserves not for their affinity with cave art, but for their money-making potential. You see, deans, a.k.a. extortionists, charge each successive generation of students for the *same damages,* never repairing them. So are the sins of the fathers visited upon the sons.

To beat the system requires action at one end or the other of your stay—for best results both:

One of the first things you'll be required to do upon moving in is fill out a condition-of-room or inventory form for the superintendent of your dorm or apartment building. Be careful to take note of the problems that actually exist, but if you're willing to sink to the super's level of scamming (and who doesn't have that goal?) feel free to use your imagination. Where are you likely to affix posters? Which wall are you likely to use as a punching bag when the gym closes for Columbus Day? Mark down all the nail holes, paint chips, wall dents, and ripped screens that you anticipate leaving the room with. If your poster gum takes off less paint than you thought it would, don't feel obligated to do the job with a fingernail; it's only when damages exceed those reported that there's a problem.

However you dealt with the super's form, you'll want to do a little patching before May move-out. The amount you can get charged for is far in excess of the actual cost of fixing the problems. Even if you don't consider yourself handy, there's nothing to lose by trying to fix:

Nail holes. If there's a hardware store and some cash convenient, treat yourself to some spackle. But if you're into pinching nickels, toothpaste (white) and crushed aspirin for texture work just as well as filler. If the walls are white, your work is finished, but if they're colored, a little Wite-out tinted with nail polish (matte) will do the trick.

Peeled paint. As above, Wite-out with or without color should work. If your walls have that slightly bumpy texture, try mixing a little wheat germ or sugar from the cafeteria into your "paint."

Environmentalism

To a certain extent, you don't have much control over your living space when you're at school or in an apartment: We didn't find out that our freshman dorm was insulated with asbestos until April, when a martial arts–happy floormate punched a hole in the wall demonstrating a move. You can't finish karate kid's work without donning a white robe yourself, and notifying the administration that there's an air pollution problem would have about the same effect as notifying them that your English prof dispensed 'shrooms with the syllabus—you're not telling them anything they don't already know.

But, as you do the maintenance described above and other chores related to life in college, there are some ways you can control your impact on your own living environment and on the larger one:

If you're not sharing a bathroom with the entire hall, put a bottle, filled with water and sealed, in the toilet tank. It will displace water, resulting in decreased usage by the john.

Arboreal as Lymon Glade O' Pine Sol is, it works by deadening receptors in your body, not by really masking the stink. A dish of vinegar and lemon juice works better, and doesn't come in an aerosol can.

Save the fish—when it finally comes time to do the wash, use a phosphate-free detergent (liquids usually are). Even if there aren't lakes or rivers nearby, phosphates can travel through the ground and eventually reach open water, where they fertilize algae and suffocate the life below.

Select the cold cycle on the washing machine. Heating water consumes most of the energy it takes to run the machine, and doesn't make for any cleaner clothes.

Instead of buying notepads, just tear up old—or current—problem sets/drafts and use the back of the scraps for phone messages.

Recycle—or, even better, fold up for reuse—all the cardboard boxes you used for shipping.

Put a sign up, if one doesn't already exist, asking people to turn the bathroom light off when they're finished.

You may not be able to stop the junk mail and fliers from flooding your mailbox, but at least you can be religious about recycling. If the paper is a color that your recycling program won't accept, use it for scratch paper and recycle any white paper that you can't find a use for.

Instead of taking a Styrofoam cup every morning, get a mug.

Most campuses have recycling programs; use them.

Many cities have curbside recycling programs. Check out the city's Web site—it will probably describe what you're able to recycle (everything from cereal boxes to many nonbeverage plastic containers), procedures, and pickup days.

18 Phys. Ed. 101: Sleep & Exercise

If you're like us, you'll give both of these up for the first couple of weeks—or years, as the case may be. But pretty soon you'll realize that Fido has it all over humans when it comes to high living: being rested, ready to go, and never at a loss for a bathroom is about as good as it gets. Experience has convinced us that exercise and sleep keep you happier, less stressed, more efficient, energetic, and better-looking.

Exercise

If you're gifted athletically or like the idea of living in a locker room, the huge time commitment required by varsity sports may be okay with you. In addition to getting in great shape, you'll have a guaranteed group of friends from the beginning. For those of us who didn't grow up on fortified Gerber's, however, intramurals—offered in everything from ultimate Frisbee to arm wrestling—or an individual workout may be more manageable options.

Burning calories, of course, isn't the only benefit from such activities, but it is the one that some of our tenth-grade minds focused on, judging from our health class notes. Here's the table that has guided us for so many years:

Calories Burned per Hour

	100 lbs.	120 lbs.	150 lbs.	180 lbs.	200 lbs.
Baseball	210	238	280	322	350
Basketball (½ court)	225	255	300	345	378
Biking	157	178	211	242	263
Billiards	97	110	130	150	163
Hiking	225	255	300	345	375
Jogging (5.5 mph)	487	552	650	748	833
Racquetball	450	510	600	690	750
Rollerblading	262	297	350	403	438
Rowing/erging	615	697	820	943	1,025
Running (10 mph)	625	765	900	1,035	1,125
Skiing, Cross-country	525	595	700	805	875
Skiing, Downhill	450	510	600	690	750
Soccer	405	459	540	621	675
Swimming (slow)	240	272	320	368	400
Swimming (fast)	420	530	630	768	846
Tennis	315	357	420	483	525
Walking	204	258	318	372	426

Dormcise

Many of the above exercises, of course, require fancy equipment, esprit de corps, a gym, a nice body, etc. But if your motivation to exercise takes you only to the door of your dorm, you're going to have to investigate other options if you want to reach that target heart rate. With these helpful hints, you can turn your dorm into the athletic center its founders intended it to be!

Brick backboard. Find a side of your building with minimal ivy. Ideally, it should also have only bathroom windows on it. Begin swinging smoothly and effortlessly, and soon you will be surrounded by fans, vandal-recruiting scouts, and campus security wearing Nikes and ready to give you a run for your money before they pull out the cuffs.

Richard Simmons. Or Jane Fonda or videotaped class lectures—it's pretty much the same thing: someone in a tank top and shorts shouting at you. Channel anger/disgust/fascination into your abs/butt/biceps.

Barcaerobics. No pricey DVD needed here—you can "barc" to everything from the *Beverly Hillbillies* theme song to Pink Panther flicks. Of course, it helps if there's a rhythm, but if you want to branch out into the world of talk shows, you can kick and flex every time Conan O'Brien pops a lemon joke or Jerry Springer's henchmen have to knock out a guest (maybe too much exercise).

Power keyboarding. (Don't try this one if you think you're at risk for carpal tunnel syndrome, chapter 12.) Turn typing into a totally trimming exercise! Just slip on some hand weights before you start that paper, and soon you'll be sweatin' and writin' all at the same time!

Fidgeting. On a similar note, dedicated fidgeters have been found to burn hundreds of extra calories per day. There are tricks of the trade, of course—avoid using props like pencils in classes where they can easily go flying; choose soft-soled shoes to avoid clicking as you jiggle your legs/feet. '80s music and caffeine help.

Real stairclimbing. You've had it with "Black Hole" and "Pikes Peak"—why not make good old-fashioned sociability your program? Make acquaintances/dates as you, perspiring, ascend and descend the stairwells of your dorm, an ambassador of sweat and goodwill from your floor!

3D reading. And you thought you needed those glasses. Silly, all you have to do to make reading funtime instead of naptime is lie back on the floor, legs elevated on a chair or couch, and do sit-ups as the verbiage flies by.

Invisible futon. All the seating in use? Do a wall-sit. Simply stand with your back against the wall and pretend there's a chair below you. Continue the fiction until you find your upper leg muscles shaking with exertion, your face purple, and everyone in the room on their cell phones to the ER. Quickly recover your posture and claim one of their seats.

Banister chin-ups. Only for use in dorms designed by prison archi-

Off-Road Arm Wrestling

If you've had it with the intramural scene, another place where sociability and sweat go together like peanut butter and fluff is the Outing Club. Not only that, but events can provide a great way to get to know the area and get off campus for an afternoon or a day, or even a week during spring break, depending upon your school. Go rock climbing! Go hiking in Bryce Canyon! Go ice fishing on the hockey arena! Even if you don't end up a superactive clubster, membership has its privileges: You might be able to borrow tents and equipment from time to time for your own "outings."

tects, as our predecessors in a more rickety dorm found out the broken bone way.

Dorm soccer. Developed by a couple of our friends, this works best in dorms with fairly long hallways, and, unless the hallways are also very wide, can only be played one-on-one. Get into your togs, stand at the midpoint of the hall, and drop the ball between you. If your hallway has two stairwells, you can each defend one goal; if it's only got one, you can designate a wall or bathroom as the other end zone. Keep track of the score as you descend, floor by floor; create extra rules as the configuration of your dorm suggests (if you have an elevator, award extra points for kicking into it).

When Sweat Central (A.K.A. the College Gym) Just Isn't Cutting It:

College gyms are usually free, but that may be about all they are; facilities for nonvarsity athletes are sometimes glittering, but often grungy. The hours are usually okay, since student labor to staff the desk is cheap, but workout machines may be scarce, the air may be stale and hot, and there may not be the kind of facilities you like to work out in (tennis courts, a track). When you're looking for other options, consider . . .

Working out with athlete friends. They usually have access to excellent facilities, and during nonpractice hours it is probably no problem for them to bring friends.

Graduate school or more remote facilities. Sometimes racquetball courts appear in the strangest places. If you go to a university with separate graduate schools, call them or look on a map to see if they have gyms. They will probably be small, but they may be classier and emptier.

Joining a health club. It may sound snotty to even suggest, but joining a private health club is an option. If you're staying in the same city you grew up in and your parents belong somewhere, you may be able to stay covered by the family membership while in school. Other health clubs may offer special deals for students or at least waive initiation fees; they know no student can afford them.

Arboretums, parks. Some universities have their own arboretums either on campus or at least in the same city; safety can be a concern (see below) if you're alone, but peace and quiet can also be delightful.

Cemeteries. It sounds strange, but some cemeteries are as beautiful as arboretums, and the only place you can find much peace in some highly urbanized student areas. There are sometimes prohibitions on running, sledding, etc.; it's worth a try if you're not too creeped out.

Out of town. One reason having a car with you is nice. Weekend rentals can be cheap, too.

Sleep

The average person, we heard somewhere, takes fifteen to thirty minutes to fall asleep at night. The average college student, along with the average narcoleptic, is out in under sixty seconds, less than that if comfortable desks permit. But despite our need for sleep, we often either can't get or want to postpone getting the rest we need. Here's how to get your habits under control:

Rest amidst Tumult

The cattle are lowing, the poor coed wakes . . . Yet again, your roommate has scheduled a wrasslin' match for three A.M. on your bedroom floor. Or maybe it's a more intimate rendezvous. Or maybe it's simply the grinding of his wolflike canine teeth as he struggles over his "history" paper on nudity on the *Titanic* (appendix A, Kate Winslet). Whatever the cause, his Neanderthal heritage is wreaking havoc with your sleep schedule. Before you take drastic measures at the A.M. end of the day, try the following nonviolent tactics:

Hold the crumpets. Noncaffeinated tea as a pre-bedtime drink can be extremely relaxing, relaxing enough to keep you calm even in your ringside seat at your roommate's latest bout.

What? Pull on some earphones, either with no music or with your Walkman tuned to talk radio. Its steady pitch and volume and stultifying subject matter ("Bob Dole's Favorite Places in Kansas") will put you to sleep in no time. You'll wake up at some point either in the middle of the night or during a test of the emergency broadcast system and unplug yourself.

Less caffeine. It stays in the body a long time; even if you're not having it anywhere near bedtime, a lot of it in your body can make it difficult to get good rest.

White noise. Sometimes the whirring of a fan placed right beside your bed is enough to shut out distractions. If this doesn't work, however, and you're truly desperate, you might invest in a white noise machine. Such devices can reproduce the lullaby-like noises of waves, birds, humpback whales, or, if you come from Manhattan, the soothing rumble of garbage trucks at three A.M.

They work for lectures, too. Available at most drugstores, earplugs can be an invaluable resource in *bed*lam. Just make sure they don't shut out the alarm clock.

Hey, what's that bug on the ceiling? As he lunges for it hungrily, slip a Valium into his brewskie. Propose a toast and let those z's take him away.

Sleep Inhibitors

Before you put the above strategies into effect, Bruno was about all the sleep inhibitor you needed. But now that he's been lying on the floor peacefully for a few days (hmm, what was the dosage on that Valium?), you can't pull all-nighters as you used to. If our persuasion has been effectual, you value your sleep, but you'd just like to control it.

The solutions to your problem are as numerous as drug lords in Colombia—unfortunately, many of them are illegal and could send the paper you're writing to places no bullshitter has gone before. But even once you've committed to caffeine, the choices are multifarious enough to send your tired little head spinning. Luckily, we're here to help you discriminate among them . . .

I like coffee, I like tea. A lot of people have tea as a relaxing, pre-bedtime drink (see previous page), but Earl Grey and green tea actually have about as much caffeine as instant coffee, which in turn has about two-thirds as much of the stimulant as the brewed version.

Cola. Jolt excepted, colas have about half as much caffeine as tea, and it takes three or four cans of Dr. Pepper to equal the amount of caffeine in just one six-ounce cup of brewed coffee. Sugar gives you a high, too, of course.

Chocolate. "Paper tonight," one of our freshman roommates would announce as she helped herself to spoonful after spoonful of Reese's Pieces from the sundae line. She got some catcalls from the poor slobs after her who faced an empty bowl, but it was a good thing for her that she wasn't shy about hogging; an ounce of milk chocolate has about one-fiftieth the caffeine of brewed coffee, and it takes a lot of Reese's to equal that.

Drugs. Only for the serious tripper. One tablet of Vivarin has 200 mg of caffeine, or as much as four Cokes; NoDoz weighs in at about half that.

A Concise Guide to Dreaming

Depending on which of the above stimulants you've OD'd on and your current level of sanity, you could be in for a pretty wacky show whenever it is you do begin sleeping/hallucinating. And since you don't need any more excuses to think about last night rather than your nine A.M. lecture, we thought we'd do you a little favor, a little act of mental wizardry such as we're known for around these corn fields, to the tune of this guide. For while the prototypal "college dreams"—of which every dream you'll have is just a mutant—seem straightforward enough in their messages, deeper psychic meanings lurk beneath the surface:

What You Dream	*What It Really Means*
I. *The Agriculture Dream* Seven fat cows and seven skinny ones are standing outside your dorm window.	For seven days dinner will be edible. Then cafeteria will close for spring break.

II. *The Bathroom Dream*
You're sitting on the toilet reading
Penthouse, calmly relieving yourself,
when it suddenly becomes painful.
You think Huggies, but then pain
subsides. You breathe a sigh of
contentment and prayer.

You will shortly break up
with your girlfriend, and this
is a good thing.

III. *The Home Dream*
You're cuddled up with someone on
a warm, comfortable couch. You hear
a familiar, jocular voice, followed
by laughter, in which you join. You
lean back and pop a handful of
Pringles into your mouth.

Bring a condom when you go
to office hours.

IV. *The Date Dream*
You're at a party, talking to an
amazing girl/guy, you're not sure
which. Nonetheless, one thing leads
to another, and pretty soon you
two are out on the grass under the
stars. He/she is licking you; you're
freaked out at first, but then begin
licking back.

You miss your dog.

19
The Glory
That Was Greece:
Fraternities
& Sororities

Thanks to cinema classics like *Animal House* and *Sorority Babes in the Slimeball Bowl-a-Rama,* and that stuffy high school class on the *Iliad,* it's easy to have a mistaken notion of what Greek life is all about. Depending on your perspective, the truth is either disappointing or refreshing; the fact is that rush, at most schools, is a lot tamer than it was in the glory days. Because of hazing casualties and accusations of gender discrimination, the Greek civilization has crumbled at many colleges, leaving behind Acropolis-like ruins that upperclass students pray to Zeus for a room in. The sororities and fraternities that remain, appropriately, have become a little classier in their images and practices.

Since rituals vary widely with region and college, and are also often secret, it's difficult for us to give you any specific information about what to expect from rush and pledging. We can offer you, however, a general picture of the advantages and disadvantages of renouncing your American citizenship for Greek, a few words about what you can expect from rush, and advice on how to face up to a keg bearing your name—if your immediate response isn't to pucker up and start swigging.

Naturalization

As is true of participation in any close-knit group, membership in frats and sororities has its disadvantages as well as its privileges. Joining up guarantees you a group of friends—a valuable commodity, particularly at big schools—but can provide you with an all-too-convenient excuse not to extend yourself socially. Pledging gives you, similarly, a sense of identity at a time when it's easy to feel lost and alone, but in doing so it denies you the rewards as well as the challenges of striking out on your own and defining yourself independently of group affiliations.

And then there's rush. For some, it's time to cash in on all those years of Miss Manners reading or practice-chugging Listerine; for others, it's a seemingly endless assault on facial muscles, self-confidence, and sobriety. The Ann Taylor–clad denizens of Mount Olympus claim not to judge on appearance or connections, but even goddesses read *Mademoiselle;* toga boys may claim that Evian's a cool substitute for the Beast, but will probably pass temperance advocates on to other temples.

We say that if Greek life is a big deal at your campus, give it a try. It's likely that the school's entire social life will revolve around the frat and sorority houses, and—especially if you're a guy—it's going to be easier to get into parties if you're on the inside. If you end up deciding it's not your cup of ambrosia, you'll still have met a lot of people; some of our friends, in fact, went through rush, knowing that they weren't going to pledge, for this very purpose. Here's what they found, and what you can expect:

From a Sorority

At most of our sororities, rush events are concentrated within a period of two weeks or less. Parties, at first, are numerous and brief; as you drop sororities and sororities drop you, soirées become longer and more elaborate, giving you and the sisters a chance to schmooze at length. Even the final parties are more low-key than the movies make them out to be, but there are a few things to keep in mind:

It's not the Miss America pageant, no matter how much that length of toilet paper resting casually—and all unnoticed—across Miss Priss's dress resembles a state banner. Don't feel you have to bring the house to tears with a little Kenny Rogers crooning or trot out any sympathetic one-liners about the rug rats in India. It sounds clichéd, but be yourself.

Similarly, don't stress about clothes unless stressing about clothes is a way of life for you. We know people who poured $1,500 or more into clothes they definitely would not have bought but for rush, with results scarcely different from ours. And even if clothes do get you into every sorority on campus, is that really the kind of success you want? Presenting yourself as something you're not is only going to get you admitted to groups you won't feel at home in; when you pledge, you're in for the long haul, and fakery just isn't sustainable.

Just as sisters are forgiving of fashion faux pas, you shouldn't be too judgmental about sororities. The worst thing you can do is sit down with your friends at the beginning of rush and decide which are the "good" and "bad" sororities. For one thing, you're probably going to be wrong; there are probably lots of groups that would suit you. Even if you're right, chances are one of you is going to end up in a sorority that your crowd nixed after a ten-minute exposure to it, and rush is competitive enough without those kinds of complications.

On a similar note: While your mother's advice may carry weight with you, don't focus on a sorority just because it was hers. The current group of girls may trace its ancestry more to felines than to her chums; sororities evolve, not always in humane directions.

Having said that, you—in consultation with your personal desires and not the consensus of your friends—will have to make some decisions. If you felt things didn't go well in general at a given house, it may be appropriate to haul out the gong, but don't knock off a sorority you like just because of a little wine cooler accident with sis. One girl's stained bustier isn't enough to keep you out; sororities are more democratic than they seem.

Fraternities

Guys' rush tends to be longer (events spread out over, say, an entire semester) and more casual (i.e., modeled on the latest Budweiser commercial).

As you might imagine, displays of SAT vocabulary are less impressive than those of masculine strength and virility—can-crushing, deep-throated guffawing, goldfish-guzzling, and the age-old contest for who can stuff the largest number of Jimmy Deans down his gullet.

Despite administration crackdowns and antihazing legislation, drinking and drugs do play a larger role in fraternities' events than in sororities. But while you may find yourself doing something equally embarrassing—like hitching a ride home naked—it *is* possible to be initiated without getting sloshed. The pledging process—as opposed to rush—is mainly a formality anyway; if you've made it this far, knowing when to say when isn't going to keep you out.

20

The Leisure Class:

Student Activities

College courses, if you don't count studying, just do not take up that much time (10–16 hours a week) and frankly, once you get into your major, do not allow you to use all sides of your personality. Nor are classes—unless small and noncompetitive—a particularly good way to meet people. You need outside interests.

For some people, that means (or has to mean) work, which has its own rewards. For some it means totally informal, spontaneous fun. If you're on a big campus, however, and/or live off campus, sometimes organized extracurriculars are the only way you're going to find similar people to be spontaneous *with*. Besides all that, extracurriculars can look better than many jobs on your résumé, provide you with real-world skills, and give you an idea of career fields to explore later. Consider the following types of activities:

Publications

Even on a small campus, you're likely to find a multitude of newspapers and 'zines. If you have the urge to write, do photography or cartooning, editing, layout, or business, these can be a great way to get training. Check out the options:

The "main" newspaper. Basically, the newspaper that comes out the most frequently, whether it's a daily or a weekly, is going to be considered the main and most "prestigious" rag. This is a good and a bad thing; good because working on it will probably give you the most opportunities to get published or, if you're on the business side, the biggest budget/operations to oversee. It will also be perhaps the best connections/alumni network for future jobs in journalism if you are so inclined and probably has the most readership and prestige value. The downside includes time demands; even being a reporter, let alone an editor, for a daily can be practically a full-time job. There's also a certain responsibility to do straight news reporting when working for the main campus newspaper; it will tend to take fewer risks.

Alternative rags. These are distinguished either by coming out less frequently and being more news magazine-ish or by having a particular point of view: liberal, conservative, feminist, etc. If your dream job is to become a pundit on *FoxNews,* this is where to cut your teeth: you'll develop opinions on a variety of world and local issues in the company of people who think similarly to you. These too, of course, have a business side; if you want to develop such skills in the company of like-minded folks, with perhaps less pressure than at a daily, give it a try.

Comedy publications. They vary in quality and aren't everywhere, but if there isn't one and you're so inclined, feel free to start one. Madison's prized *The Onion* is only the hottest; the Harvard *Lampoon* has spawned books and generations of late-night comedy and *Simpsons* writers.

Music and Theater

Any grunt can churn out a piece on the dean's wild night at the campus brew hall, but to do music and theater requires *skills* . . . or so their participants think. Sometimes it's true: perfect pitch seems to be vaguely genetic. But most campuses have a wide enough variety of options (in terms of time commitment, style, size, and gender of group) that students at all levels of proficiency can give it a try and, perhaps, lose weight and skin tone and begin wearing black all the time . . .

A cappella. These tend to be the most competitive singing groups to get into, perhaps because small size, frequent soloing, and the lack of accompaniment accentuate voices whether good or bad. There are usually all-female, all-male, and coed options; in all, be prepared to commit a good deal of time, on average two nights a week, to practice. The best groups may travel and record CDs. Many do their own arranging, adapting songs to the three or four-part a cappella format, so if you're interested in composition, this can also be a great opportunity.

Choirs. Larger and more formally run (they usually are directed by an adult music professional as opposed to students), these also have a more classical repertoire, although it is possible to find a cappella groups that focus on, say, madrigals or sacred music. There is less opportunity to improvise and goof around on stage, but it's also a larger group of people to meet and work with, and is somewhat more likely to be coed. Some schools have specialized choirs in addition to general ones, like gospel choirs or choirs that provide music for the campus chapel. Many also travel and record.

Plays. Not necessarily a pipeline to Hollywood, but where else are you going to start? College theater communities are stereotyped as incestuous and slightly snotty, which may or may not be the case where you are. Working in either production (set design or direction) or acting is at the very least an intense bonding experience, and there often is overlap in the cast of characters from play to play. Some larger campuses centralize auditions in a single place at a single time early in the fall; watch for signs or you might have to wait a semester.

Radio. Most colleges have a radio station, some with signals strong enough to actually be contenders in the community/state. If you're interested in programming, being on-air, fundraising, selling ad spots, news, or studio engineering, this can be an incredible and rewarding learning experience, and also provides an excellent excuse not to kill yourself on that exam (if your station is 24-hour, you'll probably be stuck with late shifts early on). Calls from lonely gentlemen complimenting you on your voice add to the fun.

Jocking It

Armchair calisthenics just don't cut it for some of us, and they certainly aren't social. Sports are a great way to meet people, feel great, have fun, and in some cases earn your way through school and life. If the latter is a possibility for you, you probably know all you need to know. For the rest of us, consider the following lower-key options . . .

No Tilt-a-Whirl?!
The Extracurricular Fair

Most campuses, very near the beginning of the year, will have a fair where all or most of the student groups send representatives, have sign-up sheets and materials, and generally try to convince you to join. Why not? It's easier to sign up for many things and cut some than track down the right person's e-mail address so you can join the newsgroup later. At the very least take all the information on groups you might *conceivably* be interested in. If you miss out, most campus orgs have Web sites accessible through your main college site.

Intramurals. Intramural sports often require no practice, just once-a-week games with no real commitment required. These can be a great way to blow off steam without distracting from your studies. Intramurals tend to be in traditional team, coed sports like volleyball, softball, soccer, and flag football; some dorms sponsor their own teams, but also check out the athletic center for more information.

Unusual sports. Many sports just aren't played at the high school level many places, so lack of experience is no object to even competing well. Some of our friends took up fencing, water polo, water skiing, crew, ballroom dancing, rugby, even lacrosse and field hockey for the first time in college and did excellently at them, aside from the main object of having fun.

Community Service

College life can be very selfish and disconnected from the real world of families and earning a living—which isn't a bad thing necessarily—but it can feel really good to either leave campus and find this connection, or help to find a substitute for it by counseling other students who are having problems dealing with issues on their own. The time commitment is usually low and it's highly possible to find one-time-only opportunities. Many campuses offer central clearing-houses for volunteer opportunities. Think about the following . . .

Tutoring. Can work well with your schedule, since schools and colleges often have similar vacations; college also offers you a great deal of unscheduled time during the day. Most programs require a weekly commitment at the most and involve as much play and one-on-one attention-giving to kids as actual tutoring. Schools with lots of immigrant children and not enough teachers are particularly needy.

Physical labor. Raking leaves or shoveling snow for the elderly and building homes with Habitat for Humanity are only several of the opportunities to use your brawn on behalf of people in need.

Work with the disabled. Consider doing reading for blind students and community members (either into a tape recorder or in their presence); driving people who can't drive themselves on errands; delivering food for meals on wheels; visiting nursing homes; even, if you live in a pet-friendly apartment, training a dog for the Paws program, which provides guide dogs to the disabled. (The first year of training often involves just toilet-training and socializing.)

Counseling. Many campuses have many groups doing peer-to-peer counseling and education, broken down into areas related to academics, STDs, alcohol and drugs, mental health, and rape awareness and recovery. Some groups do presentations to freshman dorms and put together learning materials; some run crisis lines and will ask you to either be on call or stay at the office a few nights a month.

Religious Groups

Colleges offer religious groups catering to almost any religion or denomination and any level of commitment. Some are informal groups that just meet and walk over to services together every week, no commitment required. If your college has a church or chapel, it is likely to have a choir and a corps of students who usher. Jewish groups often organize weekly or even nightly kosher dinners; many individual denominations offer either study groups, social functions, or community service outings.

Student Government/Activism

Head of the class. Apart from the partisan newspapers discussed on page 199, it's also easy to get involved in politics on the *action* side. Freshmen are usually represented in student government, so there's no time like the present to plan your campaign. It's hard for freshmen (voters or candidates) to really be aware of issues on campus or for candidates to be known personally to many people, so most of the campaigns we saw centered around catchy uses of candidates' names. It never hurts, of course, to look at current and back issues of the student paper (online or in the library) to get a sense of hot topics.

Take to the streets. Most colleges also have a variety of other outlets for activism, from ethnic and gender- and sexuality-issue groups to those concerned with the environment, abortion, or various international issues such as disarmament or labor exploitation.

Debate, model U.N. and Senate. So some of us have really nice voices—why shouldn't we like the sound of them? College debate comes in a variety of forms: parliamentary (very silly, vaguely improvisational topics), Lincoln-Douglas, and classical. Teams often need people to judge even if you're not particularly interested in speaking much; if yours does well, you might get to tag along to the exotic locales the world tournaments tend to be held in. Model governmental bodies (like Clinton's?) also offer a chance to speak in public, meet people from other schools while dressed in your best Men's Warehouse duds, and research important topics.

21
Wild Thing:
Sex

Whether in the form of your roommate's current mount, the Italian Stallion, the Victoria's Secret catalog on the coffee table, or your own rendezvous, sex is part of college life. We've tried, throughout this book, to give you the means of access to the world of love and relationships (see especially chapters on laundry and libraries) and a sense of its delights; there are, however, sound reasons for not giving in to the moment, throwing *all* your clothes into the washer, and doing the deed with a lint tray for a pillow.

If sex takes place primarily in your dreams or the bunk below you, you'll have less need of this information. But even if you don't want to be sleeping with anyone, someone may decide to sleep with you: Almost all of us know or know of someone who's been date raped. It's important, therefore, for everyone to be informed:

Birth Control

So you've decided, having consulted someone besides a Red Dog, to become sexually active. Circumstances may dictate that you use whatever's in the glove compartment, but for your long-term approach to

Abstinent Fun: Alternative Uses for Condoms

Once again, you promised that *this* lambskin was going to do more than sit at home in your billfold, and once again circumstances have made you a liar. How to make it up to little Mr. Trojan? Before you replace him with a younger and fresher sibling, make him feel like his life meant something by putting him to use as one of the following:

Poop sack on walk with pet
Aqua sock
Carrying case for a couple of Jimmy Deans
No-frills holster
Totally sugar-free version of Hubba Bubba
Inconspicuous barf bag
Filled with toothpaste, a safe bust enhancer
Body bag for slain bat

protection against unwanted pregnancy and sexually transmitted diseases, devote a little thought to your choice. Not having the expertise or the desire to present a comprehensive study of contraception past and present, we've simply provided brief explanations of the three most commonly used options. This is intended merely as a guide; before depending upon any one, you'll want to get detailed information from a professional, or a professional book, on proper usage.

Diaphragm

Diaphragms work by thwarting sperm in their desire to reach the cervical canal. The device is a rubber cup that must be fitted by a doctor, can be used for up to two years before replacement (though you must remove it from your body after every use), and must be slathered with a fresh coating of spermicide prior to each use. The success rate against pregnancy hovers around 85–90 percent; diaphragms also help to prevent transmission of chlamydia, gonorrhea, and upper-vaginal herpes. It's safe; the only real side effect is that it increases your vulnerability to urinary tract infections.

Condoms

Cheap, portable, and evocative of Greek and Roman mythology, latex condoms have a success rate of 90–98 percent; combined with a spermicide, it jumps close to 100 percent. While providing a safe means of birth control, they also help guard against transmission of gonorrhea, syphilis, herpes, HIV/AIDS, and trichomoniasis. Use of spermicide with a condom has, however, been shown to *decrease* the condom's effectiveness against HIV. "Natural" (lambskin) condoms are not effective against STDs; viruses can get through their larger pores. If you want to use a lubricant, make sure it is water-based, like KY-jelly; oil-based lubricants degrade condoms and make them break more easily. Ribbed condoms, in general, are sturdier than unribbed or fine, "sensitive" condoms.

Shelf life, if they're actually on the shelf, is something like five years; in the heat of your pocket, however, they may die a steamy death, becoming ineffectual.

The Pill

Available in a wide variety of shapes, colors, and tropical flavors, the (traditional female) pill works by inhibiting ovulation, implantation, and sperm travel plans. In addition to offering a success rate of close to 100 percent, the pill can make you, your roommates, and any female goldfish regular. Unfortunately, however, the pill's other influences on your system are less predictable. Many women experience few or no side effects; some experience weight gain, dizziness, headaches, depression, or acne, among other minor effects; a few fall victim to much more serious problems, including increased blood pressure, changes in sugar tolerance, changes in the blood's clotting ability, and even stroke or heart attack. You'll have to consult a doctor anyway to get the prescription; at that time he or she can analyze your risk factors (diabetes, a smoking habit, vulnerability to migraines, etc.) to determine which of the various formulas, if any, is right for you. Beware, however, that the pill provides no protection against STDs.

Pregnancy

No matter how hard you try—or *because* of how hard Mr. Sperm tries —you may find yourself with a bun in the oven. Here are the early

Voyeurism

Having to crash in someone else's room may be inconvenient, but it's better than being the sole audience to your roommate's peep show. Involuntary voyeurism is no fun for anyone; if you or your roommate is sexually active, develop a system so you know when not to disturb each other. One of us had a little smiley face on our door; if it was turned one way, that meant bed down somewhere else—no room at the inn.

symptoms that will let you know you have something more serious to think about than backless bras:

Missing a period, especially if you're on the pill
Shortening of menstrual period, or unusual lightness
Swelling or tingling in breasts
Bonding with Biffies, a.k.a. frequent pottying
Problems with digestion—nausea, vomiting, heartburn,
    constipation
Feeling of constant PMS—mood swings, bloating, cramping

If you experience some or all of these, it may be time for a test. We recommend going to a clinic; while drugstore pregnancy tests offer you privacy, they aren't as accurate as those administered by a doctor.

Even professionally performed tests are prone to error, however. While false positives are rare, false negatives are fairly common. To a certain extent it's out of your control, but there are a few things you can do to help the test turn out correctly:

The day before you take the sample, avoid aspirin and just say no to any joints passed your way—marijuana can mess up the results (stop all drinking and other sketchy imbibing if you even *might* be pregnant). The hormones in birth control pills can influence the results, too, but be careful about skipping those, or you could find yourself back where you started.

Take the urine sample right when you wake up, when your urine is the most concentrated.

Use a clean, dry container. Soap or chemical residue in old shampoo or cosmetic bottles can cause a false positive.

High School Sweethearts

You'd known each other since sixth-grade shop, but it wasn't until you ran into each other at a monster trucks convention that you realized your true feelings. Prom night a few weeks later was a blur of tires and corn-stalks; you spent July listening to the Nitty Gritty Dirt Band and "fishin' in the dark," the water sport the band so eloquently supports. One day at the end of August, you slipped a ring woven of corn silk over her finger and, over the din of the engine, pledged you'd marry.

Get the Kleenex ready cause it ain't gonna last.

Harsh, we know, but true. We literally know of only two high school relationships that lasted past freshman year, and we don't know of any that didn't interfere, to some extent, with adjustment to and enjoyment of college life. A lover is a nice security blanket in the first weeks, but while you're on the phone crying about how much you miss each other, the singles are out there meeting people and starting their new lives. Seriously, get out there too—if you and your betrothed are really right for each other, you'll get back together down the road and your relationship will be the stronger for time away. Don't close yourself to college's amazing new experiences by pining for and living in the past.

Once you've done the deed, refrigerate your sample or you could get a false negative.

Doctors can tell you what's going on in your body, but they can't tell you what to do about it, and neither can we. If your beliefs make abortion an option, there are many sources of information you'll want to look into. Web sites like www.plannedparenthood.org can give you information on pregnancy and abortion; local clinics, Planned Parenthood offices, and your campus infirmary can do the same. Also check the yellow pages sections on "abortion," "birth control," or "family planning."

Sexually Transmitted Diseases

A litter of rug rats isn't the only thing that can come from a little whoopee under the bleachers. Pregnancy is obviously a serious issue, but some STDs can have an even more devastating impact on your future and health. Untreated, some can lead to genital cancer or worse; even when properly attended to, many can make you fear a toilet like it's a medieval instrument of torture. If you experience such plumbing phobia or any of the symptoms listed below, seek diagnosis and treatment immediately. These diseases don't go away by themselves.

AIDS

Prevention. If a condom doesn't slip, tear, or leak, it entirely prevents transmission of HIV. Ribbed condoms are stronger than smooth ones; natural lambskin condoms do *not* guard against HIV the way they do against pregnancy. Spermicide has a tendency to break condoms down, so if STD prevention is more of a concern than avoidance of pregnancy, beware of that technique.

Causes. HIV is present in semen, vaginal fluid, blood, and breast milk and is transmitted through needle sharing, oral sex, anal sex, or vaginal sex, or manual sex play if there are cuts on the hand. HIV is only transmissible through kissing if there are cuts on the mouth and kissing is very vigorous (it has happened this way like once).

Symptoms. Of HIV itself, there are no apparent symptoms (although the number of T lymphocyte white blood cells may be down). The actual conversion to HIV+ status occurs up to 6 months after initial infection, and can be signaled by flu-like symptoms—sore throat, rash, glandular pain—but is often silent (and flu-like symptoms alone should certainly not make you fear you have HIV). Positive status is detected by blood tests.

Complications. Infections (cough, diarrhea, abdominal pain, mouth or rectal soreness); pneumonia; colitis (inflammation of the colon); esophagitis (inflammation of the esophagus); herpes; hepatitis B; tuberculosis; Kaposi's sarcoma; lymphoma; anal and oral carcinoma

Treatment. Sophisticated, complicated-to-keep-track-of drug "cocktails" are prescribed at various stages of the disease and are effective for a time in many people; the individual illnesses caused by AIDS are also treatable on their own.

Chlamydia

Causes. Vaginal, anal, or oral sex

Symptoms. Urethral infections, painful discharge, vaginal discharge, rectal discharge

Complications. Pelvic inflammatory disease, reproductive system damage, damage to urethra, transmission to unborn children, who can then develop pneumonia

Treatment. If diagnosed early, easily treatable with antibiotics

Crabs/lice

Causes. Close contact with someone who has them, including contact with pets, bedding, upholstery, clothing, towels

Symptoms. Sometimes none; if any, itching; little dots of blood or scratches

Complications. Skin irritation or infection; can carry typhus

Treatment. Special debugging shampoo like Nix, Rid, or A-200 under doctor's supervision; decontamination of clothing and other things that could have become infested

Gonorrhea

Causes. Vaginal, anal, or oral sex with infected partner

Symptoms. Males: burning urination and penile discharge; Females: vaginal discharge, burning urination

Complications. Pelvic inflammatory disease, cervical and anorectal infection, infection of the blood, infertility, arthritis

Treatment. Curable with antibiotics

Hepatitis B

Prevention. Three-shot series of vaccines; booster after ten years; vaccination will cause you to test positive if you are tested for Hepatitis B

Causes. Any contact between bodily openings; shared needles

Symptoms. Fatigue, nausea, jaundice, rashes, urine darkening, arthritis

Complications. Liver cancer and cirrhosis, death

Treatment. Vaccination, teetotaling, rest

Herpes

Causes. Genital, anal, or oral contact with a herpes sore (whether in the mouth or genitals); transmissible even in outbreak-free periods if you don't use protection

Symptoms. Sometimes none at all; recurrent lesions with discharge, fever, headaches; painful urination; acts up during times of stress particularly

Complications. Herpes keratitis (eye infection), cervical cancer, necessity of Caesarean section if the disease is active during delivery

Treatment. No cure, but antiviral drugs can help control outbreaks

Syphilis

Causes. Sexual relations (including kissing) through open syphilis sores or rash

Symptoms:

Stage I. 21–90 days after contact, painless sore(s) at point of initial contact; these are very infectious

Stage II. Three weeks later, fever, nausea, headaches

Stage III. Latency

Stage IV. Brain damage, blindness, death, fetal injury

Treatment. Treatable with antibiotics if caught early

Venereal warts (HPV)

Causes. Oral, anal, or vaginal sex with someone carrying the virus

Complications. Urinary tract infections, genital cancers

Treatment. Hard to get rid of the virus entirely, though surgery, freezing, and burning can get rid of individual warts; women with the virus should be sure to have regular pap smears

Yeast Infection

Possible contributing factors. Pregnancy; illness; stress; the pill; douching; tight clothing; vaginal deodorant

Symptoms. White, lumpy discharge; itching

Treatment. Medicated creams or suppositories (see your doctor if this is your first one)

Rape

While lawyers may wrangle over the definition of the crime, there's usually less ambiguity for the victim; if you feel that you've been raped, you probably have been—if not for purposes of prosecution, at least for those of your mental state. Your condition is serious, both from a physiological and a psychological standpoint, and it may take a long time for you to recover. But here's how you can get started:

Do not douche; do not shower; do not wash your clothes or throw them away. Even if you think there's no way you'd ever prosecute, it doesn't hurt to preserve the evidence in case you change your mind.

By the same token, it's in your interest to report the rape. Again, if you decide later not to prosecute, that's your prerogative; there's no way the state can press charges if you refuse to testify or don't give permission to use the evidence of rape on your person.

Go to the hospital immediately. Not only can doctors examine you for evidence if you want them to, but they'll treat any injuries, give you a pelvic exam, and treat you for the prevention of STDs and pregnancy. They can also set you up with the counseling and support networks you need.

The law's the law, but let's face it . . . most college students drink, at least occasionally, before their twenty-first birthday. Is it great? Under control? Unhealthy? Scary? At times, probably, all of the above.

Free Beer

There are other ways of getting liquor, of course, than buying it yourself at a store or bar. Parties held by either older students or underagers who've wangled a keg delivery are often awash in alcohol, their hosts charging a flat fee for all you can drink. But while it's true that the more you drink, the lower the fee per beer becomes, $3 is still too much for a night of revelry when you can get it all—plus the thrill of criminality—without coughing up a red cent. To make the beer that is out there yours until you choose to throw it up, experiment with the following techniques at parties and elsewhere:

BYOC. If the hosts only dispense beer to guests who have a certain kind of cup (the color/style being sold), you're just going to have to go home and get your own. Keep a rainbow assortment of cups in your room; send one person ahead to the party to find out the hue of choice. If you can't be bothered with such ruses, make like a coon and scrounge in the corners/wastebaskets/bathrooms for discarded plasticware.

Stamp act. That Powder Puff Girls stamp your mother gave you for graduation is going to come in handy after all! If the partymasters recognize those who've paid by a stamp on the hand, come equipped with your own. If the official stamp is significantly different from yours, do a little morphing of your own—a strategic smudge turns Buttercup into Power Ranger extraordinaire.

Coup d'keg. That bozo in the old fart baseball cap has manned the spigot long enough. It's time to end the patriarchy, replacing kegmaster with kegmistress—you! Once your ceaseless conversation about water ("And then there's the time I was drinking a bottle of Poland Springs . . .") has sent him and his bathroom dance where they belong, you can help yourself and friends, turning your attention to the queue only when the natives get restless.

Sweet nothings. If Mr. Kegmaster's bladder proves resistant, there are still ways of getting what you want. Giving his bicep a rest by pumping the keg, licking the stain on his undershirt, and asking him how much he gets paid for such a professional job will all endear you to him, the fruits of the intimacy being a taller glass for you and a broken heart for him.

Drinking Games

Parties are primo, of course, but if you'd prefer to enjoy booze in a more cultured situation and with the convenience of your own bathroom nearby, drinking games may be the way to go. Like any sport, alcohol consumption has its traditions, and as jodhpurs, toddies, and an Uzi are to the English fox hunt, so are the classic games to a good ol' American drinkfest. In the same way, however, novelty is the lifeblood of any form of athletics, so we list a few ideas of our own with the age-old favorites:

Beer Die. One long table and a couple of Dixie cups make for a small-scale basketball court; throw your die and watch those games of HORSE pay off in sobriety as teammates become progressively less coordinated.

Asshole. Especially good for tyrant wannabes, Asshole involves the assigning of positions (president, treasurer, paper shredder, etc.) based on the quality of the cards in your original draw. Once play begins, your card has to be higher than that of the person with the next highest ranking; that person may also make up any rules he/she chooses for you and the underlings below you.

Beerball. Combining two great forms of athletics, beerball requires you to either drink while or after you bat, in any case keeping a stein in your hand at all times. Real test of hand-mouth coordination.

Magic Word. Magic Word requires you to drink every time your word is said in a movie. Guard your interests when the words are chosen; don't accept "f—" if the movie is *Basic Instinct* unless you're prepared to spend the night as horizontal as the characters.

Side Effects

"*Après toi, le déluge,*" you mutter confidentially to the vintage cider cradled in your hand. You down it slowly, lovingly, and then pass out.

Bonne nuit, mon cher ami. This is one sunrise you're going to miss. Sure, a few drinks can put a smile on your yawp, but when the glow wears off, Mr. Smiley can turn into Mr. Yuck in a hurry. Life ain't all peaches and cream; here's how to deal with the vinegar that grouchy cook threw into the recipe:

Hangovers. They're a little bit like fruitcakes—the best thing to do

Drugs

On some of our campuses, Mary Jane is as common a sight as Mary Janes. And while drinking can be a quiet accompaniment to a round of bridge, it's harder to control marijuana's efforts at publicizing its presence; the smell is distinctive, sometimes attracting the attention of smoke detectors as well as neighborhood pests hungry for a fix.

Our own feelings aside, there's no question that dependence on dope or even heavier drugs can be expensive to your GPA as well as your wallet; one guy we know spends his mornings communing with squirrels by the river instead of at lectures, and a guy at another of our schools went wacko from drugs, withdrew from school, and gained about seventy-five pounds during a stay at a nearby sanitarium. Even if you're under control, the drugs may not be; impurities and lacings (with speed, etc.) abound.

is just leave them be. Aspirin or other over-the-counter remedies for head and stomach pain work okay; the main thing not to do is drown your aches in more apéritifs. To avoid getting one the next time, down glasses of water before, during, and after drinking alcohol, and take an Advil right before you go to bed.

Beer belly. For more visible symptoms of alcohol consumption—i.e., that mound preventing you from admiring your new high heels—you're going to have to take a little more active role. The solution really isn't to skip meals so you can get a better buzz and drink freely; alcohol has no nutrition. Instead, get biking, or do some other low-impact sport if you've got a hangover.

Superbuzz. If you're on any prescription medication, including antidepressants, don't drink without asking your doctor if it's okay. Combining drugs—in effect what you're doing—is loony at best, fatal at worst.

I think I'm gonna hurl. You assumed that wisdom and rhymes went hand in hand, so you accepted "beer before liquor, never been sicker; liquor before beer, you're in the clear" on faith. The reality was and is that mixing drinks is always a bit risky; for this reason, or for others, you may get real sick.

If it happens to you, you'll be concentrating on barfing and not much else, but if your friend starts vomiting, it's time to play parent. The most important thing to do is make sure your friend stays conscious and more or less upright; passing out or awkward posture could lead to choking. As you wait with the person, have someone get him or her a glass of water and, if the sick one has long hair, something to hold it back.

If the sickness seems severe, if the person's skin looks blue, or if you can't keep him or her conscious, get an ambulance and professional help. We've never heard of a student being disciplined for involvement in a case of alcohol poisoning.

Alcoholism. The incidents above are serious—for your modeling career if not always your health—but a night of nausea isn't anything compared with the damages inflicted by full-fledged addiction. It's sometimes hard to distinguish the latter from mere overindulgence, but the real thing, we think, is more common on college campuses than is recognized.

Binging all the time isn't great, but if your grades don't plummet and you have dates with entities that aren't bottled, you're probably okay for now. But if you or someone you know seems out of control, drinking every night, even before exams, and often drinking alone, please do what you can to get help. Maybe the person is just sowing a little wild corn, happy to be independent, but people do fail out, get raped, or even die on college campuses every year following bouts of overdrinking—and even if people make it through without those kind of scars, they may be forming some damn bad habits.

23
Food (?)

You kissed your parents goodbye when you left home, but maybe you should have saved your tears for your farewell to their refrigerator. Because even if you land a Singaporean roommate bearing a wok, rice cooker, hot plate, bread machine, salad shooter, and deep fryer—as a friend of ours did—chances are you're not going to be eating as well as you did at home (curried eggplant, anyone?).

Cafeteria food is monotonous and generally high in fat and sodium; if you're cooking for yourself or ordering out, the most convenient items may be even more so. And if the looming freshman fifteen (see p. 226 and your bathroom scale) isn't reason enough to watch your diet, concern for your brain should be: Sensible eating will make you more alert, energetic, and able to concentrate. Some of us found out the hard way that the only ones who benefit from overindulgence in junk foods are belt manufacturers; you pay hard-earned dough for burgeoning waistlines, and old Bessie pays with her hide.

The Plan

You've seen the pyramids, the drawings of overly friendly broccoli stalks ("Psst—wanna buy a B?"), the haunting photographs of waving corn. You know your nutritional needs—the question is how to meet them.

Sometime during the summer before college, you'll probably be asked to choose a meal plan. Your options will usually include two elements: the number of cafeteria meals you'll be entitled to, and the number of "flex points" you will be able to use at sundry campus eateries—coffee shops, grills, etc.

We recommend signing up for a plan that guarantees you at least fourteen dining hall meals per week. The cafeteria can be a great place to meet random people, bond by complaining about the B-grade asparagus, emerge two hours later blood brethren, etc. And besides, when you first get to college you'll probably be too busy to worry about cooking.

If a semester-long independent study of the potato's various forms emboldens you to strike out on your own, as it seems designed to do (it's all part of education), you can always switch to a less complete plan come January. Even if you're living in a dorm, you'll probably have access to a kitchen and pots. The best option is one that allows you semiregular access to the dining hall, a.k.a. Stop & Steal. Here's how to make the most of whatever meal plan you choose . . .

When Captain Crunch Chicken Just Won't Do It: How to Create Your Own Meal from Cafeteria Provisions

The super salad. A bowl of lettuce may not be a meal, but such vegetables as broccoli and tomatoes are filling as well as nutritious. Raisins or sliced oranges, apples, and bananas can sweeten an otherwise bland concoction; beans, wheat germ, or cheese slices provide protein. Add a splash of lemon juice or olive oil and vinegar instead of creamy salad dressings for a healthy meal.

Sick of eating rubber? We've all seen it happen . . . with every passing meal, it becomes more and more clear that the "chef" missed his calling as a Superball manufacturer, until one day your Brussels sprout takes a wrong bounce, ricochets off a few students' heads, and before you can say "Smokey Robinson" all the cafeteria windows are dust. Make your dining room safe for mankind—steam/boil your own vegetables from the salad bar by putting them in a bowl with water, covering with another bowl, and microwaving.

Vitamins and Minerals

Some of us misplaced our trusty Flintstones among the pizza boxes of first semester, and paid the price: the minor colds that vitamins can help to prevent. Breakfast is the best time to take your pills, but lunch and dinner are also fine—the main thing is to get in the habit. One daily covers most of your body's needs.

Fred and Wilma don't only contribute to general health, of course; those little tricksters work in particular ways, some of which are especially important for females. So in addition to taking multivitamins, women should make sure they're getting enough . . .

Calcium. You may not be growing anymore, but your bones should be. Late adolescence is a key time for laying down bone mass, and downing a glass of milk now decreases the risk of sports injuries and osteoporosis later. Tums or other calcium supplements are not enough; the body does not absorb these as well as natural calcium. Eating dairy products regularly is especially important if you consume large amounts of diet sodas and caffeine, since these act as "antidotes" to calcium.

Iron. Menstruation doesn't just deprive you of your dime supply and sanity; it also depletes your store of iron. If you eat red meat regularly, this should be no problem. But if you don't, go for these high-iron foods: potatoes, spinach, peas, peaches, apricots, pears, raisins, and dates. Many cereals and breads are also fortified; check boxes or packaging for complete information. Iron supplements are also available and may actually help with cramps as well.

Build your own sandwich. If the clucker of the day doesn't suit you, adapt it: a filet of chicken, sliced and mixed with mayonnaise, makes the start of a chicken salad sandwich. Egg salad, too, can be made from salad bar items. Combine cold cuts, toasted bread, and you're on your way to a warm three-decker club. Vegetarians, opt for pita melts: Stuff bread and zap.

Fresh from the grill. Microwave ovens can't brown grilled cheese sandwiches, so toast the bread first. Butter, pile with cheese, tomato, and ham slices, wrap in napkins and heat.

The best of the West. (Try this at home.) Cafeteria steak is often well on its way to desiccation when it hits your plate; it takes little encouragement to jump the fence into true beef jerkydom. The tough stuff is usually made from raw meat, but unless you're a connoisseur, your *filet mignon* will do just as well. Bring your Swiss Army knife to brunch and slice meat into long, narrow strips. Quietly pound a little salt, pepper, and garlic powder (use the end of a saltshaker or napkin dispenser) into the meat. Let strips hang out (literally) in the Toast-R-Oven or microwave until black and brittle (about four hours in a 120° oven), and enjoy.

Mama mia! Turn dry bread into delicious garlic bread. Just add margarine, shredded or sliced cheese, and garlic powder to slices and microwave.

Pita pizza. For yet another corruption of the Italian culinary tradition, pile pocket bread with tomato sauce (often available at pasta bar), shredded cheese (salad or sandwich bar), peppers, mushrooms, onion slices, chocolate-covered tofu — go nuts. Microwave.

Low-fat baked potato. Instead of piling on the sour cream, chili, and cheddar, try a simple topping of cottage cheese and chives.

Virgin fondue. Unless your clothing accommodates a flask of Beaujolais, you're not going to be able to make cheese fondue — using cafeteria facilities — *comme les Français*. But you can still make a nice dip for broccoli or bread by microwaving cheese with a little water.

Like Quaker without Wilford Brimley. Microwaved Grape-Nuts make a crunchy alternative to soup. Another nontraditional grain dish consists of plain yogurt, sugar or honey, cereal, and raisins or sliced fruit.

The soda fountain without the jerk. Let's face it, cafeteria ice cream isn't Ben & Jerry's (unless you go to Middlebury) — it sometimes needs embellishment. Root beer and vanilla make a float; Coke gives you the makings of a soda. And if you're lucky, brownies may be available; add peanut butter for a Reese's-style sundae.

Homemade Hershey's. If your only source of chocolate is the hot cocoa machine, don't be discouraged; simply remove the top of the machine, help yourself to cocoa powder, mix it with a little milk, and you have syrup worthy of Willy Wonka. Use it on ice cream or as dip for bananas, oranges, and raisins.

Getting Your Money's Worth

Some cafeterias are generous and/or self-service, but what do you do when the lady in the hairnet shortchanges you on peas? The only response to such consistent stinginess is to take matters into your own hands. Here's how to make sure that you never have to go back for seconds:

I want to shake your hand. Make like Hansel and offer a stick instead of your hand when you and Mrs. Bifocals cement your friendship. Watch her murmur "Uff da, another anorexic," and slyly slip a choice piece of lard into your heaping portion of sticky rice.

Blitzed out. Borrow a roommate's football uniform and pads to wear to dinner. Douse yourself with some oil and emit a couple of growls when you reach the head of the line.

"Just checking out the campus..." Wear a fake mustache to lunch if you're known around the cafeteria, then introduce yourself as a pre-frosh.

Reverse psychology. Ask for "jus' a smidgin" of roast beast. Some servers get the only power trip of their lives from doing exactly the opposite of what students ask.

The games we play. Engage employee in game of Twister. When she sets down spatula to better reach the ice dispenser, that tray of ziti's yours.

Granny Smith rises from the dead. It's February, and the only place apples are fresh is New Zealand. But you can rejuvenate your cafeteria's aged provisions with the following tricks:

Baked apples. Slice apples, add cinnamon, sugar, and margarine (optional), and microwave.

Lunch-in-an-apple. Hollow out an apple and fill with raisins, sunflower seeds, or chicken salad for a portable, no-trash lunch.

Fruit salad. Combine apple and orange chunks, banana slices, and whatever other canned or fresh fruits are available. Cover with a mixture of yogurt, milk (for thinning), and honey for a light, tangy dessert.

Dessert pizza. Along these same lines, try piling butter, cinnamon, and sugar on an open-faced loaf of pita bread and microwave.

The Art and Craft of the Swipe

"Sure," you say, kneeling, "your suggestions are genius. But, Swami, you know how it is—the old lady wants to eat in now and then. How'm I gonna make out?"

Depending on your meaning, pardner, you may be on your own. But if by "make out" you mean "grub," then the answer's simple. You're paying for the chuck; it should be up to you where and when you eat it. The food's yours for the taking if you know the right . . .

Method. The blatant approach sometimes works; one of our roommates fills two-liter bottles from the drink machine, and has no qualms about loading brownies straight from the serving plate into her waiting Tupperware. Once interrupted in her pilfering by an overly possessive cook, she muttered something bitterly in Japanese (she is Hispanic) and resumed her activity. If your foreign language proficiency is low (or if your stomach for confrontation is weaker than your stomach for confections), you may want to consider more subtle tactics. Pack up at your table rather than in the cafeteria line, or forgo Tupperware for baggy, shoplifter-style clothing.

Materials. In addition to filling your snacking needs, the cafeteria can also provide you with needed ingredients for recipes. Why buy and carry a heavy bag of sugar from the grocery, for example, when a simple twist of the cap and a flick of your wrist can score you enough of the sweet stuff for a batch of congo bars? Salt, oil, honey, margarine, milk, raisins, spices of all kinds, and fruit (hello, banana bread) are also readily available in most dining halls.

Home Cookin'

Cooking at least some of your own meals is often the best and cheapest option—even if your morals dictate actually buying most or all of the ingredients. It can also be easy and fun, as the title of the book that should be your new bible—*The Joy of Cooking*—indicates. As you grow intimate with this and other friendly sources, you will develop your own favorite methods and recipes. But here are some foolproof (believe us . . .) ideas to start you off:

Vegetables. Your two simplest options are boiling and steaming. To boil, add raw vegetables to enough boiling water to cover them (excess water leaches vitamins) and cook for 8–10 minutes. To steam, fill the bottom of a pot or vegetable steamer with room temperature water, place vegetables in the top, and cover. Activate the burner; turn off after 12–15 minutes, depending on the size of the vegetables.

Pasta. Add to boiling water (4 quarts per pound of pasta) and cook for 3–10 minutes, depending upon the size of the pasta (the package will have directions). Stir periodically; when firm to the bite, drain immediately and serve.

Baked potatoes. Wash, pare blemishes, and make a few tiny but deep slits in the potato's skin (these release steam during cooking, ensuring that the potato won't explode). Cook at 350° for about 90 minutes or zap.

Baked chicken breasts. Either leave skin on or remove it and coat the fowl in a simple sauce to seal in moisture. Cook at 325° for about one and one-quarter hours.

Waste Not, Want Not

Some of our freshman dormmates liked grocery stores. They went, dressed in a variety of costumes—tuxedos, togas—about once a week at two A.M., buying large supplies of whatever was on sale. Once it was bleach; another time it was cake mix (they would eat a 950-calorie box dry, for a snack); other times it was exotic tropical fruits, which they taped to one of our doors in a gesture of courtship toward a roommate. Another time—well, we won't go into the bacterial details. The lesson's clear: Food wasn't meant for teeth alone. Here, a guide to its alternate uses:

"I would rather sit on a pumpkin and have it all to myself than be crowded on a velvet cushion." Make good on Thoreau's assertion and avoid filling the coffers of Barcalounger, Inc. For a cozier fit for your derriere, cut vegetable in half, clean off pulp, and you'll be snug as a bug in a rug.

The celery blues. Salad sent you under the table trying to get the strings out of your teeth? Mourn no longer the insufficient supply of toothpicks; simply borrow a stick of raw linguine and kiss unsightly food remnants *arrivederci.*

Sugar & spice & everything nice. And you thought cinnamon was just for drawing designs in on the table. Register your vote against animal cruelty by rejecting Cover Girl for Durkee: Cinnamon makes ideal eye shadow or foundation (lighten by combination with powdered sugar if you're Caucasian).

I simply remember my favorite things . . . Clogged toilets, much like Julie Andrews in *The Sound of Music,* cheer up quickly when their eyes fall upon melons; scrape away fruit from skin and flexible hull becomes powerful suction plunger.

The quicker picker-upper. Better than Bounty, a fresh English muffin makes an ideal sponge when the corn oil's heading for your CD player.

The great American pastime. In the absence of Wiffle Balls, turn to rice cakes for a lightweight, safe flying object for in-dorm baseball. For added fun/nourishment, spread with jam/glue/honey/butter.

Wonderbra. Why contribute to the tabletop pornography ring of Victoria's Secret when you can get the same amazing effects with a slightly more perishable padding—Wonder *Bread?* Simply add slices to achieve desired volume; remove when they become toasted.

Guarding against Bacteria

Food is your friend, but, as encounters with the incognito meat in the cafeteria line have no doubt taught you, it can have its ugly side. To prevent introduction and ingestion of unhealthy bacteria, take the following precautions in storing and preparing food:

Always wash your hands thoroughly before and after handling raw meat. Immediately wash with soap, also, any surface that meat touches. Bacteria from uncooked meat can contaminate other food.

Take a closer look at that can of beans before you pop off the lid and take a swig. If any container or carton looks six months' pregnant, smells odd, or froths unnaturally when you shake it, the contents may be contaminated with botulism. Get rid of it before it gets rid of you. Signs of other, less deadly contaminations include brown or soft spots, visible mold, cracks in eggs, sliminess on meat, foul stenches, etc.

Beware of dishes—some mousses and puddings, caesar salad, steak tartare—whose recipes do not call for the cooking of eggs and meats. Salmonella and E. coli bacteria are potentially deadly.

Always thoroughly wash containers that have held milk and especially oil or butter. These products can easily go rancid when trapped in cracks and corners of improperly cleaned dishes.

Peanut butter travels okay, but sandwich fillings like egg or chicken salad are meant for the fridge, not the open road. Don't pack them in bag lunches unless you know you're going to be eating them quickly (within a few hours).

Fighting the Freshman Fifteen

Call it pregnancy, call it a stowed basketball, call it whatever you like—it's a beer belly. But while food is rarely the main cause of freshman weight gain, that steak à la mode isn't going to burn anything except your heart. To keep the abortion protesters from accosting you when you go in for a throat culture, keep your eating, if not your drinking, sensible:

Eat breakfast. Studies—formal as well as our own—have shown that eating more food earlier in the day not only gets your brain in action, but curbs your appetite later on.

Don't skip meals. Abstention only results in gorging later on and can slow your metabolism, sometimes permanently.

There will be a vending machine somewhere that, like a lovelorn ex, just keeps calling your name. But when you feel that late-night urge to crunch, skip the Snickers and go for low-fat pretzels, popcorn, Junior Mints, or Rolos. If it's an all-night convenience store sending you come-hither glances, your best bets are Snackwell's, Fruit Newtons, ginger snaps, or Nilla wafers. Remember, however, that "nonfat" isn't synonymous with "all you can eat," and calories can catch up with you.

If your dining hall staff does not display nutritional information for dishes served, they may have it available upon request. Otherwise, keep in mind the following rules of thumb for evaluating the healthfulness of offerings:

Cereals. Generally high in sugar, low in fat, and fortified with minerals and vitamins. Granola is an exception; it can have more fat than a hunk of pie.

Muffins and quick breads. May seem healthier than those donut holes lounging nearby, but don't be deceived; they're probably equally high in fat.

Rolls/breads. Generally better than cereals. The wheatier, the better. Desert delight, a.k.a. pita bread, is often lowest in sugar and fat.

Meats and fish. Broiled or baked is better than breaded.

Sweet nothings. Sugar and fat often go together, but they don't have to; honey, Jell-O, jams, and syrups, are almost always fat-free.

It isn't Philly. Dining-hall pastas and meat dishes are often loaded with cheese, and while it can function as a good source of protein, the type of cheese your cafeteria uses is probably higher in oil than nutrition. The cream cheese available, for example, is usually higher in fat (which guarantees a longer shelf life) than many grocery store brands. Spring for mozzarella and parmesan sprinkles; leave the rest for mice.

Protein without the pork. Meat, peanut butter, eggs, cheese, and nuts of all kinds are excellent sources of protein; they're also excellent sources of fat. For "lighter" muscle-building material, opt for beans (often available at the salad bar), cottage cheese, and cold cuts.

24
Turkey in a Toast-R-Oven & Other Trappings of Celebration:
Holidays

Take a long drag on that candy cigarette, relax, and lend us your imaginations. Think about a world in which dentist neighbors could always be counted on to dispense mint floss at the sound of "trick or treat"; in which whoopee cushions, instead of sissy embroidered ones, were standard fare in proctologists' waiting areas; in which proper reverence was shown for corn in all its manifold forms, not just the plumped-up, surgically altered, Britney Spears-like guise in which microwave popcorn manufacturers prefer to present it.

Unfortunately, if you want to retain this vision for any length of time, you're going to have to scrounge your carryalls for something a little stronger than that candy cig. Alas, the world is a cruel place for dreamers without connections to South American drug cartels. But, brothers and sisters, it's up to you to keep suckin' sugar and keep the dream kickin' by doing all the celebrating you can do in this cold world. Otherwise you're gonna wake up one morning in November and the only turkey you'll see will be when you look in the mirror. Here, a few ideas for how to let the celebrations begin.

Halloween

When you professed your acting ambitions, did people always say you'd be a natural for *The Addams Family*? Has your life been a story of humiliations, laboring under the curse of poor fashion sense ("But, honey, this isn't a *costume* party!")? Well, it's time to show that I'm-too-good-for-green-mascara crowd a thing or two—Halloween is *your* day! But before you unleash your God-given taste for hideous clothing, spend a little time in preparation . . .

How to Cook Pumpkin Seeds

After you've cleansed the seeds of slime, you've got a couple of options. Access to a kitchen is necessary for the first; the second can be done either in a regular stove or in a Toast-R-Oven. It takes a certain amount of fat to make them crispy; if you're not a greasehound, blot them dry before eating or storing.

Fryin'. Put the seeds in a skillet with enough margarine to cover them. Cook over medium heat, stirring to make sure that seeds get turned over regularly. Add salt to taste while they're cooking and, if they turn out too bland, immediately after they've browned.

Bakin'. This is still a form of frying, but it uses less oil. Preheat oven to 350° and arrange the seeds on a cookie sheet (or piece of tinfoil) in a single layer. Sprinkle with melted margarine and salt; if the seeds don't seem to be browning, add more margarine as needed. Check the seeds every minute or so; when the undersides have acquired a nice Hawaiian Tropic glow, turn them over to give the tops a chance to brown too.

Papier-mâché

Whatever effect you're trying to achieve, papier-mâché can help.

If you don't subscribe to the newspaper, raid the recycling bin. Soak strips of newspaper in wallpaper paste (one part paste to ten parts water) or glue (one part glue to one part water). Apply to an inflated balloon, bucket, wastebasket, or other object approximating the size and shape of the mask you want to make; allow to dry and repeat the process several times, until the form is the thickness you want.

Thanksgiving

Most college students celebrate Thanksgiving by going home. But if the Pilgrim spirit hits while you're still at school, or if you will be spending Turkey Day in the dorm, here are some ways to say *muchas gracias* with pizzazz!

Turkey in a Toast-R-Oven

Before you remove the wrapper, check the weight written on it.

Preheat your oven (see temperature guidelines below).

Unwrap bird. Swallow your modesty and take a peek in front and back cavities; remove any shrink-wrapped items such as neck, giblets, concealed weapons.

Stuff it with something (keeps bird from drying out, cooks whatever's inside flavorfully).

If the whole bird fits into your little range, use the table below for figuring cooking time:

weight of bird	cooking temperature	cooking time
12–16 lbs.	325°	3 hrs.
16–20 lbs.	325°	3¼–3½ hrs.
24–28 lbs.	300°	5½–6 hrs.
28–32 lbs.	300°	6½–7½ hrs.
32–50 lbs.	send your "bird" in for an autopsy, unless you're cool w/cannibalism	

Tent the bird in tinfoil to keep from getting dry. Administer Gatorade as necessary.

For the last 20–30 minutes of cooking, "unzip" the tent to brown the skin. Baste the turkey with oil/shortening about every five minutes during this period.

Garnish with "cranberries" (diced Jell-O), "potatoes" (just add water), and "pumpkin pie" (the now-collapsed jack-o'-lantern requires no cooking).

Make Yo'sef a Corncob Pipe

How to look and talk like Huckleberry Finn. We're not advocates of smoking, but we are advocates of corn — and if you smoke already, what better way to celebrate de season while diverting profits away from Marlboro and toward Farmer Bob?

You'll want a dry ear — preferably one that has never been cooked, but if you've taken our advice about cafeteria filching to heart, an unbuttered one saved from dinner will do. To dehydrate it, put it in an oven/Toast-R-Oven at 120° to 140° for 8–12 hours (monitor to forestall incineration) or, if de heat's on in yo' dorm, on top of de radiator for a few days.

Cut a 2-inch-long cross section of de cob. Hollow it out, but make sure to leave de walls and bottom about one half inch thick.

Drill/excavate a small hole a little ways above de bottom of de cob. Insert a small piece of bamboo (if none is readily available, a drinking straw or a pen with de ink tube removed) so that it fits snug, and fill in de cracks with glue, preferably epoxy.

Depending on yo' level of pretension, varnish and/or sandpaper yo' cob. As fer us, we'll leave sech prettifying to de morticians!

Christmas/Hanukkah

At one of our schools, where Christmas spirit is synonymous with sex drive, the week before vacation culminates in Incest Fest, a no-repercussions dance at which strangers convey holiday cheer to each other through exchanges of saliva rather than words.

If your tastes run to the pornographic, you can approximate the experience of this event by investing heavily in mistletoe, flicking on some old episodes of *Pee Wee's Playhouse,* and settling down with a good book about mono. If, on the other hand, you prefer to save smooching for your reunion with your schnauzer, try these more traditional modes of celebration:

Gingerbread/Biology Review

Study . . . or cook? Cook . . . or study? To resolve your existential dilemma before it drives you to the edge, do both at the same time! Here's what you'll need:

½ cup butter or margarine
½ cup molasses
½ teaspoon salt
½ teaspoon baking soda

½ cup sugar
2½ cups flour
2 teaspoons ginger
¼ cup hot water

Melt the butter in a hot pot, coffeemaker, or microwave oven (last choice). Stir in sugar, then molasses. Dissolve baking soda in hot water. Mix remaining dry ingredients and alternate adding them and the soda water to butter mixture. Chill in fridge/windowsill/roommate's bed for 2–3 hours.

Preheat oven to 350°. Roll out dough to about ⅛ inch. As a means of creative exam preparation, hold a competition for the most anatomically correct, opposite sex cardboard cut-out, using the winning figure to form cookies. While the men, women, or androgynes—depending upon your recollection of biology—bake for 10–12 minutes, whip up 2 egg whites and 3 cups confectioner's sugar for a creamy finish.

Latkes on the Cheap

You really don't need much other than common stationery supplies and dorm furniture to make the rough-hewn latke of old. Find, grow, or buy

1 large onion
4 large eggs
¼ tsp. pepper
⅓ cup matzo meal
2½ lbs. potatoes
oil for the electric pan

Beat the eggs with a fork or used-up pen. Pound matzos to make meal with a paperweight or fist. Grate the onions on the side of your desk or other area where the wood has gotten very rough. Peel potatoes with one blade of your scissors and grate them either the same way as the onions or, if necessary, with the aid of a staple remover. Combine all ingredients and mix well. Measure out approximately ¼ cup of mixture and pat it down flat on pan or radiator. Cook until as gold as your rusty tap water.

Insta-stocking

Who wants to pay $10 a go for some fancy embroidered stocking that's just going to serve as a barf bag the next time you guys have a party? Throw an old tube sock in with the colored load and presto change-o —festively colored stocking!

The Giving Tree

If a tabletop tree is all you care to manage, you should be able to find one—perhaps potted or on a wooden stand—at a local flower store or grocery. But if you've had a Charlie Brown Christmas one time too many and want something flashier, you'll need a saw rather than a pocketbook. Ten dollars is one thing, but the $30–$50 a six-foot tree will cost you is money better spent otherwise. Why shell out when you can get a tree for free from behind the bio labs?

Trees need water as Coke needs rum. If you've got a tabletopper implanted in a wooden base, try placing wet sponges or washcloths where the tree meets the board. If the tree still seems to be drying out, remove it from the base and insert it into a container of water.

Depending on the size of your conifer, anything from a shot glass to a used keg may be necessary to accommodate its girth and the water it requires. If the container tends to topple with the weight of the tree, try either throwing a few marbles in, surrounding the base with stones or textbooks, or duct taping the container to the floor or table.

Unless you've actually got it immersed in the fish tank, your tree's still something of a fire hazard. To avoid being faced with a biblical-style burning bush, position your tree far from fireplaces, menorahs, TVs, lamps, stereos, radiators, or other sources of heat. Unplug any strings of lights, as well, when you leave the room.

High-Tech Holidays

Solitaire is so old hat. Drive your professor's nagging voice out of your head as you play

Dreidel. The Web site www.billybear4kids.com/holidays/hanukkah/hanukkah.htm offers cyberdreidel, as does www.chanukah2000.com/lights/gamesIndex.html.

Exams you can pass. Www.chanukah2000.com/lights/gamesIndex

.html asks some fairly sophisticated questions about the history of the festival of lights; the Web site www.geocities.com/Heartland/7134/Christmas/chrtest.htm offers the official young elf exam.

How to Elicit Presents without Giving Any

Gifts?! As though that tree wasn't enough to break the bank. What's a poor slob to do? Well, there's always the option of giving away the things you receive to different people, but what happens when roommate Betty opens a bracelet you failed to notice was engraved with your name? Besides, that leaves you up a crick empty-handed present-wise. And since Mom and Dad measure your social progress by the size of your haul, that thar's bad news.

Time to get smart, cookie. As a *Sesame Street* character once said, Christmas means the *spirit* of giving—not the actual thing. Here, then, is how to handle the system of gift exchanges to your advantage:

Raid the recycling bin for shopping bags, empty boxes. Fold them up and stuff in backpack before you wave goodbye to roommates, credit card conspicuously held between your teeth. When you return hours later weighed down with "presents," make a circuit of the dorm, wishing holiday greetings to friends before you smile slyly and make for the closet.

During loud, fake phone conversation with parents (no need to waste money by actually calling them), comment on *generosity* of roommates and friends within earshot.

Recount all the awesome things you and your high school friends gave each other. Then say, "But I feel so much closer to you guys" and give 'em a hug.

Pack your suitcase to go home, but leave a big space in it with a Post-It Note "to yourself" saying "Leave room for *presents!*"

Vicarious Celebration

If it's sap you crave, we refer you to Grinch flicks or nearby sugar maples. But if you're man enough to handle the real story on the holiday (it's nicknamed X-mas for a reason), snuggle up with these docudramas:

Silent Night, Deadly Night 5: The Toymaker
It's a Bundyful Life

Black Christmas
Christmas Raccoons
Bloodbeat
Who Slew Auntie Roo?

Valentine's Day

February 14—the very date evokes images of champagne, roses, and celebrations for vibrator salesmen. But if the traditional dinner-and-futon evening has gotten to be old hat, or if you're immobilized by the loss of your "romantic things to say" list, it can be hard to know what to do with all that love a bubblin' out of your heart! Hard to know, that is, until in the following pages you reap the benefit of more creative romantic minds. With the help of these tools for celebration, this night gonna be one to remember:

Romantic Movies

A dimly lit room, candles, a couple rolls of Sweet Tarts . . . what could be more romantic? Nothing, unless you add in one of these little-known but potent cinematic love potions . . .

Has Anyone Seen My Pants?
'Tis a Pity She's a Whore
Nice Girls Don't Explode
Man Is Not a Bird
A Girl, a Guy, and a Gob
Can I Do It . . . Till I Need Glasses?
The Happy Hooker Goes to Washington
Sorority Babes in the Slimeball Bowl-a-Rama
Gimme an F
A Woman, Her Men and Her Futon

Eat Me

The way to most people's hearts is through their stomachs; here's the classic recipe for homemade cookies that earn you, and not Betty Crocker, the love of your mate:

2½ cups flour
1½ teaspoons baking powder
¾ teaspoon salt
1 cup sugar

¾ cup shortening
2 eggs
1 teaspoon vanilla
granulated sugar, to sprinkle

After preheating the oven to 375°, sift together the first three dry ingredients and set them aside. Then combine sugar and shortening, adding to them the eggs and then the vanilla, mixing well after each addition. Finally, add the dry ingredients, mix thoroughly, and shape the dough into balls. Roll them in granulated sugar and bake 10–12 minutes on a lightly greased cookie sheet or piece of tinfoil.

How to Pretend You Have a Valentine

You down a stein of pink beer — the only kind available at the campus grill. Another Valentine's Day, another night spent sloshed and humming the pig Latin versions of the messages on those little candy hearts to unreceptive audiences. "Osay inefay!" — you howl, trailing off as a volley of cooked carrots greets your aria. You begin symbolically sawing one of the hearts in half with your teeth — sawing, sawing to ease the pain.

"So it has been, and so shall it be," you begin to mumble, glancing thoughtfully at the sharp toothpick by your plate. But as soon as the thought of suicide crosses your mind, you pull back from the edge: God almighty, it's time to end the humiliation! If your parents can fake love, why can't you? Unfortunately, your mind has lost its usual nimbleness, and you're at a loss. Here's what to do, first for Mr. Lonelyhearts and then for Miss:

Ma petite amie. Borrow or find a large trench coat, one in which there's room to conceal that Animatronic Betsy Ross you stole from Epcot. As you waltz into a popular restaurant, "fiancée" snuggled tenderly inside your outerwear, alternate between low and squeaky voices to simulate conversation, and do what you can to make those buckle-shoed feet sticking out from under the hem look like they're moving. Ask for booth for two and squirm around in corner throughout meal.

Just a gigolo. Arrange to have the college escort service pick you up at your dorm. Feign either amnesia about destination or trouble with the English language to extend walking time. Secretly inject his right side with Novocain so that he doesn't notice when you slip your arm in his. When people pass by, say things like "Thanks for the roses!" If he asks what's up, say your multiple personalities are having an affair.

Special delivery. Say, wonder what that flowering plant's doing sitting by the podium in Greek Poetry 101? Could it be for you, from a secret admirer (a.k.a. yourself)? Blush becomingly as you accept it from your professor, and admiring studs begin comparing you to Helen of Troy and flashing you glimpses of what's under their togas while the absent-minded Ph.D. attends to the blackboard.

April Fool's Day

There's nothing like a prank or two to teach everyone you know to consult the wall calendar immediately upon waking. Sure, you can use the old standbys—whoopee cushions, disappearing ink, fake vomit (maybe that wouldn't be such a shocker), but you've got the rest of your life to compose variations on the theme of a Bronx cheer. Now's the time to utilize to the fullest the resources at your fingertips for some truly humorous action. All of these were actually done:

Fun with Macintosh. Either remove all files from your roommate's hard drive (transferring them to disk), or switch all of their names around. With any luck he'll print up what was once labeled "Sexual Chronicles, Chapter One" and hand it in to his chem prof without proofreading.

L'Oreal. In a slightly kinder variation on the above, spike hairspray or other hair products with temporary hair dye, preferably "Grey Poupon yellow" or another shade that clashes with the predominant color of your victim's wardrobe.

While you were out. Fake phone messages are fun, especially when you're there to hear the embarrassing "return" call your roommate hastily makes. False notifications of sweepstakes or best butt contest victories will stoke his ego; if he's cruising for a bruising, go for something less flattering and more realistic, like whoring charges or plagiarism accusations.

"I've been watching you in 'rocks for jocks' lecture . . ." Along these same lines, a fake phone call from an admirer can do the trick. Here's where knowledge of your friend's romantic tastes comes into play: The dupe works better if the caller pretends to be someone she's actually interested in but hasn't talked to enough to mistrust the classic "I've got a cold" excuse for a strange voice.

Deconstruction. To really surprise your roommate—or signal he'll have to look elsewhere for future living arrangements—take apart his bed and reconstruct it in the bathroom, preferably the one belonging to the opposite sex. If you have time to kill, go for the dresser as well, but make a few strategic replacements: feminine undies for his boxers, tampons for his Trojan collection, and Disney stuffed animals for his G.I. Joe figures.

Easter

Sure, you can use the Paas everything-in-the-goddamn-little-box approach, but what's college about if not resourcefulness in the face of adversity? Life is a challenge, and so ought Easter egg making to be. Listen, learn, and get those creative juices sloshing! Bottoms up, boys!

Au naturel. Buy your eggs a good month in advance of the holy day and put them in a nice warm place, like the top of the radiator, or atop your computer. Simply wait and watch as they assume various earth-tone colors.

Just like Ma used to do in Ukraine. You'll need hard-boiled eggs, a crayon or a candle, and vegetable dyes/food coloring. Dip the eggs in vinegar (which will act as a fixative), dry them, and then wax over whatever parts of the egg you wish to remain white. Dip the egg in the lightest color you intend to use on it, leaving it in for about five minutes. Without removing the first set of wax designs, cover with wax the areas you wish to remain the light color. Continue this procedure with progressively darker dyes until the pattern you desire is complete. Then pop the eggs in a warm oven/Toast-R-Oven with the door open until the wax looks shiny. You can then wipe it off.

Just like Jimi Hendrix used to do in the 'hood. A less anal way of producing designs is to simply mix each dye pot with vegetable oil (raid the salad bar). When you dip the egg in, blobs of oil will randomly adhere to it, blocking the adhesion of dye. Continue dipping the egg in progressively darker dyes until it looks like it's from the '60s.

Delicacy. For eggs less vulnerable to the ravages of rotting, dye them uncooked, then prick a hole at each end. Blow out the insides, thread with string, and hang.

Conclusion:
Looking Ahead

All great companionships must come to an end, and ours is no exception. Now you are as knowledgeable as we are; our Jedi friends, you have attained the sum of wisdom. If we were paid by the page, we might wax eloquent and subjective on relationships, ambition, and the meaning of life, issues which will increasingly concern you as your college career proceeds. But unlike some writers of guidebooks for college students, we would rather part ways than preach to pad our text. We are, after all, not experts; no one is.

But before we leave you standing on a high cliff, looking ahead and perhaps trying to determine whether the bathers out at sea are actually nude, a few sentimental words to remind you of us when we are gone.

While decisions about sophomore rooming probably aren't worth losing friendships over, they are important. If you're not happy with your living arrangements, it's going to be pretty hard to be happy in general. Be as kind as you can, but don't be a martyr; don't take on charity cases or sign on with people just because you want to be nice. It will end up being bad not only for you, probably, but for everyone involved.

Look early for summer jobs.

Go abroad if you possibly can (there are lots of grants if you look hard enough).

Spend some time in nature. You don't have to follow Thoreau into the woods if that isn't your style, but at least make time in your life for some bonding with that oak tree next to the Porta Potti. Especially in times of crisis (failed test, failed relationship), it can be reassuring to remember that something in the world is at peace and hasn't changed.

"Live all you can," as an aged character in a Henry James novel said. Life's not all downhill from college, but you're never again going to have a chance to sample so many activities and forms of friendship, and you're never again going to have such a good excuse for being unfocused and for hanging out.

As you're enjoying some indecision, slacking, and flailing, however, keep an eye out for something that you feel passionate about, something that you think would be worth devoting at least a couple of years of your life to. It can be hard to find things to believe in, and if you listened to the pundits you'd think that no one in our generation has any faith in anything. We have not found this to be true of ourselves (corn, if nothing else . . .), and we hope that it is not true of you.

Party on, lords and ladies.

Acknowledgments

Peanut butter without banana, Cancun without Kaopectate, and this book without the help of so many people are all distressing propositions. I'm grateful to my editors, Marnie Patterson and Susan Canavan, and Jeannie Hanson, my agent and mother, for their suggestions and enthusiasm; to Heloise, whose hints have long gotten me through household crises too big for a little Stain Stick action to resolve; to my now-deceased dog, Butterscotch, for his companionship on a "working vacation" at my cabin; to my Macintosh, for acting as a backup buddy when Prozac moments interfered with B-scotch's usually charming demeanor.

But thanks most of all to my humanoid friends from high school and roommates from college: Cindy Alvarez, Spencer Bershow, Erin Bix, Debbie Herman, Jane Hirt, Holly Milbrath, Caryn Olson, Katie Richards, Hillary Ross, Christine Sheppard-Sawyer, Susan Shin, Sheila Swaroop, and Becky Watson. Thanks for your ideas, your insights, your tips, your time, your tall tales from the trenches of college, and your support through drain cloggages and printer snafus, battles with roommates and Belgian waffles. Thanks especially, Hillary, for being so generous with your creativity and humor; you set a standard of silliness I will always be trying to reach. I hope that I will never cease to collaborate in one form or another (Pictionary, anyone? Whoops, that's Hillary's line) with all of you. Thanks for letting me learn from you and share your lives.

Jennifer